New Hampshire's 52 With A View: A Hiker's Guide

SECOND EDITION

Ken MacGray

Copyright © 2019, 2020 by Ken MacGray
Second Edition, First Printing, June 2020

ISBN-13: 978-0-578-70176-9

All rights reserved. No part of this book may be reproduced in any form or by any electronic or mechanical means including storage and retrieval systems without written permission from the publisher, except by a reviewer who may quote brief passages.

Disclaimer: Every effort was made to ensure the accuracy of the information in this book at the time of publication. However, trail conditions and routes are constantly subject to change. The author welcomes hearing of any changes, discrepancies or updates via email at 52wavbook@gmail.com. Readers should also note that hiking in the mountains is a potentially hazardous activity. Weather and trail conditions can change very quickly, and hikers should be fully prepared with proper gear, clothing, physical conditioning and researched knowledge. Readers are responsible for their own actions and are urged to exercise caution and use sound judgement. Use of this guide is at the reader's own risk and is not a substitute for thorough research. The author assumes no responsibility or liability.

Photography and book design by Ken MacGray.

Front cover: A hiker takes in the vista from the fantastic open ledges along Chippewa Trail on Black Mountain in Benton. Back cover: Baldface Circle Trail leading to South Baldface.

Typeset in Valkyrie and Concourse by Matthew Butterick (practicaltypography.com).

The cliffs of Rogers Ledge, which was added to the 52WAV list in 2020.

Contents

Acknowledgments 7
Introduction 8
How To Use This Book 10
Hiker Resources 13
Frequently Asked Questions 20
The Peaks 22
Locator Map 24

SOUTHERN NEW HAMPSHIRE   25
Mt. Kearsarge 25
Mt. Monadnock 29

LAKES REGION/SANDWICH RANGE/WATERVILLE VALLEY   37
Hedgehog Mountain 37
Jennings Peak 41
Middle Sister 44
Mt. Chocorua 48
Mt. Israel 55
Mt. Morgan/Mt. Percival ** 59
Mt. Paugus (South Peak) 64
Mt. Roberts 68
Mt. Shaw 71
Potash Mountain 74
Sandwich Dome 77
Welch Mountain/Dickey Mountain * 82

WESTERN NEW HAMPSHIRE   87
Black Mountain (Benton) 87
Blueberry Mountain 91
Mt. Cardigan 96
Mt. Cube (South Peak) 103
Smarts Mountain 108
Stinson Mountain 113

CENTRAL WHITE MOUNTAINS/CRAWFORD NOTCH — 117

- Middle Sugarloaf 117
- Mt. Avalon 120
- Mt. Crawford 122
- Mt. Parker 126
- Mt. Pemigewasset 129
- Mt. Resolution 132
- Mt. Tremont 138
- Mt. Webster 142
- Mt. Willard 145
- Stairs Mountain 149

EASTERN WHITE MOUNTAINS — 154

- Eagle Crag 154
- Eastman Mountain 157
- Imp Face 160
- Mt. Kearsarge North 163
- North Doublehead/South Doublehead * 167
- North Moat Mountain 171
- Shelburne Moriah Mountain 175
- South Baldface/North Baldface ** 179
- South Moat Mountain 185
- Table Mountain 188

NORTHERN NEW HAMPSHIRE — 193

- The Horn 193
- Magalloway Mountain 197
- Mt. Hayes 200
- Mt. Martha (Cherry Mountain) 203
- Mt. Starr King 208
- Mt. Success 210
- North Percy Peak 215
- Pine Mountain (Gorham) 219
- Rogers Ledge 225
- Sugarloaf (Stratford) 230

DELISTED PEAKS	**234**
Black Mountain (Jackson)	234
Carr Mountain	235
Hibbard Mountain	237
Iron Mountain	238
Mt. Wolf	240
Square Ledge (Albany)	241
West Royce Mountain	242
References	244
About The Author	245

* *Two neighboring peaks combined into one hike for the purposes of the list.*
** *Two separate peaks on the list but commonly hiked together.*

Acknowledgments

First off, this book would not have been possible without Lib Bates, Catherine Crooker (Lib's daughter), Tracy Ripkey, all of the Over The Hill Hikers past and present, and their vision of a group of scenic peaks away from the more popular 4,000 footers. They chose well and as hikers we are forever indebted to them for selecting these beautiful and scenic destinations.

My friends and extended hiking family have been there for many of the 52WAV journeys, as well as others. We've laughed and we've cried at the beauty of the mountains and we've overcome our challenges, one cairn at a time. I wouldn't trade those experiences for anything.

Hiking guru Steve Smith of The Mountain Wanderer and AMC's 4,000 Footer Committee has been invaluable as a mentor in this whole book writing endeavor and for graciously sharing some of his research which appears here. His support and guidance helped to make this project the best it could be. A huge thanks to Steve.

If it weren't for my work on the Southern New Hampshire Trail Guide for Appalachian Mountain Club, this book may not have appeared until much later. Working on that guide created the spark to put together this one. Special thanks to AMC Cartographer Larry Garland for providing the most recent LIDAR elevations for the peaks on this list.

Thanks also to the members of the NH 52 With A View Facebook group, who have provided invaluable support and updates from the field.

To my good friend Maureen Kittredge as well as Mike Dickerman at Bondcliff Books, a huge thanks for investing in this project and for your continued confidence in making it a success.

To Ed Rolfe at Wilderness Map Company of Franconia, NH, I extend my thanks for the creation of the excellent peak locator map.

Special thanks go out to Tim Hughes and Tivvi Pare at the Horton Center for their guidance on hiking Pine Mountain safely and for allowing continued public access to this scenic peak.

And lastly I would like to thank my dad, who, when I was a young child, introduced me to the neighboring town forest just down the street from our house. In reality, this forest is only a few square miles in size, but as a child it seemed like a vast wilderness and filled me with wonder. It was here where my love for being in the woods and my connection to nature was born.

Introduction

The story of the Over The Hill Hikers — a group of retirees in their 50s and 60s who moved to the small town of Sandwich, NH in the late 1970s — brought together a group of people who would quickly become close friends. They all gathered in this small town, drawn from around the United States and even the United Kingdom — by a deep love and respect for the mountains and a newly shared passion for hiking. Their outings began fairly modestly in 1979 with a leisurely hike to Great Falls for a picnic. Eventually they would move on to more challenging peaks in the nearby Sandwich Range and further north in the White Mountains.

Originally, the group was organized in a somewhat loose fashion, but all that changed with the arrival in Sandwich of Elizabeth MacGregor Crooker, a retired school teacher and her late husband Charlie, a preacher, in 1981. Better known as Lib Bates (after marrying orthopedic surgeon Frank Bates after Charlie passed in 1994), she stepped in to organize events and grow the informal organization beyond its local Sandwich roots. Her introduction, motivation and leadership — which made her affectionately known as the "Den Mother" — brought a unique bond and new sense of community to the group. It was at this point they became the Over The Hill Hikers.

Lib was the daughter of one of the first AMC hutmasters, Red MacGregor, and grew up hiking the mountains of New Hampshire with her father. Her first "hike" was as a toddler to Carter Notch, carried in an Adirondack basket by Red. As leader of the OTHH, she was eager to show her new friends what the mountains had to offer. Under her guidance, the group was reborn in a sense and blossomed.

Tuesday was the day settled upon for hiking, and they kept up a frantic pace, bagging the NH 4,000 Footers while also adding in overnights at AMC huts as well as ski trips. In the mid-1980s, they ventured outside of New Hampshire to Mt. Katahdin in Maine's Baxter State Park. They would later make excursions into Vermont's Green Mountains and the Adirondacks in New York, tackle the Maine 4,000 Footers, visit Montana, and even hike in the Alps. The group had swelled to over 100 people, many of whom have climbed the NH 4000 Footers multiple times, some doing so over the age of 70. Today, a few members continue to pursue the grid and the ambitious goal of redlining all the trails in the AMC White Mountain Guide.

By 1991, with so many amazing accomplishments under the group's belt, Lib began thinking about what might be next, and started researching peaks which fell short of the 4,000 ft. mark but which could complement that list to create an even 100 peaks. Initially, there was a decision to either keep these additional hikes local to the Sandwich area or to extend them statewide. The latter won out. It was around this time that the AMC Hundred Highest list was being worked on by ardent peakbaggers, but many of the peaks on that list had no trailed access and no view. Lib proposed a new list which consisted only of peaks with a trail and a view. The destinations were then plotted out and organized by decreasing elevation, starting at the highest end with Sandwich Dome then moving down to the lowest peak, Hedgehog Mountain. These mountains truly spanned the entire state as far south as Mt. Monadnock and up to the furthest reaches of the North Country with Magalloway Mountain.

The 52 With A View list had been born.

One day in 1997, at the age of 78, Lib made the difficult and heart-wrenching decision to step down from her role as leader and organizer. She found she was slowing down, her first husband had died, and other demands outside of the group were taking up more of her time. The group carried on however, following a strict list of duties she had compiled which was known as, *"how the work gets done"*.

While Lib was out of the leadership role, she still continued to hike, although at a slower pace than her quicker friends. In ill health by 2010, an oxygen tank was her constant companion, but even this didn't stop her from hitting the trails — she devised a pack which would hold two oxygen bottles so she could keep at it.

In 2011, Lib passed away, but she left behind a legacy and a sense of camaraderie amongst friends that has remained unsurpassed. The Over The Hill hikers still get out there today, carrying on in the spirit instilled by their original Den Mother. For the rest of us, we have the good fortune to hike to the beautiful destinations selected by her and described in this guide, for which we can all be very grateful.

"Mountain trails feel like home to me." — Lib Bates

Visit the Over The Hill Hikers at overthehillhikers.blogspot.com

How To Use This Book

PEAK DESCRIPTIONS

All peaks are grouped together by geographic region, then alphabetically within. The standard description format is name and elevation, location, introduction and historical tidbits, parking and driving details, detailed description of the recommended route, any additional routes (if applicable) that may be of interest with a brief summary, overnight/camping options (if applicable), and tips for hiking the peak in winter.

While the mass of a given mountain may span across multiple geographic areas, the location provided in the description is where the highest point is. The summit elevations for each peak have been revised in this edition to reflect the updated New Hampshire LIDAR survey data released in 2019. In almost all cases, the elevation changes are minimal.

The view highlights provided with each description are intended to be a general summary of what you are looking at from each peak, and not a completely detailed guide.

ROUTES

The recommended route given is usually the most traveled or accessible route, but not always (in the case of peaks with only one access point, only that route will be provided). The parking and driving details described are for the recommended hiking route — this information is described in lesser detail for additional routes. Additional routes are suggested options and in many cases do not include all possible routes. Hikers should refer to Appalachian Mountain Club's White Mountain Guide or Southern New Hampshire Trail Guide and the various maps for a given peak regarding details on all available options.

Route descriptions may simply be one trail or a combination of trails. All routes include either round-trip (out-and-back) or complete loop/traverse mileage along with total elevation gain, which includes any applicable gain on the way back. Loop hikes are also specified as being either clockwise or counter-clockwise. Mileage segments are provided within the descriptions at key points, but are kept somewhat to a minimum to reduce complexity.

Trail blaze colors are included in the descriptions where applicable, but these blazes may not always be clear, consistent or easy to follow. Above treeline, trails are usually but not always marked by stone cairns. Please do not dismantle cairns or build additional ones, as they are an essential navigation aid, especially at times of low visibility.

In some cases, the route provided does not travel over the actual high point of the mountain. In such cases, details on where the high point is are noted within each peak description.

MAPS

The maps indicated with each description are a subjective choice by the author as the most informative for that particular peak, although several different maps may overlap to cover the same area. See the Hiker Resources section of this book for details on the available maps.

A note on USGS quadrangle maps: These topographic maps are often very useful, but sometimes contain inaccurate or outdated information. In many cases trails are indicated but may not be accurate due to being closed or relocated. In some cases older, historical trails are still indicated even though they no longer exist. Using the USGS maps is fine, but it is best to use them with a current printed map of the same region.

CAMPING

Peak-specific overnight options for backpackers are listed within individual trail descriptions where applicable. For peaks within the White Mountain National Forest, backcountry camping is also allowed in some locations. See fs.usda.gov for a complete list of rules and regulations and where you can and cannot camp.

Camping is not allowed in the Ossipee Range (Mt. Shaw, Mt. Roberts), Nash Stream Forest (North Percy Peak, Sugarloaf), Warner and Rollins State Parks (Mt. Kearsarge) Mt. Willard, or Mt. Cardigan (aside from AMC Cardigan Lodge and designated sites). Camping is also prohibited at the site of the former Resolution Shelter off Davis Path near Mt. Resolution and Stairs Mountain. Camping on any private land is prohibited without the express permission of the landowner.

WINTER

The winter advice included with each peak description includes general guidelines for winter access, hiking routes and parking. See the Hiker Resources section of this book for more general information on hiking during winter.

ABBREVIATIONS USED IN THIS BOOK

AMC	Appalachian Mountain Club
AT	Appalachian Trail
CITC	Castle In The Clouds
CRT	Cross Rivendell Trail
CTA	Chatham Trails Association
LRCT	Lakes Region Conservation Trust
MSG	Monadnock-Sunapee Greenway
NG	National Geographic
NHDP	New Hampshire Division of Parks and Recreation
OTHH	Over The Hill Hikers
RMC	Randolph Mountain Club
SPNHF	Society For The Protection Of New Hampshire Forests
SRKG	Sunapee-Ragged-Kearsarge Greenway
TCTA	The Cohos Trail Association
USDA	United States Department of Agriculture
USFS	United States Forest Service
WMNF	White Mountain National Forest
WVAIA	Waterville Valley Athletic & Improvement Association

Hiker Resources

TRAILS AND TRAIL CONDITIONS

Most of the trails in this guide are located on public land or land owned by various state agencies and conservation organizations. Hikers should observe all posted regulations to protect the land itself and the rights of the respective landowners. Hikers are also urged to travel responsibly in respect to the land and fellow hikers, and dog owners should keep their pets under control at all times. Please note that the only 52WAV peak where dogs are not allowed is Mt. Monadnock.

Two very good websites exist for researching trail conditions before heading out and both are free and easy to use. Use of these sites as both a researcher and submitter is encouraged as they are very beneficial to hikers who hit the trails after you. Both sites are especially valuable in winter when conditions can change rapidly. New England Trail Conditions (newenglandtrailconditions.com) requires no registration for hikers to post reports after their hikes. TrailsNH (trailsnh.com) is unique in that it aggregates reports from NETC, Views From The Top and various blogs that it tracks into one comprehensive source.

WEATHER

Mountain weather can change quickly, creating variable and sometimes dangerous conditions. Hikers should always watch the forecast starting a few days out, and then right up until hike time, for any last minute changes. Please keep in mind that while conditions may be favorable in a valley or at lower elevations, they could be quite different at the summit. The National Weather Service website (weather.gov) is an excellent resource, allowing you to enter a peak name or specific location in the search field to get a point forecast for that area. Mountain Forecast (mountain-forecast.com) offers the option of searching for a peak and getting a forecast for both the base and summit. Mount Washington Observatory's Higher Summits Forecast is often recommended as a weather resource, but isn't really applicable outside the Presidential Range.

SEASONAL ROAD CLOSURES

Many White Mountain National Forest roads and other access roads around the state are gated or not maintained in winter, making certain peaks more difficult to reach or in some cases cutting them off completely. Each peak description in this book contains a section on winter travel. Please refer to these sections for any specific details on winter access and parking. For the latest status of road closures and openings, visit trailsnh.com.

MAPS

As the 52WAV peaks are spread out around the entire state, there is no one map which includes them all. However, a variety of maps do exist which cover most of the peaks and are available through The Mountain Wanderer (mountainwanderer.com) in Lincoln, AMC Pinkham Notch Visitor Center and Highland Center (outdoors.org), in various local bookstores, or directly through the publishers. Below is a selection of maps which cover the peaks in this guide.

AMC Southern New Hampshire waterproof map (includes Mt. Cardigan, Mt. Monadnock), published by Appalachian Mountain Club (AMC; outdoors.org)

AMC White Mountains trail map set, published by Appalachian Mountain Club (AMC; outdoors.org)

Appalachian Trail New Hampshire/Vermont map set (includes Smarts Mountain, Mt. Cube), published by Appalachian Trail Conservancy (AT; appalachiantrail.org)

Castle in the Clouds Conservation Area Hiking Trails map (includes Mt. Roberts, Mt. Shaw), published by Lakes Region Conservation Trust (CITC; lrct.org)

Chatham Trails Association map (includes South and North Baldface, Eagle Crag, Eastman Mountain), published by Chatham Trails Association (CTA; chathamtrails.org)

Cohos Trail map (includes Sugarloaf (Stratford) and North Percy Peak; Magollaway Mountain is depicted but its trails are not indicated), published by Cohos Trail Association (TCTA; cohostrail.org)

Crawford Notch Map and Guide (includes Mt. Willard, Mt. Crawford, Mt. Avalon, Stairs Mountain, Mt. Resolution), published by Wilderness Map Company (bondcliffbooks.com)

Cross Rivendell Trail map (includes Mt. Cube), published by Rivendell Trails Association (CRT; rivendelltrail.squarespace.com)

Exploring New Hampshire's White Mountains Topographic Map and Guide, published by Wilderness Map Company (bondcliffbooks.com)

Franconia Notch Map and Guide (includes Mt. Pemigewasset), published by Wilderness Map Company (bondcliffbooks.com)

Kancamagus Highway Pocket Map and Guide (includes Potash Mountain, Hedgehog Mountain, Mt. Tremont, Mt. Paugus, Mt. Chocorua, Middle Sister, Moat Range), published by Map Adventures (MA; mapadventures.com)

Map of Hiking Trails in the Waterville Valley (includes Dickey Mountain, Jennings Peak, Sandwich Dome, Welch Mountain), published by Waterville Valley Athletic & Improvement Association (WVAIA; wvaia.org)

Monadnock-Sunapee Greenway SuperMap (includes Mt. Monadnock), published by Monadnock-Sunapee Greenway Trail Club (MSG; msgtc.org)

Mount Monadnock waterproof map, published by Map Adventures (MA; mapadventures.com)

Randolph Valley and Northern Peaks of the Presidential Range Trail Map (2016), published by Randolph Mountain Club (RMC; randolphmountainclub.org)

Squam Trail Guide (includes Mt. Israel, Mt. Morgan, Mt. Percival), published by Squam Lakes Association (SLA; squamlakes.org)

Sunapee-Ragged-Kearsarge Greenway Guide (includes Mt. Kearsarge), published by Sunapee-Ragged-Kearsarge Greenway Coalition (SRKGC; srkg.com)

White Mountains waterproof map, published by Map Adventures (MA; mapadventures.com)

White Mountain National Forest West Trail Map, (includes Mt. Cube, Smarts Mountain), Published by National Geographic (NG; shop.nationalgeographic.com)

Wonalancet Out Door Club Mount Monadnock map, published by Wonalancet Out Door Club (WODC; wodc.org)

Wonalancet Out Door Club Sandwich Range map (includes Sandwich Dome, Jennings Peak, Potash Mountain, Hedgehog Mountain, Mt. Paugus, Mt. Chocorua, Middle Sister, northern approach to Mt. Israel), published by Wonalancet Out Door Club (WODC; wodc.org)

In addition, The New Hampshire Division of Parks and Recreation (NHDP) offers maps of varying quality on their websites for Cardigan Mountain State Park (Mt. Cardigan), Crawford Notch State Park (Mt. Willard), Franconia Notch State Park (Mt. Pemigewasset), Monadnock State Park (Mt. Monadnock) and Rollins and Winslow State Parks (Mt. Kearsarge). These maps can be downloaded from nhstateparks.org.

BOOKS

50 Hikes North of the White Mountains, by Kim Nilsen, published by Countryman Press (countrymanpress.com)

AMC Southern New Hampshire Trail Guide, 5th Edition, by Ken MacGray, published by Appalachian Mountain Club (outdoors.org)

AMC White Mountain Guide, 30th Edition, by Steven D. Smith, published by Appalachian Mountain Club (outdoors.org)

The Adventures of Buffalo and Tough Cookie: A Hiking Journey of Discovery Through New Hampshire's "52 With a View" Mountain List, by Dan Szczesny, published by Bondcliff Books (bondcliffbooks.com)

WEBSITES

FranklinSites - 52 With A View (franklinsites.com)
Hiking the 52 With A View List (newenglandwaterfalls.com)
NH Mountain Hiking - 52 With A View (nhmountainhiking.com)
Over the Hill Hikers (creators of the 52WAV list) (overthehillhikers.blogspot.com)
Redline Guiding - Hiking NH's 52 With A View (redlineguiding.com)

HIKESAFE HIKER RESPONSIBILITY CODE

You are responsible for yourself, so be prepared:

With knowledge and gear. Become self-reliant by learning about the terrain, conditions, local weather and your equipment before you start.

To leave your plans. Tell someone where you are going, the trails you are hiking, when you will return and your emergency plans.

To stay together. When you start as a group, hike as a group, end as a group. Pace your hike to the slowest person.

To turn back. Weather changes quickly in the mountains. Fatigue and unexpected conditions can also affect your hike. Know your limitations and when to postpone your hike. The mountains will be there another day.

For emergencies. Even if you are headed out for just an hour, an injury, severe weather or a wrong turn could become life threatening. Don't assume you will be rescued; know how to rescue yourself.

To share the hiker code with others.

STATE OF NEW HAMPSHIRE HIKESAFE CARD

Hikers in possession of this card are not held liable for costs incurred should they need to be rescued due to negligence on their part. They may however be responsible for such expenses if it has been determined they acted recklessly or intentionally created a situation requiring an emergency response. Those who carry a current New Hampshire Fish and Game hunting or fishing license, or possess a valid registration for an off-road vehicle, snowmobile or boat, will also not be held liable for costs incurred by rescue due to negligence on their part.

As of 2020, the cost for the card is $25 per year for individuals and $35 per year for families. All revenues aside from a small transaction fee go toward NHF&G's Search and Rescue Fund. The card can be ordered online at hikesafe.com where more information on the program is also available.

LEAVE NO TRACE SEVEN PRINCIPLES

1. Plan Ahead and Prepare
2. Travel and Camp on Durable Surfaces
3. Dispose of Waste Properly
4. Leave What You Find
5. Minimize Campfire Impacts
6. Respect Wildlife
7. Be Considerate of Other Visitors

© 1999 by the Leave No Trace Center for Outdoor Ethics: www.LNT.org

THE TEN ESSENTIALS

The Ten Essentials are a collection of survival items that are recommended for every hiker to ensure safety on the trail and in emergency situations. This list first appeared in the third edition of Mountaineering: The Freedom of the Hills, published in January 1974. The items consist of:

1. *Navigation* - Printed maps in waterproof container, compass and optional GPS app or handheld receiver.

2. *Sun protection* - Sunscreen, sunglasses, wide-brim hat and long clothing.

3. *Insulation* - Jacket, wool hat, gloves or mittens, rain shell and thermal base layers.

4. *Illumination* - Flashlight or headlamp with extra batteries. An LED headlamp is preferable for extended battery life.

5. *First aid* - First aid supplies and bug repellent.

6. *Fire* - Butane lighter, matches in a waterproof container, or other fire starting material.

7. *Repair kit and tools* - Pocket knife or multi-tool, scissors, pliers, screwdriver, trowel or shovel, duct tape and zip ties.

8. *Nutrition* - Extra food for one additional day in case of emergencies.

9. *Hydration* - Two extra liters of water for one additional day in case of emergencies.

10. *Emergency shelter* - Tarp, ultralight tent, bivy sack, space blanket, contractor bags, ponchos, sleeping bag or insulated sleeping pad.

WINTER

Both weather and trail conditions can change by the hour or even the minute in winter. Things may be fine at the trailhead, but could drastically change at elevation. Acquiring a current weather forecast is critical before heading out. Days are very short in the early winter, with darkness falling around 4pm. Be sure to factor in enough time to complete your hike given the conditions and shorter daylight.

Navigation skills are essential, especially if a trail is not broken out. Blazing and signage may be obscured by snow, and trail corridors may not always be obvious to see. In general, out-and-back hikes are easier in winter than loops, as you will at least have a track to follow back. Many of the peaks on this list are well-traveled in winter, but others are less so. Water crossings should be approached with caution if not well-frozen.

Appropriate clothing and gear should be worn in winter, in the form of synthetic fabrics, which wick away moisture. Layering is a critical skill to learn which takes practice. The goal is to avoid overheating and excessive perspiration, which can soak clothing and lead to hypothermia. For footwear, regular summer hiking boots are not sufficient. Insulated winter boots will keep your feet warm and dry. A headlamp should be in every winter hiker's pack for short winter days as well as emergencies. If you carry water bottles, it is best to store them upside down or in an insulated carrier to prevent freezing. Water intake should also be increased during winter, as the much drier air increases the chances of dehydration. Air temperatures are cold enough, but adding wind on top of that presents a very real risk of frostbite to exposed skin. Venturing above treeline in windy conditions during winter is recommended only for experienced hikers with the appropriate gear.

Snowshoes or skis should be used in heavy snow conditions, although more popular trails are usually broken out fairly quickly after a storm. Breaking trail, enjoyable for some, can be strenuous and tiring. This difficulty is compounded by the relative steepness of a given trail. Snowshoes should be worn on trails that are unbroken or just loosely broken out in order to consolidate a base. Barebooting soft trails is especially exhausting and potentially a source of injury both for yourself and for those who hike after you. Postholes can freeze later, presenting an ankle-twisting hazard. Snowshoes are also recommended to be carried even if a trail is packed out in case drifting is encountered or for emergencies.

In icy conditions, microspikes will suffice in most cases, but on open ledge areas or steeper trails, full mountaineering crampons may be needed. Also be prepared to change in and out of various traction depending on trail conditions. While the 52WAV peaks are smaller than their more well-known higher siblings, they should not be underestimated. It is best to turn back if icy trails cannot be safely negotiated.

Some trailhead parking areas are not plowed in winter, resulting in more limited room. If it is necessary to park along the side of a major roadway, a good practice is to get all four wheels out of the travel lanes, otherwise there is a risk of being ticketed or towed. Parking roadside is not recommended during or immediately after a snow event due to plowing. If in doubt, see the local rules and regulations for the town in which the parking is located.

HIKING IN THE ERA OF COVID-19

At the time of this guide's publication, the world was still dealing with the COVID-19 pandemic. Hikers are urged to heed the latest recommendations of the Centers for Disease Control (cdc.gov), Appalachian Mountain Club (outdoors.org), USDA/USFS (fs.usda.gov/whitemountain) and any applicable local trail organizations in regards to staying safe and healthy on the trail, including physical distancing, sanitization, and wearing of masks.

52 WITH A VIEW PATCH

Like other popular hiking lists, a patch is available for the 52WAV list as well. To register as a finisher and to receive your patch, mail a completed checklist with the dates you hiked the peaks and which one you finished on with a self-addressed stamped envelope and $5 (cash please, no checks) to:

Catherine Crooker, 73 Dale Rd., Sandwich, NH 03227
Questions? Email catherinecrooker@gmail.com

The 52WAV checklist is available online at the following locations:

facebook.com/groups/nh52wav/
kenmacgray.org/52/

Frequently Asked Questions

Who Created The 52WAV List?
The list was created by a list of hikers from the Sandwich, NH area known as the Over The Hill Hikers. First formed in 1979, the group was organized a few years later by the first OTHH "Den Mother" Lib Bates and her late husband Charlie Crooker. In 1990, she came up with the idea of creating a new list of hikes with scenic views outside the more popular 4,000 footers, and the 52WAV list was born. The group is still active today and hikes regularly.

How were the peaks originally chosen for the list? Why are there 52 of them?
The peaks were chosen simply for their scenic vistas and the number 52 was chosen to complement the 48 4,000 Footers. Both lists combine to make an even 100 peaks.

Will new peaks be added to the list at all?
Yes, the list will get revised from time to time (a period of years) as views diminish due to tree growth. For descriptions of hikes that used to be on the list, see the Delisted Peaks section of this book.

The 4,000 footers have a separate winter patch. Is there a winter patch for the 52WAV?
There is no separate patch for hiking the 52WAV in winter like there is for the 4,000 Footers, but there's nothing stopping one from ordering an additional patch. Just about every peak on this list is accessible in winter. The toughest ones to get to due to seasonal road closures and somewhat remote locations are North Percy Peak, Sugarloaf (Stratford) and Magalloway Mountain. Every trail description in this guide provides details and tips for winter treks.

Is there a separate patch for dogs?
No, but like with winter, you can always order an additional patch for your four-legged friend. Mt. Monadnock is the only peak on this list that does not allow dogs per regulations, but that does not preclude them from finishing the list and getting their patch.

What are some of the harder 52WAV peaks?
This is somewhat subjective, but the loop over the Baldfaces is probably the toughest, mainly due to the steep, strenuous scrambling up to South Baldface, lots of above treeline exposure to the weather, and the substantial elevation gain, which is more than many 4,000 Footers. Mt. Chocorua is a peak that should not be underestimated — it has significant elevation gain depending on the chosen route, and its completely exposed summit ledges offer no protection from the weather. Shelburne Moriah can be difficult due to a steep and rough climb to the ridge and the long overall distance. Kearsarge North, while very well-traveled, is a bit more difficult than the numbers might suggest, again due to a lot of elevation gain. Mt. Tremont, which hikers either love or hate, is also challenging in its upper half, with very steep grades and rough, eroded footing.

What are some of the easiest?
Generally, Mt. Willard with its mellow grades and short distance is considered the easiest 52WAV peak. It's an excellent hike for those just starting out, or those of us not so young anymore, or families with kids. It's a good half-day hike and a frequent first time "big mountain" experience. Other peaks on the easier end include Mt. Cardigan via West Ridge Trail (the easiest and shortest route to this stellar peak), Blueberry Mountain, Mt. Pemigewasset, and Mt. Roberts.

Which peaks can be combined?
Hedgehog Mountain, Potash Mountain (two separates hikes which leave from the same trailhead)
    Eastman Mountain, South Baldface, North Baldface, Eagle Crag
    Hedgehog Mountain, Potash Mountain (two separates hikes which leave from the same trailhead)
    Jennings Peak, Sandwich Dome
    Middle Sister, Mt. Chocorua
    Mt. Avalon, Mt. Willard (two separate hikes from the same trailhead)
    Mt. Crawford, Mt. Parker, Mt. Resolution, Stairs Mountain
    Mt. Cube, Smarts Mountain
    Mt. Morgan, Mt. Percival
    Mt. Roberts, Mt. Shaw
    South Moat Mountain, North Moat Mountain

The Peaks

The trail descriptions in this guide are grouped together by geographic region and then alphabetically within those regions, beginning in the southern part of the state, then west to east, and finishing way up in the North Country.

SOUTHERN NEW HAMPSHIRE

This is the area of the state south of the Lakes Region. There are only two 52WAV peaks in southern New Hampshire, the bald and very popular Mts. Kearsarge and Monadnock. Mt. Cardigan is sometimes considered to be in this area, but for the purposes of this guide it is included in the Western New Hampshire section due to its closer location to peaks in that region.

LAKES REGION / SANDWICH RANGE / WATERVILLE VALLEY

The peaks in this section lie within the Ossipee Range near Lake Winnipesaukee and the Sandwich Range, the southernmost range of the White Mountains, and also extend westward toward Waterville Valley. Peaks in this area include Mts. Roberts and Shaw and their broad views, the classic loop over Mts. Morgan and Percival, the majestic Mt. Chocorua, Sandwich Dome, the ledgy Hedgehog and Potash Mountains and one of the best short hikes in the Whites, Welch-Dickey.

WESTERN NEW HAMPSHIRE

This area is described as being west of I-93, the Plymouth/Rumney/Warren area, the Benton Range west of Mt. Moosilauke, and the upper Connecticut River Valley, and includes bare Mt. Cardigan, Black Mountain — crown jewel of the Benton Range, Mt. Cube and the wild and rugged Smarts Mountain with its fire tower.

CENTRAL WHITE MOUNTAINS / CRAWFORD NOTCH

Located closer to the core of the White Mountain National Forest, this region stretches from Franconia Notch around to and down through the US 302 corridor from Carroll to Bartlett, reaching into the Presidential Range-Dry River Wilderness along the way. Starting with the popular Mt. Pemigewasset, this area heads east toward Middle Sugarloaf, then down through Crawford Notch to Mt. Crawford and the more remote Mts. Resolution and Parker.

EASTERN WHITE MOUNTAINS

This region generally encompasses the Conway, Jackson and Evans Notch areas, but also steps over into the Carter-Moriah Range for Imp Face and Shelburne Moriah Mountain. Other peaks in this section include the spectacular Baldfaces, the high, scenic Moat Range, and Mt. Kearsarge North with its historic fire tower. Table Mountain is also included here.

NORTHERN NEW HAMPSHIRE

This area extends northward from US 302 in Bethlehem to the Cherry-Dartmouth Range, the Pliny Range, the Mahoosucs and Nash Stream Forest, culminating in the furthest reaches of the North Country in Pittsburg. Among the mountains in this section are Mt. Martha, The Horn — the watchtower of the Kilkenny Region, steep-sided North Percy Peak, Mt. Success, Pine Mountain in Gorham, Rogers Ledge, and the very remote and wild Magalloway Mountain, just 20 mi. shy of the Canadian border.

DELISTED PEAKS

On occasion, the 52WAV list will be revised by the Over The Hill Hikers as nature slowly reclaims the views over time. This has happened previously with Carr Mountain being removed in 2001 and Mt. Wolf being removed in 2010. A decade later in 2020, the list was once again revised with the removal of five peaks: Black Mountain (Jackson), Hibbard Mountain, Iron Mountain, Square Ledge (Albany), and West Royce Mountain were taken off the list and replaced by Mt. Morgan, Mt. Percival, Pine Mountain, Rogers Ledge, and Table Mountain. In addition, North Doublehead was combined with its neighbor South Doublehead (which has the better views) to create one hike (for the purposes of the list), similar to Welch-Dickey.

This edition of the guide reflects the most recent changes and includes all of the 52WAV peaks past and present for both historical purposes and for anyone looking to hike the former mountains.

Locations of the 52 With A View

1 - Black Mountain (Benton)
2 - Blueberry Mountain
3 - Eagle Crag
4 - Eastman Mountain
5 - Hedgehog Mountain
6 - The Horn
7 - Imp Face
8 - Jennings Peak
9 - Magalloway Mountain
10 - Middle Sister
11 - Middle Sugarloaf
12 - Mt. Avalon
13 - Mt. Cardigan
14 - Mt. Chocorua
15 - Mt. Crawford
16 - Mt. Cube (South Peak)
17 - Mt. Hayes
18 - Mt. Israel
19 - Mt. Kearsarge
20 - Mt. Kearsarge North
21 - Mt. Martha (Cherry Mountain)
22 - Mt. Monadnock
23 - Mt. Morgan
24 - Mt. Percival
25 - Mt. Parker
26 - Mt. Paugus (South Peak)
27 - Mt. Pemigewasset
28 - Mt. Resolution
29 - Mt. Roberts
30 - Mt. Shaw
31 - Mt. Starr King
32 - Mt. Success
33 - Mt. Tremont
34 - Mt. Webster
35 - Mt. Willard
36 - North & South Doublehead
37 - North Moat Mountain
38 - North Percy Peak
39 - Pine Mountain (Gorham)
40 - Potash Mountain
41 - Rogers Ledge
42 - Sandwich Dome
43 - Shelburne Moriah Mountain
44 - Smarts Mountain
45 - South Baldface
46 - North Baldface
47 - South Moat Mountain
48 - Stairs Mountain
49 - Stinson Mountain
50 - Sugarloaf (Stratford)
51 - Table Mountain
52 - Welch & Dickey Mountains

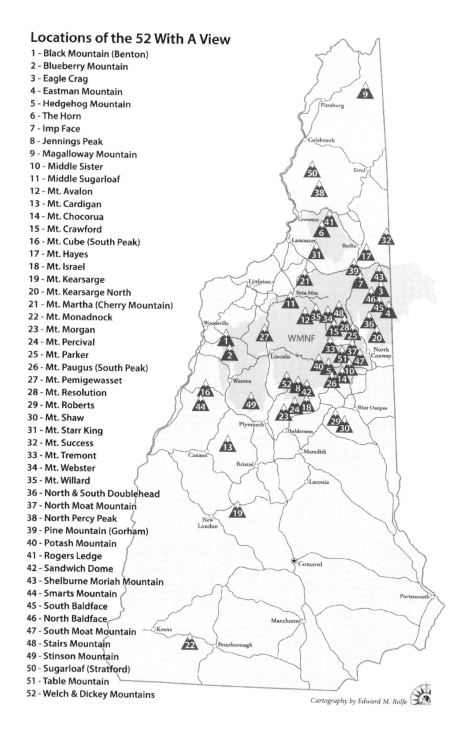

Cartography by Edward M. Rolfe

Southern New Hampshire

Mt. Kearsarge

Elevation: 2,935 ft.
Location: Towns of Wilmot and Warner
Map: SRKG map, NHDP Winslow State Park map
Locator map: 19

Hikers atop Mt. Kearsarge's bald summit.

Mt. Kearsarge (not to be confused with its larger sibling Mt. Kearsarge North near Conway), is one of the most prominent and isolated mountains in New Hampshire, rising some 2,100 ft. above the surrounding landscape. Its sprawling mass is visible from many locations in the southern part of the state. The summit — also the high point of both Warner and Wilmot — was bared by a 1796 forest fire which resulted in stunning views, and is also home to a communications tower and an active fire tower.

Two state parks are located on the mountain. Winslow State Park is on the northwest slope, and a picnic area situated on an 1,820 ft. plateau with views of the White Mountains was once the site of a 19th century hotel known as the Winslow House — all that remains today is a cellar hole. The hotel was named after Admiral John Winslow who commanded the USS Kearsarge during the Civil War, which was constructed from timbers harvested from the slopes of Mt. Kearsarge. While the ship itself was sunk in battle, Admiral Winslow went on to become a national hero for his efforts during the war.

On the south slope is Rollins State Park, reached by a 3.5 mi. scenic auto road which rises to a trailhead and picnic area historically known as the "Garden", located in a naturally-wooded glen. This auto road was originally chartered in 1866 as a toll road from Warner Village to the summit with construction beginning in 1873, traversing the partly open Mission Ridge. By 1900, the road fell into such a state of repair that it became impassable but was later reopened in the 1930s along with what would become today's Rollins Trail. More information on both state parks is available at nhstateparks.org.

The mountain's name first appeared on a 17th century map as "Carasarga", an Abenaki or Penacook term roughly translating to "notchpointed mountain of pines". "Kearsarge" was adopted in 1816.

GETTING THERE

Parking is available at Winslow State Park at the end of Kearsarge Mountain Rd. in Wilmot (note that this is a different road than the Kearsarge Mountain Rd. in Warner on the opposite side of the mountain which leads to Rollins State Park) with an entrance fee collected in season. To reach the trailhead from NH 11 in Wilmot, take Kearsarge Valley Rd. south. In 1.5 mi., turn left onto Kearsarge Mountain Rd., then turn right after 1.6 mi. (sign for Winslow State Park) and continue 0.7 mi. to the trailhead and parking area.

RECOMMENDED ROUTE

Winslow Trail, Barlow Trail (Sunapee-Ragged-Kearsarge Greenway)

2.8 mi. counter-clockwise loop with 1,100 ft. elevation gain

This loop over the summit of Mt. Kearsarge uses the steeper, more rugged and direct Winslow Trail for the ascent and the more gradual Barlow Trail for the descent. Winslow has some fairly rough footing in its middle section. Barlow has a few steep ledgy pitches before fully dropping back into the forest and is especially scenic in its upper reaches.

Both trails leave from a kiosk at the upper end of the parking area (here, Winslow Trail is also signed as Northside Trail). From the kiosk, red-blazed Winslow Trail departs right at easy grades at first with decent footing. It crosses a powerline cut sometimes used by backcountry skiers in winter, then begins to climb more steadily. The trail swings right and ascends very steeply past "Halfway Rock" on the right, a small trailside boulder with a faded blue "1/2" painted on it. Above the rock, the trail swings left up a steep pitch via rock steps, then grades ease. It reaches an open ledge on the left with a view to the north at 0.7 mi., then continues a moderate ascent on a winding route over wooded ledges to reach a junction with Barlow Trail on the left at 1.0 mi. Here, both trails overlap and continue to the bare summit ledges and fire tower at 1.1 mi. A large cairn sits atop the southern knob, but the high point is where the tower is. A small dip lined with scrub on one side between the fire tower and southern knob provides protection from the wind.

Backtracking to the trail junction, yellow-blazed Barlow Trail, a section of the Sunapee-Ragged-Kearsarge Greenway, traverses the summit ridge through scrub and over open ledges with fine views, then curves left through bands of scrub and ledge. It passes a unique alpine bog on the left (sign) and then emerges on lofty, open ledges at 1.3 mi., with panoramic views to the north. The trail drops down these ledges to turn sharply left and continues descending moderately with several twists and turns before re-entering the forest for good. It continues an easy to moderate descent, briefly swinging out into the town of Andover, crossing the orange-blazed town line at 1.9 mi., then returns to Wilmot, crossing the border again at 2.1 mi. The trail now descends gradually, crosses a footbridge over a seasonal brook and returns to the trailhead and the junction with Winslow Trail at 2.8 mi.

VIEW HIGHLIGHTS

Views from the bare summit of Mt. Kearsarge are some of the finest in southern New Hampshire, although you have to roam around the summit a bit to get the full 360-degree panorama. Also, being so isolated, most of Kearsarge's views are fairly distant.

Starting due north, the bald dome of Mt. Cardigan can be seen, followed to the right by Mt. Moosilauke, the Kinsmans, Franconia Ridge, Mt. Tecumseh, the Sandwich Range, and Mt. Washington on exceptionally clear days. Further right, the Ossipee and Belknap Ranges can be seen before the eastern vista becomes quite flat, looking far out into Maine. Close by to the southeast is Sawyer Hill, seen beyond Kearsarge's Mission Ridge, which the Rollins State Park auto road traverses.

Directly south are the Mink Hills and Stewarts Peak in Warner, with Mt. Monadnock popping up in the distance to the right. Swinging to the southwest, the view moves over to the smaller peaks of the southwest New

Hampshire region, including Pitcher Mountain and Lovewell Mountain. Looking west, several peaks in southern Vermont become visible, such as Equinox Mountain, Mt. Ascutney, Killington Peak, Bread Loaf Mountain, and Camels Hump, before the vista arrives back at Mt. Cardigan.

ADDITIONAL ROUTES

Rollins Trail
1.2 mi. round-trip with 350 ft. elevation gain
The shortest route on the mountain, unblazed Rollins Trail follows a rugged, rocky former carriage road which departs from the parking area at the top of the Rollins State Park auto road (fee charged in season), 3.5 mi. from the toll gate. From NH 103 in Warner Village, follow Kearsarge Mountain Rd. north for 5.0 mi. to the state park entrance.

Link Trail, Lincoln Trail (Sunapee-Ragged-Kearsarge Greenway)
9.2 mi. round-trip with 2,200 ft. elevation gain
The longest route to the summit with a very steep and rough section near the top, white-blazed Lincoln Trail is a segment of the Sunapee-Ragged-Kearsarge Greenway. In 2018, the trailhead on Kearsarge Valley Rd. was disrupted by a logging operation which was completed in May 2019. Follow markings and signage in this area carefully. Parking is available in a roadside pull-off along Kearsarge Valley Rd., 0.4 mi. north of its junction with North Rd. (AKA "Shingle Mill Corner") in Sutton.

WINTER

In winter, Kearsarge Mountain Rd. is gated 0.7 mi. below the trailhead. Limited plowed parking is available outside the gate. Parking is not allowed along the south side of either Kearsarge Mountain Rd. or adjacent Twist Hill Rd. per posted signs; violators will be ticketed. Total distance for this loop from the gate is 4.2 mi. with 1,520 ft. elevation gain. The access road is often used by skiers and snowmobiles; hikers should keep to the side.

Kearsarge can make for a challenging winter climb depending on conditions and should not be underestimated. Winslow Trail is north-facing and usually collects a lot of thick ice in its middle section early in the season and holds onto it. The iciest pitch is usually the steep section around Halfway Rock and the stone staircase above it, where full crampons may be required. Crampons may also be needed on the bare summit ledges in icy or crusty conditions. In deep snow, Barlow Trail can be difficult to follow on the open ledges near the summit if it has not been broken out as most of the blazes are on the ledges themselves, although there are several cairns in this section. The vistas from Kearsarge's bald summit are spectacular in the clear winter air, but there is little shelter aside from the fire tower foundation and picnic area and high winds often batter the exposed ledges.

Rollins Trail is inaccessible by vehicle in winter as the auto road is gated. It is however accessible by ski and snowmobile and is sometimes used by hikers who opt for the long 3.5 mi. walk from the gate. Limited roadside parking is available where plowing stops at the Rollins State Park entrance.

Limited roadside parking is available for Lincoln Trail at the plowed pull-off along Kearsarge Valley Rd., but the route itself is not frequently hiked in winter and may require long and strenuous trail breaking.

Mt. Monadnock

Elevation: 3,170 ft.
Location: Town of Jaffrey
Map: NHDP map, MSG map, AMC Southern New Hampshire Trail Guide map, MA Mt. Monadnock map, WODC Mt. Monadnock map
Locator map: 22

A hiker takes in the view of the main summit of Mt. Monadnock from Bald Rock.

Often referred to as one of the most hiked mountains in the world — having been climbed since 1725 — Mt. Monadnock offers sweeping views in all directions from its high, lofty summit and open ridgelines, bared by a series of fires in the early 19th century, both of which were intentionally set by farmers. The purpose of the first fire in 1800 was to clear the lower slopes of the mountain for pasture. The second fire has a more colorful history in legend. Sometime around 1820, the peak was allegedly set ablaze again to drive out marauding wolves who the farmers believed were denning in the blowdowns from the first fire. This intense second fire would burn for many days, scorching even the soil down to bare bedrock. The accuracy of this story has been open to interpretation as it is believed that wolves were largely absent from the area at that time.

Monadnock is one of southern New Hampshire's most prominent peaks, rising some 2,000 ft. above the surrounding landscape and 1,000 ft. above any mountain within 30 mi. It is also the highest point in Cheshire County and the Town of Jaffrey. A 2,834 ft. elevation along Pumpelly Ridge is the highest point in Dublin. In addition to a complex network of trails which cover nearly 40 mi. on the mountain itself, three long-distance hiking trails also reach the summit: the 50 mi. Wantastiquet Monadnock Trail from Brattleboro, VT, the 110 mi. Metacomet-Monadnock Trail from the MA/CT border, and the 50 mi. Monadnock-Sunapee Greenway From Mt. Sunapee in Newbury, NH.

Monadnock's popularity, ease of access and close proximity to population centers comes along with an exceptionally high number of visitors (an estimated 100,000+ per year), especially on summer weekends, which may not appeal to everyone. Still, hikers can find relative solitude on some of the peak's lesser-traveled routes. A feature-length documentary film on the mountain and its popular appeal was slated to be released in 2013 but as of 2020, the project is still underway.

A small fire warden's hut was located on the summit from 1911 to 1948. This hut was later repurposed into a snack bar and hiker shelter in 1969, and was ultimately removed in 1972. Today, part of the hut's foundation remains and is often used as a wind shelter. On one wall are numerous etchings from visitors over the centuries.

In the mid-1800s, the mountain was greatly admired by Ralph Waldo Emerson and Henry David Thoreau, both of whom wrote fondly of it. Emerson in particular was a regular visitor and penned one of his famous poems, *"Monadnoc"*, during his experiences here. A ledgy lookout along Cliff Walk, "Emerson's Seat", is named after him. Thoreau was a less frequent visitor, but between 1844 and 1850 he took great interest in the natural features of the mountain, cataloging them extensively. His observations are thought to be one of the first naturalist inventories of Monadnock. He was also honored in name by two natural features: a bog near the summit and the "Thoreau's Seat" viewpoint along Cliff Walk.

It was around this same time that the mountain became a major destination for New Englanders. First constructed in 1864 and later expanded, the Halfway House, a grand hotel, drew visitors from around the region and became the hub for a network of trails leading to scenic destinations on the mountain. The hotel burned to the ground in 1954, but today the Old Half Way House Trail ascends to the clearing where the hotel once stood. Many of the shorter trails which branched out from this location have since been lost to nature, but several still survive.

The broad, rich history of Mt. Monadnock would require a whole book in itself to cover, but one of the most notable figures in the modern history of the mountain is Larry Davis. Davis, a photographer from Jaffrey, made it a personal goal in 1984 to climb Monadnock 84 times that year. He would surpass that by climbing it 106 times. Between 1990 and 2000, he logged a staggering 2,850 consecutive ascents, sometimes ascending more than once a day. Most of these hikes were solo, many in severe weather, and a few were while in less than perfect health (one ascent was made during a bout of food poisoning, and another was done on crutches). As of 2019, it is estimated that he has climbed the mountain over 8,000 times.

Today, the term "monadnock" is used to describe a prominent mountain which rises far above the terrain that surrounds it. Its original meaning is thought to go back to an Abenaki word which roughly translates to "mountain that stands alone". The mountain is also sometimes referred to as Grand Monadnock. Other peaks bearing the Monadnock name are Pack Monadnock and North Pack Monadnock ("Pack" is a Native American world for little) in the Wapack Range, nearby Little Monadnock Mountain in Troy and Monadnock Mountain in Vermont's Northeast Kingdom.

A note regarding dogs: For hikers working the 52WAV list who usually bring their dogs along, you will unfortunately have to leave them at home for this one. Dogs are not allowed anywhere on the mountain or on any trails per state park regulations. This however does not prevent them from completing the list.

GETTING THERE

From NH 101, 0.3 mi. west of the Dublin traffic circle, turn south onto Lake Rd. for 0.4 mi. to start off Pumpelly Trail on the left (sign is set back into the woods). There is very limited roadside parking here; do not block the road. As of 2020, the north side of the road is posted against parking.

RECOMMENDED ROUTE

Pumpelly Trail

8.8 mi. round-trip with 1,950 ft. elevation gain

Out of the myriad of trails on Mt. Monadnock, this is the longest and probably quietest route to the summit but is also incredibly scenic with the second half being mostly out in the open, offering spectacular views along Monadnock's northeast ridge. Grades and footing are easy at first, but become quite steep and rugged in places along the ridge. The first part of this trail is on private property; please stay on the marked trail and obey all posted signage.

From Lake Rd., white-blazed Pumpelly Trail begins along an old woods road, quickly turns right off it, then turns right again onto a second old road at 0.2 mi. The road proceeds at easy grades, gradually diminishing into a footpath. At a sharp left turn at 1.8 mi., the trail abruptly becomes more rough and much steeper as it ascends the rugged north end of the ridge. At the top of the climb, the trail reaches the first of many open ledges where views increase as you climb higher. Pumpelly Trail traverses the ridge over numerous minor ups and downs to pass a junction with Cascade Link at 3.0 mi. (this trail descends to the state park headquarters) on the left, then passes just to the right of Town Line Peak, a 2,884 ft. rocky nubble located near the boundary of Dublin and Jaffrey.

The trail descends to a junction with Spellman Trail (steepest route on the mountain) on the left at 3.7 mi. then climbs past an enormous coffin-like boulder known as the Sarcophagus on the right. The trail continues up the increasingly open ridge, passing a junction on the left with Red Spot Trail at 4.0 mi., descends into a steep-walled, wooded notch which provides a bit of protection from bad weather, then scrambles up the other side. From this point, Pumpelly Trail runs completely in the open (follow blazes and cairns carefully) and reaches the bare summit at 4.4 mi.; a USGS benchmark is at the highest point. Leaving the summit, Pumpelly Trail departs to the east; watch paint markings and cairns carefully to avoid wandering onto a different trail.

VIEW HIGHLIGHTS

With nothing higher around it for many miles, Mt. Monadnock's lofty summit offers unobstructed vistas in every direction, mainly over the relatively flat terrain and smaller hills of southern New Hampshire, but on clear days it is possible to see into all six New England states.

Stretching out to the northeast is the long Pumpelly Ridge, which Pumpelly Trail traverses, with Dublin Lake to the left. Above the ridge and far in the distance is a look out toward the Belknap and Ossipee Ranges and the Blue Hills of Strafford. Further right are the Pawtuckaway Mountains, the Uncanoonucs, and Joe English Hill.

Closer in the foreground is the long ridge of the Wapack Range, stretching from North Pack Monadnock on the left to Mt. Watatic in Massachusetts on the right. Almost directly south is the rocky nubble of Bald Rock (2,626 ft.), one of Monadnock's subpeaks. The other, Monte Rosa (2,515 ft.), is seen to the right of it. To the southeast, Wachusett Mountain rises prominently on the horizon and the skyscrapers of Boston may sometimes be seen, 62 mi. away. Close by to the southwest are the twin summits of Gap Mountain, connected to Monadnock via the Metacomet-Monadnock Trail. Little Monadnock Mountain is visible to the right of Gap, and further west and distant is the highest point in Massachusetts, Mt. Greylock.

Swinging more to the west, several major peaks in southern Vermont come into view, including Stratton Mountain, Mt. Equinox, and Bromley and Dorset Mountains. The view northwest looks out to Killington Peak, Mts. Abraham and Ellen, Mt. Mansfield, and Camel's Hump in the Green Mountains. The prominent Mt. Ascutney can be seen closer in. Looking north, Silver Mountain, Croydon Peak, Lovewell Mountain, and Mt. Kearsarge are seen, then the view moves around toward the White Mountains to Mt. Moosilauke, the Kinsman Range, Franconia Ridge, the Sandwich Range, and Mt. Washington, 105 mi. in the distance.

ADDITIONAL ROUTES

White Dot Trail, White Cross Trail

4.0 mi. counter-clockwise loop with 1,800 ft. elevation gain

Starting and ending at the main state park entrance on Poole Rd. in Jaffrey (per person fee charged year-round), this is the most direct route to and from the summit, making it the most popular and heavily-used. You will definitely not be alone here. Sections of these white-blazed trails are quite steep with several scrambles. To reach Poole Rd., take Dublin Rd. north for

1.2 mi. from NH 124 in Jaffrey or Upper Jaffrey Rd. south for 4.9 mi. from NH 101 in Dublin.

Dublin Trail
4.2 mi. round-trip with 1,800 ft. elevation gain
This northwestern approach (a segment of the Monadnock-Sunapee Greenway) is one of the oldest routes on the mountain, dating back to around 1840, and is considered the easiest ascent to the summit by Monadnock standards. It is blazed in white. From Jim's Junction near Dublin Peak, Dublin Trail coincides with Marlboro Trail for the final 0.2 mi. to the summit. It begins at a trailhead on Old Troy Rd., 1.9 mi. south of Old Marlborough Rd. in Dublin (the last mile of this road is rough and narrow).

Marlboro Trail
4.2 mi. round-trip with 1,850 ft. elevation gain
This sole route to the summit from the west, blazed in white, dates back to around 1825 and has some very rough and steep climbing in areas. The last 0.2 mi. to the summit coincides with Dublin Trail. It begins at a trailhead at the end of Shaker Farm Rd. South off NH 124, 5.1 mi. east of NH 101 in Marlborough. The last half of this road is rough and often not passable in mud season but may be improved in the future by SPNHF for timber harvests. High-clearance is recommended.

Old Half Way House Trail, White Arrow Trail
4.6 mi. round-trip with 1,700 ft. elevation gain
This heavily-traveled route from the Old Toll Rd. trailhead in Jaffrey on NH 124 (per person fee charged in season) is steep, rough and exposed in its upper half with several potentially difficult scrambles, but offers stunning scenery for the hard work. Old Half Way House Trail is unmarked but easy to follow; White Arrow Trail is blazed in white. To reach the trailhead, take NH 124 east for 7.1 mi. from NH 101 in Dublin.

White Dot Trail, Cascade Link, Spellman Trail, Pumpelly Trail, Red Spot Trail
5.3 mi. counter-clockwise loop with 1,780 ft. elevation gain
This is one of the more rugged routes on the mountain, ascending to Pumpelly Ridge via Spellman Trail and descending via Red Spot. Spellman is the steepest route on Monadnock, climbing 600 ft. in 0.6 mi. Most of this

gain is in the middle section, which requires hand over foot scrambling with some exposure. This trail is not recommended for descent or if wet or icy. Most trails are blazed in white except for Cascade Link which is marked yellow and Red Spot Trail which is marked red. This loop begins and ends at the state park headquarters on Poole Rd.

OVERNIGHT OPTIONS

Monadnock State Park provides two campgrounds. The first is located near the state park headquarters at the end of Poole Rd. in Jaffrey. In summer, it is reserved for youth camping only. In late fall through early spring, it is available to adults and families on a first come, first served basis. For more information, call 603-532-8862. Gilson Pond Campground, with a total of 40 sites, is located off Dublin Rd. in Jaffrey. More information is available at reserveamerica.com. Dogs are not allowed at either campground and camping is prohibited elsewhere on the mountain.

WINTER

Mt. Monadnock is frequently climbed in winter, but not so much via Pumpelly Trail. Parking along Lake Rd. may be non-existent with high snow banks, and a winter trek along this route could involve long, strenuous trail breaking.

As much of the upper mountain is bare ledge, conditions can become quite icy and full crampons may be required. Monadnock's lack of surrounding terrain and exposure above treeline offers little protection from the wind, and in poor visibility it can be difficult to initially follow the various trails down from the summit. While relatively low compared to the White Mountains, Mt. Monadnock can be a formidable and potentially dangerous peak in winter and should not be underestimated. In windy conditions, some shelter at the summit can be found in the foundation of the former fire warden's hut but this should not be relied on for emergencies.

The most accessible and most traveled route in winter is the White Dot/White Cross loop, where plowed parking is available at the state park headquarters on Poole Rd. In lean snow years, this route can be very icy and combined with steep grades on White Dot Trail, conditions can be challenging. Also leaving from this trailhead is the loop using Spellman, Pumpelly and Red Spot Trails. Spellman Trail is not recommended for winter use and could be potentially dangerous in icy or loose snow conditions.

The Old Toll Rd. parking area is partially plowed with room for several vehicles. The going is usually easy up to the Halfway House site, but beyond there White Arrow Trail also collects a lot of ice, especially along one steep scramble. The section of trail above treeline can also be tricky due to steep climbing below the summit.

Old Troy Rd. is plowed only as far as the large farm about a mile before the Dublin trailhead, so this route is usually inaccessible in winter. If snow depths are light, high clearance vehicles may be able to make it to the trailhead with care. Due to these access issues, Dublin Trail is not frequently hiked in winter and trail breaking will likely be required. The upper section of Dublin Trail along Monadnock's northwest ridge is completely out in the open and fully exposed to the weather.

Marlboro Trail is lesser-used in winter, as Shaker Farm Rd. South is not plowed all the way to the trailhead. High-clearance vehicles may be able to make it if snow depths are thin.

Additional plowed parking is also available at the entrance to Gilson Pond Campground, which provides access to Birchtoft Trail. This parking area is along Dublin Rd. in Jaffrey, 2.7 mi. north of NH 124.

On the eastern slopes of the mountain is an additional 8 mi. network of trails maintained for Nordic skiing, marked with blue blazes. These trails are ungroomed and require a minimum of 12 in. of natural snow cover. All trails are classified as moderate, but some do have steeper sections and sharp turns better suited for more advanced skiers. It is recommended that novice skiers use the Gilson Pond Campground loop and picnic area trails. Equipment rentals are not available so skiers must provide all of their own gear. A map of the trails and more information is available at nhstateparks.org.

Sunset on Mt. Monadnock.

Lakes Region/Sandwich Range/Waterville Valley

Hedgehog Mountain

Elevation: 2,543 ft.
Location: Town of Albany
Map: WODC map, AMC map - Crawford Notch/Sandwich Range
Locator map: 05

Hedgehog Mountain's East Ledges and neighboring Mt. Passaconaway.

Hedgehog Mountain, next door neighbor to fellow 52WAV peak Potash Mountain, was the lowest peak on the list until Mt. Percival was added, but it's no slouch when it comes to excellent views from the East Ledges — the largest expanse of open rock on the mountain — Allen's Ledge, and various points along UNH Trail, the sole route over the peak.

Hedgehog get its name from dark spruces along its ridgecrest and prickly appearance from afar. This Hedgehog is sometimes referred to as "Albany Hedgehog", to differentiate it from the unofficially named "Wonalancet Hedgehog", a spur of Mt. Passaconaway, 3 mi. to the south.

Allen's Ledge bears the name of Jack Allen, a hunter, trapper, guide, teller of tales, and Civil War veteran, who frequented the Albany Intervale area in the late 1800s and early 1900s.

GETTING THERE

Parking is available in a large lot which provides access to UNH Trail, Downes Brook Trail, and Mt. Potash Trail in Albany, located at the end of an access road (sign for all three trails) off NH 112 (Kancamagus Highway), 2.0 mi. west of Bear Notch Rd.

RECOMMENDED ROUTE
UNH Trail, Allen's Ledge Spur
4.8 mi. clockwise loop with 1,400 ft. elevation gain
UNH Trail allows for a loop hike over Hedgehog, visiting the scenic East Ledges on the way in, and a quick side trip to the Allen's Ledge viewpoint on the way back. Grades vary from easy to moderate with generally good footing along the loop, although there are a few steep and eroded sections.

From the parking area, head up a wide gravel road past a gate and quickly bear left onto yellow-blazed UNH Trail (sign), which runs level along the grade of the old Swift River Logging Railroad. At 0.2 mi., the trail turns right off the railroad grade and onto a section relocated in 2012 (the former route continues ahead as a cross-country ski trail and is closed to hiking), and ascends at easy to moderate grades to a junction at 0.8 mi. with the eastern section of the UNH Trail loop.

Turn left here and descend on a newer section of footpath at easy grades, then at 1.1 mi. turn right onto the original route of UNH Trail to begin a moderate climb, ascending over a small knoll, then dipping to cross White Brook at 1.3 mi. Past the brook, the trail ascends through an area of boulders, then makes its way up the slope via a series of switchbacks. At 1.8 mi., the trail turns right with a view across Albany Intervale on the left, then climbs with one short scramble to arrive at the East Ledges at 2.0 mi. Use caution atop these high cliffs and keep children and pets close.

The trail exits the ledges back into the woods and descends to traverse the edge of a high cliff (use caution), followed by open ledges with Mt. Passaconaway looming ahead, and the summit of Hedgehog up on the right. At the far end of the ledges, the trail again enters the woods and descends along rough footing through boulders, passes large cliffs on the right, then ascends steeply through a series of short switchbacks with several scrambles;

watch blazes carefully in this section. At 2.9 mi., the trail passes over the summit (high point is marked by faded yellow X on ledge), and nearby ledges provide good views.

From the summit, the trail turns left, then bears right where a side path on the left leads to an outlook. Descend easily through an open stretch with views north, then steeply with rough footing to a junction at 3.6 mi. with a side path on the right, which leads to a view of Mt. Chocorua. Where UNH Trail turns sharply left at 3.7 mi., a side trail on the right (sign: "Allen's Ledge") climbs steeply over roots for 60 yds. up to Allen's Ledge. Just before reaching the main ledge, a short side path leaves left and descends to a lower ledge with a better vista.

The main trail descends to cross a brook then turns right to join an old logging road, which it follows back to the loop junction at 3.9 mi. Bear left to descend 0.8 mi. back to the trailhead and parking area.

VIEW HIGHLIGHTS

East Ledges: Hedgehog's East Ledges are perhaps the most scenic spot on the mountain, with a nearly 180-degree panorama featuring a close look into the Sandwich Range. Highlights from left to right include Bear Mountain, Table Mountain, Big Attitash Mountain, the Moat Range, and Mt. Chocorua and the Sisters, followed by the lumpy ridge of Mt. Paugus. Perhaps the most impressive view is looking up to towering Mt. Passaconaway, less than two miles away, with its lower spurs dropping off to the left. Directly below the East Ledges and stretching out to many of these points is the valley of Oliverian Brook.

Summit view: The summit of Hedgehog is not completely open, but various ledges around the summit provide views in most directions. A ledge on the northwest side offers a standup view west and north. Seen from this perspective is a long look up Downes Brook Valley to the rolling ridge of the Sleepers, with the Tripyramids to their right. Extending from the Sleepers is a long ridge leading to Hedgehog's neighbor Potash Mountain. More distant peaks in view are sections of Franconia Ridge, the Hancocks, Mt. Carrigain, the Bonds, the Twins, and the Nancy and Willey Ranges.

Exploring ledges to the south opens up views to the heart of the eastern Sandwich Range, including Mts. Chocorua and Paugus. To the right is Paugus Pass, located at the head of Oliverian Brook Valley. In the distance beyond the pass, peaks in the Ossipee Range can be seen, including Mt.

Shaw. High on the right and watching over everything is the huge mass of Mt. Passaconaway, just a mile and a half away and rising 1,500 ft. above.

North outlook: About 0.1 mi. north of the summit along UNH Trail is an open ledgy area with good views to the north. The vista here takes in Mt. Huntington, the Hancocks, Mt. Carrigain, the Bonds, South Twin Mountain, and Mt. Guyot. Lying low below Carrigain is the ledgy Greens Cliff. The view swings around to the Nancy and Willey Ranges, then onto the southern Presidential Range peaks of Mts. Webster and Jackson, extending right to Mts. Monroe and Washington. Seen below Washington are Mt. Crawford, Stairs Mountain, and rust-colored Mt. Resolution.

Allen's Ledge: This open ledge offers excellent perspectives northeast and east over the Albany Intervale. The widest views are reached by carefully descending left along the ledges 30 yds. to a flat shelf atop a cliff. Highlights from this vantage point include Mt. Carrigain on the far left, followed by the Nancy Range and Mt. Tremont. Further right are Iron Mountain and Black Mountain in Jackson. The long ridge of the Moat Range also comes into view, as do the Three Sisters, Mt. Chocorua, and Mt. Paugus.

ADDITIONAL ROUTES

Hedgehog Mountain summit via UNH Trail (western section)
3.8 mi. round-trip with 1,250 ft. elevation gain
This shorter option allows for an out-and-back visit to the summit of Hedgehog, but skips the East Ledges.

Allen's Ledge via UNH Trail (western section), Allen's Ledge Spur
2.2 mi. round-trip with 650 ft. elevation gain
For hikers with little time or simply seeking a shorter objective with great views, this out-and-back trip to Allen's Ledge is a good option.

East Ledges via UNH Trail (eastern section)
4.0 mi. round-trip with 1,150 ft. elevation gain
This fine out-and-back trek leads to Hedgehog's East Ledges and their spectacular views to the south. This route does not reach the summit.

WINTER

Hedgehog is an excellent winter hike, with mostly moderate grades and a few steep pitches along the way. Crampons may be needed on the East Ledges if conditions are crusty or icy; stay back from the edges. The parking area is accessible in winter, but may not be plowed immediately after a storm.

Jennings Peak

Elevation: 3,493 ft.
Location: Town of Waterville Valley
Map: WODC map, WVAIA map, AMC map - Crawford Notch/Sandwich Range
Locator map: 08

Peering down into the valley of Smarts Brook from Jennings Peak.

Jennings Peak is a sharp spire along a northwest ridge of Sandwich Dome and is prominently seen from many areas, especially while driving east along NH 49 toward Waterville Valley, and from the first ledges along the Welch-Dickey loop. Its summit is mostly wooded aside from a large cliff which offers excellent views south and east over Smarts Brook Valley.

Jennings is also no stranger to White Mountain air disasters. On March 19, 1966, a Cessna aircraft with a lone pilot crashed into the peak at around 2,800 ft. The plane was traveling from Burlington, VT to Portland, ME and was reported missing when it never arrived. Despite an intensive search, the wreckage would remain undiscovered until a hiker stumbled across it six weeks later.

The peak was named after "Captivity" Jennings, a baby girl born in Canada after her mother was kidnapped by Indians and taken there. Both mother and daughter were later returned home after a ransom was paid. Jennings Peak was also once known as Dennisons Peak, the name of an early hunter in the Waterville Valley area.

GETTING THERE

Parking is available in a small lot for Sandwich Mountain Trail off NH 49 in Waterville Valley, located 10.2 mi. east of Exit 28 off I-93 and 0.4 mi. west of Tripoli Rd.

RECOMMENDED ROUTE

Sandwich Mountain Trail, Jennings Peak Spur
6.0 mi. round-trip with 2,100 ft. elevation gain
This route provides a steep ascent up to the ridge and Noon Peak viewpoint, followed by an easier traverse to the spur trail to Jennings. The last 0.1 mi. of the spur trail is steep and rough.

Yellow-blazed Sandwich Mountain Trail first descends steeply to cross Drakes Brook, which may be difficult at times of high water. To avoid this crossing, walk back out to the highway and head west, crossing the bridge over the brook. Just past the bridge, turn left onto a rough herd path on the opposite side of the brook and continue for 0.1 mi. back to the trail. The entrance to this herd path has been marked by flagging in recent years.

From the brook, the trail first ascends moderately, entering the Sandwich Range Wilderness at 0.6 mi., then very steeply with alternating easier sections, to the northern end of the ridge and a view ledge on the left, with a vista east and northeast toward the Osceolas, the Hancocks, the Tripyramids, and Mt. Carrigain. This is a good spot for a breather after the stiff climb. Past this outlook, the trail descends slightly, then climbs over Noon Peak (2,976 ft.), with another excellent view ledge on the left just past the summit. It then descends briefly and ascends gradually along the beautiful ridge, passing through an expansive ledgy area, to a junction with Drakes Brook Trail on the left at 2.7 mi., and then a junction with Jennings Peak Spur on the right 0.1 mi. further, where Sandwich Mountain Trail swings left.

This 0.2 mi. spur trail ascends easily at first, then becomes quite steep and rugged with some minor scrambling, passes an outlook on the left, then reaches the summit of Jennings Peak and the outlook ledges atop a high cliff (use caution with children and pets or if wet as this cliff drops straight down) just past the wooded high point.

VIEW HIGHLIGHTS

Main summit ledge: Jennings' clifftop viewpoint provides a unique perspective over the secluded Smarts Brook Valley far below. The dominant feature from this vista is the enormous mass of Sandwich Dome just a mile away, and its broad ridge which Sandwich Mountain Trail traverses. To the right of the Dome, a long ridge extends over one of Sandwich's two Black Mountains, traversed by the Algonquin Trail.

As the ridge dips to the horizon, Mts. Monadnock and Kearsarge come into the view in the far distance with the Campton Range closer in. Just shy of west is Mt. Cardigan, with Vermont's Mt. Ascutney further out. Stinson Mountain is about due west and under Stinson, lining one edge of the Smarts Brook Valley, is the prominent Aceton Ridge, with ledgy Sachem Peak poking up at the eastern end. This rocky nubble mimics the shape of Jennings Peak from some angles, and has also been referred to as a miniature Mt. Chocorua.

Southeast outlook: This view ledge just before the summit offers wide views to the Sandwich Range. Starting on the right at Sandwich Dome is a look down into the upper valley of Smarts Brook with the northern Flat Mountain and Mts. Whiteface and Passaconaway beyond. To the left of Passaconaway, the Sleeper Ridge extends over to the Tripyramids with the South Slide fully visible. Snows Mountain in Waterville Valley is seen below the slide, and to the left of North Tripyramid, a long ridge stretches to Scaur Peak. Over this ridge, the Carters and Wildcats come into view, and Mt. Washington rises just to the left of Scaur Peak over remote Livermore Pass.

Mts. Clay and Jefferson appear to the left of Washington with Mts. Monroe, Franklin and Eisenhower below. Seen under the Presidentials is the Nancy Range — Mts. Bemis, Nancy, Anderson and Lowell — with Mts. Pierce and Jackson beyond Lowell. Mt. Carrigain towers to the left of the Presidentials followed by Mt. Field and the Hancocks.

ADDITIONAL ROUTES

Sandwich Mountain Trail, Jennings Peak Spur, Drakes Brook Trail
8.2 mi. counter-clockwise loop with 2,950 ft. elevation gain
Many hikers do this popular loop which visits both Jennings Peak and Sandwich Dome. This route requires crossing Drakes Brook twice; both of

these crossings may be difficult or impassable in high water. Both trails leave from the Sandwich Mountain Trail parking area.

Smarts Brook Trail, Sandwich Mountain Trail, Jennings Peak Spur
11.6 mi. round-trip with 2,750 ft. elevation gain
This longer western approach starting from a trailhead on NH 49 in Thornton, 4.0 mi. east of NH 175, ascends at easy to moderate grades up the beautiful and secluded Smarts Brook Valley alongside glacial boulders and cascades to the ridge between Jennings Peak and Sandwich Dome. This is a quieter alternative to the busier Sandwich Mountain Trail approach.

WINTER
Jennings can be a strenuous snowshoe trek due to the steep grind up to the ridge. The crossing of Drakes Brook can be difficult if not well frozen. In such cases, the bypass route should be used. Crampons may be needed on the short, steep ascent to Jennings Peak and on the summit ledges if icy. The parking area is not always plowed reliably or fully and space may be more limited. Do not block access to the adjacent electrical substation.

Plowed parking is available at the Smarts Brook trailhead, which is accessed mainly for local ski trails, but the hiking trail itself is lesser-used in winter and may likely require long, strenuous trail breaking.

Middle Sister

Elevation: 3,340 ft.
Location: Town of Albany
Map: WODC map, AMC map - Crawford Notch/Sandwich Range
Locator map: 10

Middle Sister, as its name suggests, is the central peak along the triple-bumped Three Sisters ridge, extending northeast from Mt. Chocorua. Along with siblings First Sister (3,354 ft.; high point of the ridge) and the minor bump of Third Sister, all three combine to offer stellar views. The walk over the open ridge of the Three Sisters is one of the best traverses in the White Mountains. Middle Sister can be climbed on its own or combined with a loop hike over Chocorua, and offers a quieter alternative to that peak's summer weekend crowds.

A fire lookout station occupied the summit from 1927 to 1948, the stone foundation of which remains today. This station was originally intended to be located on Mt. Chocorua to replace an earlier 1911 station there, but strong opposition by Chocorua Mountain Club, AMC and SPNHF resulted in it being moved over to Middle Sister. Unlike typical tall fire towers, the Middle Sister station was intentionally constructed to be short and squat so it would not be obtrusive when seen from the valleys below. During World War II, the station was staffed by experienced hiker Elizabeth Sampson, part of a group of women recruited by USFS to serve as fire lookouts. This group was known as the WOOFs, or Women Observers of the Forest. A horse trail which was originally constructed to access the station from Champney Falls Trail is the current Champney Falls Cut-Off. Today, a small USFS radio repeater is also located near the station's foundation and steps.

The Three Sisters were originally named Bald Mountain, an obvious reference to their bare summits and a common name for treeless peaks in New Hampshire. That name still exists for a ledgy spur at the end of Mt. Chocorua's southern ridge which the Hammond Trail traverses.

Jagged ledges and fire tower relics atop Middle Sister.

GETTING THERE

Parking and restrooms are available in a large lot for Champney Falls Trail/Bolles Trail (WMNF fee area) along NH 112 (Kancamagus Highway) in Albany, 1.6 mi. east of Bear Notch Rd. and 10.6 mi. west of NH 16 in Conway.

RECOMMENDED ROUTE

Champney Falls Trail, Champney Falls Cut-Off, Middle Sister Trail
7.0 mi. round-trip with 2,100 ft. elevation gain

Yellow-blazed Champney Falls Trail offers easy to moderate grades and mainly follows an old logging road up the valley before transitioning to several long switchbacks which are rougher and rockier. The trail is eroded in many areas from heavy use. Champney Falls Cut-Off provides a 0.3 mi. shortcut to Middle Sister, bypassing the climb over First Sister (also a wonderful destination on its own).

From the parking area, Champney Falls Trail enters the woods (sign) and immediately crosses Twin Brook, which may be difficult at high water (a former footbridge here was washed out in a storm; if unable to cross, walk back out to the highway, turn right to cross the bridge over the brook, then turn right again onto an old logging road and follow it a short distance to rejoin the trail on the other side). The trail bears right onto an old logging road and ascends at very easy grades, quickly passing a junction with Bolles Trail on the right. Easy walking continues as the trail swings left at 0.5 mi. to make the first of two crossings of Champney Brook (may be difficult at times of high water; a former relocation which turned right here and avoided both crossings was closed in 2019 and the trail was restored to its former route). On the other side of the brook, the trail swings right and ascends easily to cross the brook a second time, and then passes the other end of the former relocation on the right at 0.7 mi. The trail continues ascending at easy to moderate grades to the lower junction of Champney Falls Loop on the left at 1.4 mi. See the Mt. Chocorua section for the description of this loop.

From the junction, Champney Falls Trail ascends more moderately above the falls over sections of older rock steps with many water bars, climbing over one slippery ledge. At 1.7 mi., the upper end of Champney Falls loop rejoins on the left. The main trail continues a moderate climb up through the valley, where footing is eroded and rocky in places. Look up to the left for glimpses of Middle and First Sisters through the trees. The trail traverses a particularly rocky section with a seasonal waterfall on the right, then turns sharply right to enter the first of several long but never steep switchbacks, where footing becomes rougher and awkward on side-sloping ledges. At the fourth switchback at 3.0 mi., it reaches a junction with Champney Falls Cut-Off which continues straight ahead as Champney Falls Trail turns right.

Lightly used Champney Falls Cut-Off, blazed in yellow, ascends easily at first, then moderately, along the west side of First Sister, crosses open ledges with views north, then swings right to arrive at the saddle between Middle and First Sisters at 3.3 mi. Turn left onto Middle Sister Trail (also blazed in yellow) for a moderate 0.1 mi. climb to the summit.

VIEW HIGHLIGHTS

The panorama from Middle Sister's summit is on par with that of Mt. Chocorua although slightly lower, but the views are very similar. See the Mt. Chocorua section for details. Unlike Chocorua, it takes a little bit of wandering around the summit ledges to get the full 360-degree view. What is impressive from Middle Sister, and First Sister especially, is the view back to the sharp, majestic horn of Chocorua. In addition, Mt. Moosilauke, not quite visible from Chocorua, is clearly seen from Middle Sister.

ADDITIONAL ROUTES

Piper Trail, Nickerson Ledge Trail, Carter Ledge Trail, Middle Sister Trail, Champney Falls Trail

7.1 mi. counter-clockwise loop with 2,750 ft. elevation gain

Steep and rugged in places with several difficult scrambles, this very scenic yellow-blazed route allows for a loop hike over Carter Ledge and the Three Sisters ridge with stunning views along the way, starting and ending at the Piper Trail parking area off NH 16 in Albany, 6.2 mi. south of the eastern terminus of NH 112 (Kancamagus Highway).

Piper Trail, Middle Sister Trail, Carter Ledge Trail

8.8 mi. clockwise loop with 2,800 ft. elevation gain

This is a variation on the route described above, using Piper Trail for the ascent and the entire Middle Sister Trail and eastern section of Carter Ledge Trail for the descent. It begins at the Piper trailhead but ends at White Ledge Campground a bit further north on NH 16, so a short car spot is needed.

OVERNIGHT OPTIONS

Hikers doing a loop over Middle Sister and Mt. Chocorua can utilize either Camp Penacook Shelter or Jim Liberty Cabin. See the Mt. Chocorua section for details.

WINTER

Much like neighboring Mt. Chocorua, Middle Sister can be a challenging hike in winter, especially along the open summit ledges which are fully exposed to the weather and may be icy. Crampons should be carried. Route-finding along these areas may also be challenging as the yellow blazes are painted on the ledges. The easy to moderate grades of Champney Falls Trail make it ideal for snowshoeing although in lean snow years the trail can be quite icy. The crossing of Twin Brook at the start is usually well frozen. Champney Falls Trail is heavily-traveled in winter and is usually broken out quickly after a storm but the Cut-Off and Middle Sister Trail may not be. The parking area along NH 112 is plowed but can be icy.

On the south side of the mountain, the Piper trailhead parking area is not plowed by USFS, but in recent years an adjacent resident has been plowing out room for hikers to park on their property for a fee. Parking is prohibited at Davies General Store on NH 16. Piper Trail is traveled in winter but less so than the Champney Falls approach. The entrance road for White Ledge Campground is not plowed, but sometimes there is limited room to park near the gate or at nearby pull-offs along the highway. Carter Ledge Trail is not recommended in winter due to the steep scrambles in its upper section, the trickiest of which could be dangerous in icy conditions. Middle Sister Trail from the campground is rarely hiked in winter.

Mt. Chocorua

Elevation: 3,490 ft.
Location: Town of Albany
Map: WODC map, AMC map - Crawford Notch/Sandwich Range
Locator map: 14

Mt. Chocorua is the most majestic of the Sandwich Range peaks, whose striking summit cone offers panoramic vistas in all directions. The mountain has been highly revered by artists, poets and writers since the early 1800s.

Artistic luminaries like Henry Wadsworth Longfellow, Thomas Cole, Lucy Larcom, and Benjamin Champney have extolled the virtues and beauty of Mt. Chocorua and its surrounding landscape.

Hikers have been ascending the peak since around the same time. The mountain is blessed with over 35 miles of trails, too numerous to cover in complete detail here. Most routes involve significant climbing on par with much higher peaks, and the final stretch above treeline is completely exposed to the elements. While the ascent to Chocorua is not easy, its famous views make it a very popular destination and well worth the effort. With that comes the crowds. On nice summer weekends, the parking area can be overflowing and the main routes can be very busy — don't expect to be alone at the summit. However, depending on how you time it and which route you choose, you can still approach the peak in relative solitude.

Around 1815, a large fire swept over the mountain, burning the upper reaches down to bare rock, the evidence of which we still see today. In 1911, a fire lookout station was established on the summit. This was not a typical fire tower, but rather a simple table that the observer would place his map and alidade (device that allows one to sight a distant object and use the line of sight to indicate the location on a map) on. During the time this station was in operation, another fire broke out in 1915 between Mts. Paugus and Chocorua on land that had been heavily logged. The Chocorua station remained in service until 1926, when it was moved next door to Middle Sister. See the Middle Sister section for details.

Along Piper Trail near the summit of Mt. Chocorua.

The mountain is steeped in rich history, but one of Chocorua's wilder stories occurred in 1915 when the Peak House was quite literally blown off the mountain during a late autumn windstorm. This hostelry, originally built in 1892, featured a kitchen, dining room, bedrooms, a bridal suite and a parlor for entertainment. The structure was built in a very exposed location along today's Liberty Trail about a half mile below the summit. In an attempt to protect against harsh weather, the Peak House was physically chained to the ledges, but this didn't keep the building from being blown from its moorings on September 26. The next day, climbers discovered the remains of the building and its contents scattered across the slopes — the broken chains were still affixed to the ledges. Fortunately, the Peak House had closed for the season just a few days earlier so there were no injuries. The Jim Liberty Cabin is located on the site today, and it too is also chained to the mountain to hopefully avoid the same fate.

This section wouldn't be complete without mentioning one of the greatest figures in White Mountains lore. Chocorua was a Pigwacket (Pequawket) chief who allegedly met his fate at the summit of the mountain sometime during the 1700s. How exactly that came to be depends on which version of the legend you go with.

One account states that Chocorua fell to his death by falling off a high rock while hunting. This interpretation was later published in an 1825 poem by Henry Wadsworth Longfellow entitled *"Jeckoyva"*.

Another account suggests he was murdered by a bounty hunter. Chocorua pleaded for his life with the hunter but he was unrelenting. Before he could take action, the chief defiantly jumped to his death from the mountain after laying a curse on the land.

The more widely circulated story involves a tale of revenge and a father's grief. The legend states that Chocorua was away in Quebec visiting relatives, and in his absence, his son died after accidentally ingesting poison originally intended for nuisance foxes. Upon the chief's return, he was so enraged at the settlers who were supposed to be caring for his son that he killed the wife and children of a man named Cornelius Campbell in retaliation. Campbell and several friends in return pursued Chocorua to the summit, gunning him down in cold blood.

The amount of truth contained in any of these accounts is open to interpretation, but the legend of Chocorua is one of the greatest tales in the rich and colorful history of the peak. Today, visitors to the summit can view

"Cow Rock", a large boulder protruding from the east side. It was from this rock that Chocorua allegedly jumped to his death.

The Chocorua name was applied to the mountain as early as 1755 and appeared on Jeremy Belknap's 1791 map of New Hampshire. Philip Carrigain called it "Corway Peak Mt." on his 1816 map. A nearby lake, river and a village within Tamworth also bear the Chocorua name.

GETTING THERE
Parking and restrooms are available in a large lot for Champney Falls Trail/Bolles Trail (WMNF fee area) along NH 112 (Kancamagus Highway) in Albany, 1.6 mi. east of Bear Notch Rd. and 10.6 mi. west of NH 16 in Conway.

RECOMMENDED ROUTE
Champney Falls Trail, Champney Falls Loop, Piper Trail
7.6 mi. round-trip with 2,250 ft. elevation gain

Of the many trails to Mt. Chocorua, this route is probably the easiest and most traveled with mostly easy to moderate grades aside from the steep pitches and scrambling above treeline. Yellow-blazed Champney Falls Trail mainly follows an old logging road up the valley before transitioning to several long switchbacks which are rougher and rockier. The trail is eroded in many areas from heavy use. This trail also provides access to a short loop path which visits Champney and Pitcher Falls, both impressive at times of high water. The short section of Piper Trail from the ridge to the summit climbs easily until treeline, where it may be difficult to follow on the open ledges due to sparse markings. In recent years, cairns have also been built to guide the way.

From the parking area, Champney Falls Trail enters the woods (sign) and immediately crosses Twin Brook, which may be difficult at high water (a former footbridge here was washed out in a storm; if unable to cross, walk back out to the highway, turn right to cross the bridge over the brook, then turn right again onto an old logging road and follow it a short distance to rejoin the trail). The trail bears right onto an old logging road and ascends at very easy grades, quickly passing a junction with Bolles Trail on the right. Easy walking continues as the trail swings left at 0.5 mi. to make the first of two crossings of Champney Brook (may be difficult at times of high water; a former relocation which turned right here and avoided both crossings was closed in 2019 and the trail was restored to its former route). On the other side of the brook, the trail swings right and ascends easily to cross the brook a second time, and then passes the other end of the former relocation on the right at 0.7 mi. The trail continues ascending at easy to moderate grades to the lower junction of Champney Falls Loop on the left at 1.4 mi.

This 0.4 mi. loop path descends easily to the base of cascading Champney Falls, named in honor of 19th century artist Benjamin Champney. Champney was a prolific painter whose name became synonymous with White Mountains art of the time. To the left about 200 ft. is a high rock wall over which Pitcher Falls tumbles. Both falls are best experienced in spring or after heavy rain events. From the bottom of Champney Falls, the path ascends steeply up a recently reconstructed section on stone steps, and then alongside the upper end of the cascades on the left. Above here, the loop path swings right and climbs easily back to a junction with Champney Falls Trail, 0.3 mi. above the point where it departed.

From the upper junction with the falls loop, Champney Falls Trail ascends moderately up through the valley over sections of older rock steps with many water bars, where footing is eroded and rocky in places. Look up to the left for glimpses of Middle and First Sisters through the trees. The trail traverses a particularly rocky section with a seasonal waterfall on the right, then turns sharply right to enter the first of several long but never steep switchbacks where footing becomes rougher and awkward on side-sloping ledges. At the fourth switchback at 3.1 mi. is a junction with Champney Falls Cut-Off which leaves on the left.

Champney Falls Trail turns sharply right and continues a moderate climb through switchbacks. In the final switchback, a short side path on the right (sign: "View") hops up one minor scramble to a large open ledge with wide views north and an interesting look up to First Sister. Experienced "ledgewhackers" may want to venture further southwest along these ledges, being mindful to not trample vegetation, where views are higher and more open. The main trail now ascends easily with a few twists and turns to a junction on the left with Middle Sister Trail, and then it ends at a junction with Piper Trail at 3.3 mi.

Turn right onto Piper Trail for mostly easy walking with a brief ascent to a junction with West Side Trail at 3.5 mi., a bad weather route which bypasses the summit. Turn left to continue on Piper Trail and shortly break out above treeline. Here, the trail scrambles up exposed ledges with tremendous views behind you back to the Three Sisters and the White Mountains beyond. Follow yellow blazes painted on the ledges and cairns carefully in this section. Continue a winding ascent across the open ridgecrest with several ups and downs, eventually dropping to the west of it, to reach a junction with Brook Trail on the right at 3.8 mi. Scramble up a steep ledge (taller hikers have an advantage here) and turn left to enter an exposed, rocky gully which scrambles steeply to the summit; use caution if wet. The highest point and a USGS benchmark are on a large table-like ledge on the left.

VIEW HIGHLIGHTS

The views from the top of Chocorua's sharp horn are some of the best in the White Mountains, and these views have been celebrated for as long as people have been climbing here. A completely detailed guide of everything you can see from Chocorua would fill an entire book unto itself but below are some of the highlights.

Starting with the view directly north, the most prominent feature is the Three Sisters ridge, just a half mile away. The former fire lookout foundation on Middle Sister can be seen on the summit. The Wildcats and Carters with deep Carter Notch are seen to the distant right over it. Further right and far in the distance is the Mahoosuc Range, West Royce Mountain, and Eastman Mountain in Evans Notch, along with the cone of Kearsarge North. Under Kearsarge is the Moat Range. Next up is Black Cap and Middle Mountain in Conway, followed by a wide expanse of peaks and hills in southern Maine, as the view turns east. Moving around to the south and southeast, Effingham's Green Mountain comes into view along with the Ossipee and Belknap Ranges. Almost directly south-southeast, the Atlantic Ocean may be visible on very clear days with the right light. Nearby to the south is Chocorua Lake (one of the most iconic views of the mountain is from this lake) with Ossipee Lake beyond.

On exceptionally clear days, a very distant Mt. Monadnock can be seen to the southwest along with Mt. Kearsarge and Ragged Mountain. Mt. Israel is just about directly southwest, with Mt. Cardigan to its right. Swinging around to the west is a look straight down the Sandwich Range with the lumpy Mt. Paugus a short distance away. Behind Paugus are Whiteface, Passaconaway, and the Tripyramids. Next to the right are the Osceolas, the Kinsmans, and a touch of Franconia Ridge, before moving over to the Hancocks-Carrigain region. Coming back around toward the north is the Crawford Notch area, including Mt. Crawford, Stairs Mountain, and Mt. Resolution. Beyond those three peaks the long ridge of the southern Presidentials and Mt. Washington rise in the distance.

ADDITIONAL ROUTES
Piper Trail
8.4 mi. round-trip with 2,700 ft. elevation gain
This longer southeastern approach, one of the oldest routes on the mountain which was laid out by Joshua Piper in the mid to late 1800s, is very scenic in its upper half. There are also some steep and rough sections. Parking is available in a large lot off NH 16 in Albany, 6.2 mi. south of the eastern terminus of NH 112 (Kancamagus Highway).

Piper Trail, Nickerson Ledge Trail, Carter Ledge Trail, Middle Sister Trail, Champney Falls Trail
9.5 mi. counter-clockwise loop with 3,390 ft. elevation gain
This is a steep, rugged and strenuous loop, but is perhaps the most scenic grand tour of the Chocorua area, traversing the open Three Sisters ridge along the way with stunning vistas, as well as providing excellent views from Carter Ledge. It begins from the Piper Trail parking area.

Brook Trail, Liberty Trail
7.4 mi. clockwise loop with 2,750 ft. elevation gain
Brook Trail provides excellent views from its upper ledges which are steep, rough and require some difficult scrambling in places. Descent is via the easier and more gradual Liberty Trail. Both trails leave from a parking area on Paugus Rd. (WMNF Forest Rd. 68) in Albany. This road branches north from Fowler's Mill Rd., 1.2 mi. north of NH 113A in Tamworth.

OVERNIGHT OPTIONS
Backpackers approaching via Piper Trail can utilize historic Camp Penacook Shelter, located on a side path 0.2 mi. off that trail, 0.8 mi. below the junction with Champney Falls Trail. This three-sided shelter, constructed in 1916 by Chocorua Mountain Club, has a tent platform behind it and a pit toilet nearby. An unreliable stream a short distance west of the shelter may provide water; it is recommended that hikers carry in what they need.

Historic Jim Liberty Cabin, originally built in 1932 on the site of the former Peak House, is located along Liberty Trail, 0.5 mi. southwest of the summit. The cabin is a one room structure with bunks for nine people and an outhouse is located a short distance down Liberty Trail. Fires are not allowed. There is a water source, but it is unreliable.

More information on both shelters is available at fs.usda.gov.

WINTER

Mt. Chocorua can be a challenging hike in winter, where the open summit ledges may be icy, and the exposure to the wind and weather above treeline is significant. These ledges often require full crampons to negotiate. The last steep pitch up the gully to the summit can be especially tricky and potentially dangerous if icy. A winter ascent to this peak should not be underestimated. Champney Falls Trail offers easy to moderate grades for snowshoeing and the crossing of Twin Brook is usually well frozen. The trail is well-traveled and is usually broken out fairly quickly after a storm. The parking area along NH 112 is plowed but can be icy.

Champney and Pitcher Falls are a wonderful destination in winter, either as a side trip on the way to or from the summit or just by themselves. When well frozen, Pitcher Falls is a high wall of ice and complete work of art by nature; chances are very good you'll see ice climbers at play here. Use extreme caution along the loop above Champney Falls, as the ledges slope down toward the brook and can be icy; there have been injuries here.

On the south side of the mountain, the Piper trailhead parking area is not plowed by USFS, but in recent years an adjacent resident has been plowing out room for hikers to park on their property for a fee. Parking is prohibited at the closed Davies General Store on NH 16. Piper Trail is traveled in winter but less so than the Champney Falls approach. Carter Ledge Trail is not recommended in winter due to the steep scrambles in its upper section, the trickiest of which could be dangerous in icy conditions.

For Liberty and Brook Trails, Paugus Rd. is only plowed to the last house, 0.1 mi. from Fowler's Mill Rd. There is usually room for a few cars here along the roadside, but do not park next to the house or block access. From this point it's a 0.6 mi. walk to the trailhead.

Mt. Israel

Elevation: 2,636 ft.
Location: Town of Sandwich
Map: SLA map, AMC map - Crawford Notch/Sandwich Range
Locator map: 18

Mt. Israel occupies a unique location within the White Mountains, straddling the area between the Sandwich Range and the Lakes Region, with views to each. Israel's open, ledgy summit area offers a wide vista to the Sandwich Range, while a viewpoint part of the way up looks out to the lakes. Additional ledge outlooks can be visited by following beaten but obscure paths beyond the summit.

A fire lookout station was established on Mt. Israel around 1912, which was accessed by an old trail up the steep east face of the mountain. This station was replaced by the fire tower on nearby Red Hill in the late 1920s. The peak was named after Israel Gilman, an early settler in the intervale south of the mountain during the 1760s.

GETTING THERE

Parking is available at Mead Conservation Center in Sandwich. To reach the trailhead from NH 113 in Center Sandwich, take Grove St. northwest for 0.4 mi., then bear left onto Diamond Ledge Rd. and continue 2.0 mi. to a fork where historic Sandwich Notch Rd. diverges left. Bear right and continue for 0.4 mi. to the parking in front of the main conservation center building.

Mt. Israel's stunning northwest panorama.

RECOMMENDED ROUTE
Wentworth Trail
4.2 mi. round-trip with 1,700 ft. elevation gain
Of the two main routes up Mt. Israel, Wentworth Trail, maintained by Squam Lakes Association, is more strenuous and far more popular than the

lightly traveled Mead Trail. Grades are mostly moderate at first but become steeper and rougher in the upper half, with one rocky scramble just above the lakes outlook.

The yellow-blazed trail begins to the left of the main building and quickly enters the woods to ascend moderately, passing through several old stone walls. It turns sharply right and continues at easy grades to cross a small brook, then turns left to parallel it. It soon bears right away from the brook to climb steadily and then more steeply via several twists and turns. At 1.5 mi., the trail passes a rock face to reach a southern-facing outlook ledge a few yards on the left.

From this viewpoint, the trail turns right and climbs a steep and rough scramble, after which grades and footing become easier. The ledgy southwest summit of Israel is soon reached at 1.8 mi., where there are good views north. The trail then turns sharply right along open ledges, descends easily along more ledges (follow blazes carefully through here), then climbs gradually to a junction with Mead Trail on the left at 2.1 mi. The true summit of Israel is just 75 yds. ahead, a prominent uplifted ledge crowned with a large cairn.

VIEW HIGHLIGHTS

South outlook: The open ledge 1.5 mi. up Wentworth Trail provides a restricted view to the south over the Lakes Region, best seen while standing with a bit of moving around. The view starts on the far left with the Ossipee Range, then moves over to the more distant Moose Mountains and Copple Crown Mountain. Further right is Moultonborough Bay and Blue Job Mountain far beyond. Sprawling Red Hill appears next, followed by Mt. Major and the eastern Belknap Range peaks of East and West Quarry Mountains and Mt. Klem. The higher western peaks of Belknap, Gunstock, and Piper Mountains are visible to the left of Red Hill. To the right of Red Hill is Squam Lake, with distant Pack Monadnock and Crotched Mountains seen far in the distance. Mt. Kearsarge pokes up over East Rattlesnake, and Ragged Mountain is visible over West Rattlesnake. On the far right is Mt. Livermore in the Squam Range.

Main summit: The true summit of Mt. Israel offers one of the best views of the entire Sandwich Range and several points beyond from one spot. Visible on the far left is Mt. Cardigan followed by Stinson Mountain, with several peaks in the Green Mountains of Vermont seen further out. To the right of Stinson, Carr Mountain and Mt. Kineo spread out above the closer Campton

Range. Further right is Mt. Cushman before the massive Mt. Moosilauke becomes the dominant landscape feature in this direction.

Next up, the Sandwich Range panorama begins with Sandwich Dome, just 4 mi. away. Its broad southeast ridge reaches over toward the northern Flat Mountain, then continues up to the higher peaks of the Tripyramids, with the South Peak's slides on display. Continuing right, the Sleepers come into view, as do Mts. Whiteface and Passaconaway. Extending right from Passaconaway are its spurs Nanamocomuck and Wonalancet Hedgehog, with Hibbard Mountain and Mt. Wonalancet below. Further right is Mt. Paugus and then the magnificent Mt. Chocorua, which anchors the eastern end of the range. To the right of Chocorua are the distant Streaked and Pleasant Mountains in western Maine.

East and southeast outlooks: The ledge viewpoints reached by a side path from the summit open up additional outlooks to the east and southeast. This side path continues beyond the summit, descends a short steep pitch with a convenient tree for a handhold, then runs through a brief stretch of woods to emerge at the east viewpoint. From this point, additional views open up to the southeast from various ledges, although no clear paths lead to them. The east view provides an even more open panorama of the Sandwich Range than the main summit. The views here also include additional looks toward Pleasant Mountain, Burnt Meadow Mountain, and Sebago Lake, all in Maine. Seen to the southeast is the volcanic ring dike of the Ossipee Range, followed by the Moose Mountains, Copple Crown, the Blue Hills Range in Strafford, the Belknap Range, and Red Hill.

ADDITIONAL ROUTES

Guinea Pond Trail, Mead Trail
6.6 mi. round-trip with 1,300 ft. elevation gain
This fairly easy route from Sandwich Notch Rd. in Sandwich uses part of Guinea Pond Trail, a former railroad bed, and the lightly traveled Mead Trail, to ascend the northwest side of the mountain. Guinea Pond Trail is often wet and Mead Trail takes care to follow in places. There is no parking available at the start of Guinea Pond Trail, but hikers can park in a designated area on Beebe River Rd. (WMNF Forest Rd. 400), approx. 3.0 mi. northwest of the fork where Sandwich Notch Rd. and Diamond Ledge Rd. divide. This parking area is about 100 yds. west of the Guinea Pond trailhead.

Wentworth Trail, Mead Trail, Guinea Pond Trail, Sandwich Notch Rd., Bearcamp River Trail
8.2 mi. counter-clockwise loop with 1,850 ft. elevation gain
This loop hike, which starts at Mead Conservation Center, is a grand tour of Mt. Israel, visiting nearby natural features such as Beede Falls and Cow Cave on the return trip and includes a walk along the historic Sandwich Notch Rd.

OVERNIGHT OPTIONS

Mead Base Conservation Center at the start of Wentworth Trail offers three campsites which are available by reservation only. Seasonal water (turned off in winter) and a year-round toilet are also available. More information is available at meadbase.org.

WINTER

Wentworth Trail provides a bit of a challenge in winter due to its steep sections. If snow cover is thin, parts of the trail, especially the scramble above the lakes viewpoint and the open summit ledges, could be icy and may require crampons. The route is mostly protected from the weather but there is some exposure to the wind on the open summit. The parking area is usually well-plowed.

The approach via Guinea Pond Trail/Mead Trail is not impossible but is essentially the same as the loop hike option, as Sandwich Notch Rd. is closed to vehicles in winter. It is however usually packed down by snowmobiles. Guinea Pond Trail may be broken out by skiers, but Mead Trail will likely require trail breaking to reach the summit.

Mt. Morgan/Mt. Percival

Elevations: 2,213 ft. / 2,200 ft.
Location: Town of Campton
Map: SLA map, AMC map - Crawford Notch/Sandwich Range
Locator map: 23/24

Note: These are two separate peaks for the purposes of the 52WAV list and can be climbed individually, but are commonly hiked together as a loop and are described as such below. Individual routes are also noted.

Mts. Morgan and Percival are two of the highest peaks in the Squam Range, a relatively low but deceivingly-rugged 12 mi. ridgeline which runs southwest to northwest from Holderness to Sandwich. Both peaks offer excellent views over the Lake Winnipesaukee region from their open, rocky summits and from various cliffs and ledges. Hikers can do a simpler and somewhat easier loop over the peaks or they can make things more adventurous by utilizing two short alternate routes shortly below the summits which climb up cliffs via ladders and through rugged boulder caves. These alternate routes have earned Morgan and Percival their rightful place on the "Terrifying 25" hiking list. Both peaks were added to the 52WAV list in 2020.

Much of the Squam Range is located within private property protected by conservation easements held by Lakes Region Conservation Trust and Squam Lakes Conservation Society. Access to day hikers is graciously granted by the landowners and overnight camping is not permitted.
The range gets its name from nearby Squam Lake, just to the south. The lake was originally known as Keeseenunknipee, which translates to "the goose lake in the highlands", but early settlers shortened the name to "Casumpa", "Kusumpy", or "Kesumpe" in the late 18th century. In the early 1800s, the lake was re-christened as Asquam, meaning "water", and was later shortened to its current name in the early 20th century. The lake's claim to fame was when Hollywood came to Center Harbor in 1981 to film the Oscar-winning *On Golden Pond*, starring Katherine Hepburn and Henry Fonda.

GETTING THERE

The Mt. Morgan trailhead is located along the north side of NH 113 in Holderness, opposite the parking area for East and West Rattlesnake. This is 5.4 mi. northeast of US 3 in Holderness and 6.1 mi. southwest of NH 109 in Center Sandwich. The parking area here is small and tends to fill up quickly, so hikers are urged to arrive early in summer. If full, additional parking is available at the trailhead for Mt. Percival Trail, 0.3 mi. further northeast along NH 113 (to reach Mt. Morgan Trail from this trailhead, follow Mt. Percival Trail and Morse Trail). Parking is prohibited along NH 113.

A note on spring parking: Squam Lakes Association usually closes the above parking areas as well as these trails during mud season. Refer to squamlakes.org for additional details.

ROUTE

Mt. Morgan Trail, Crawford-Ridgepole Trail, Mt. Percival Trail, Morse Trail
5.7 mi. clockwise loop with 1,600 ft. elevation gain

This yellow-blazed route makes a loop over the bare tops of Morgan and Percival and provides excellent views at or near the summits and from nearby open ledges. As is the general character of the Squam Range, portions of this route are very steep and rugged, particularly on the Mt. Percival Trail. The alternate ladder and cave routes described below require caution, are best suited for more experienced hikers, and may not be suitable for some dogs. The loop can be done in either direction, but the ladder route up to Mt. Morgan is recommended for ascent only.

Looking out over Lake Winnipesaukee from the Mt. Morgan ledges.

From the parking area, Mt. Morgan Trail ascends easily along an old woods road, passing a junction on the right with Morse Trail at 0.1 mi. At 0.4 mi., the trail quickly turns right and continues ascending through a fine hardwood forest. It crosses a brook at 1.0 mi., runs through a wet and muddy section, then resumes climbing again, crossing two small streams in succession at 1.4 mi. After a steep climb to the ridgecrest, the trail descends slightly to a T-junction with Crawford Ridgepole Trail at 1.8 mi.

Turning right, Mt. Morgan Trail and Crawford Ridgepole Trail coincide, ascend easily, swing left up a steep pitch, then swing right and continue up to a junction at 2.0 mi. Here, an alternate route (use caution if wet or icy; recommended for ascent only) turns left and ascends steeply up exposed cliffs via a set of three ladders, with a somewhat tricky move where one must shift sideways between the second and third ladder. Above the ladders, the trail squeezes through a boulder cave and scrambles up steep exposed ledges before reaching an outlook below the summit of Mt. Morgan.

From the junction with the alternate route, Mt. Morgan Trail continues straight ahead and climbs to a junction at 2.1 mi., where Crawford Ridgepole Trail departs on the right. Mt. Morgan Trail bears left here and runs mostly level, passing a side path on the right at 2.2 mi. (sign: "Summit"), which climbs steeply for 50 yds. to the mostly wooded true summit of Mt. Morgan. The main trail continues ahead a short distance and ends at open ledges with excellent views over Lake Winnipesaukee (the upper end of the alternate ladder route joins in here on the right).

To continue to Mt. Percival, backtrack to the junction with Crawford Ridgepole Trail noted above and turn left. This ridgecrest route heads generally northeast, zigzagging across the undulating ridge with many ups and downs. At around 2.5 mi., the trail passes just to the west of the highest point in the Squam Range (2,238 ft.), known as The Sawtooth; a short but somewhat scrappy bushwhack leads to the wooded high point which is marked by a cairn. At 2.6 mi., the main trail passes over ledges with restricted views to the south, then makes a long gradual descent to a low point. The trail climbs steeply over a rocky knob and after one scramble out of the woods, it emerges onto the summit of Mt. Percival at 3.1 mi.; the true summit (marked by a drill hole) is atop an uplifted ledge behind the summit sign.

Three routes leave the summit, so choosing the correct one requires some attention as the current signage is not clear: Crawford Ridgepole Trail turns left, Mt. Percival Trail continues ahead, and the alternate cave route bears right. This alternate route descends over ledges, then turns sharply left and drops very steeply with rocky footing over cliffs and through rugged boulder caves, where it is often necessary to remove your pack to squeeze through the tight openings. It emerges from the caves and rejoins Mt. Percival Trail in 0.1 mi. Use caution on this route if wet or icy.

From the summit, Mt. Percival Trail descends over ledges, turns left where more ledges on the right provide excellent views to the south, then turns sharply right to scramble down cliffs, reaching the lower junction with the cave route at 3.2 mi. The main trail turns left here and continues a steep and rough descent with several scrambles. It drops through a rocky gully and at 3.5 mi., swings right to traverse a boulder field. At 3.6 mi., the trail crosses a small stream, quickly crosses it again, then makes a long gradual ascent to cross a wider brook at 4.2 mi. It soon joins an old woods road which offers easy walking, and at 5.1 mi., it reaches a junction with Morse Trail on the right (Mt. Percival Trail continues ahead for 0.2 mi. to its trailhead).

Morse Trail — a connecting route created to eliminate a road walk on NH 113 between the Mt. Morgan and Mt. Percival trailheads — turns right and runs mostly level over gently rolling terrain, crosses a brook on a footbridge, then a second brook (no bridge), then an old logging road, before gently ascending to a junction with Mt. Morgan Trail. Turn left here for an easy 0.1 mi. walk back to the trailhead.

VIEW HIGHLIGHTS

Mt. Morgan ledges: These ledges, just beyond the spur path to the summit at the top of the ladder alternate route, provide big views over Lake Winnipesaukee and out to many peaks in this region as well as across southern New Hampshire.

Starting on the far left is a distant look out to southwestern Maine, followed by the volcanic ring dike of the Ossipee Range rising from the surrounding terrain. Next to the right and closer in is the long ridge of Red Hill with its fire tower visible, with the Moose Mountains, Copple Crown Mountain, Caverly Mountain, and other small peaks in the Merrymeeting Lake area in the distance. Closer still and visible right down from the ledges are the double humps of East and West Rattlesnake. Far in the distance, the Belknap Range rises on the other side of the lake, followed to the right by a flatter expanse of southern New Hampshire punctuated with peaks such as Joe English Hill, Rose Mountain, Pack Monadnock Mountain, and Hersey Mountain. Next to the right, the Squam Range ridgeline extends into the distance beyond Mt. Webster, looking out to Mt. Kearsarge, Ragged Mountain, Forbes Mountain, Plymouth Mountain, nearby Mt. Prospect in Holderness, and Mt. Cardigan beyond.

Mt. Morgan summit: The true summit of Mt. Morgan is located atop a rocky knob surrounded by trees which block most of the views. However, peeks through these trees reveal looks to Mt. Moosilauke to the northwest and Sandwich Dome to the northeast.

Mt. Percival summit: The vista from the summit of Percival is much the same as that of Mt. Morgan but adds on additional views to the northwest and west, including Mt. Moosilauke, The Osceolas, Mt. Tecumseh, Jennings Peak and Sandwich Dome, Mt. Chocorua, Mt. Israel, and Mts. Squam and Doublehead in the Squam Range. For the widest view over the lake from Mt.

Percival, descend slightly from the summit to the ledges at the top of the alternate boulder caves route.

INDIVIDUAL PEAK ROUTES
Mt. Morgan only via Mt. Morgan Trail
4.2 mi. round-trip with 1,400 ft. elevation gain

Mt. Percival only via Mt. Morgan Trail, Morse Trail, Mt. Percival Trail
4.8 mi. round-trip with 1,500 ft. elevation gain

WINTER
These can be challenging peaks to hike in winter if the steep sections below the ridge are icy; full crampons may be required. That said, it is a popular route in winter and the trails are usually broken out quite quickly after a storm. There is some exposure to the wind on both summits, but on bright days the south-facing ledges on each provide sunny warmth. Deep snow improves the view over the trees at the true summit of Mt. Morgan.
The alternate ladder and cave routes could be tricky if icy and depending on snowfall and ice amounts, passage through the boulder caves may not be possible. If in doubt, stick to the safer main hiking trail. SLA signage at junctions is also quite low to the ground so it may be buried in times of deep snow, however all of the trails described here are well-blazed.

Mt. Paugus (South Peak)

Elevation: 3,100 ft.
Location: Town of Albany
Map: WODC map, AMC map - Crawford Notch/Sandwich Range
Locator map: 26

Less frequented by White Mountain hikers, Mt. Paugus is a wild and rugged mountain located mostly within the Sandwich Range Wilderness. Its steep terrain and rust-colored cliffs and slides give it a unique appearance when seen from adjacent peaks. From some perspectives, Paugus looks like a peak you would find more in the western US rather than in New England. For the purposes of this list, hikers must climb to the south summit of the mountain, but bushwhackers may wish to visit the true summit (3,185 ft.), 0.3 mi. to the north though thick, scrappy woods. The south summit is mostly wooded but a large open ledge nearby offers excellent views.

Mt. Paugus was named in honor of a chief of the Pequawket tribe and great grandson of the mighty sachem Passaconaway, who had settled in what is now Conway, NH. He was killed during a 1725 battle which also took the life of Captain John Lovewell who led the attack. The word Paugus roughly translates to "the oak".

The mountain was also once known as Old Shag due to its abundant ledges and cliffs. A former hiker shelter a short distance below the south summit bore this name before it was removed in the mid-1980s. The 1889 History of Carroll County states that Paugus went by many other names over the years including Hunchback (because of its low, massive shape), Deer (because of the herds that roamed it), Frog, Middle (because it is located between Mts. Chocorua and Passaconaway), Berry, and Bald (because of its bare ledges). In 1875, the current name was suggested by poet Lucy Larcom, a frequent visitor to the Tamworth area, just south of the Sandwich Range. Two small peaks in the Ossipee Range are named after her.

Looking west along the Sandwich Range from Mt. Paugus' southwest ledges.

GETTING THERE

The parking area and trailhead are located at the end of Ferncroft Rd. in Albany. This trailhead, located on private land, is very popular and is often overflowing due to hikers bound for Mts. Whiteface and Passaconaway. Due to heavy use, a possible expansion is being proposed for the future. Beyond the turn for the designated parking area, no parking is allowed along the main road. Please observe all posted signs and do not obstruct access to nearby private residences. An outhouse is also located at the far end of the parking lot. From Center Sandwich, take NH 113 east for 3.7 mi., then bear left onto NH 113A (use caution with oncoming traffic here as the intersection is somewhat obscured) and continue 6.7 mi. to picturesque Wonalancet Village. At the sharp right turn in the road, turn left onto Ferncroft Rd. and continue to the trailhead and parking on the right in 0.5 mi.

RECOMMENDED ROUTE

Kelley Trail, Lawrence Trail, Old Mast Rd.
8.5 mi. counter-clockwise loop with 2,450 ft. elevation gain
This route to Paugus begins with an easy walk then becomes more rugged as you approach the peak. Footing is rough in places, especially within Kelley Trail's box canyon. Views are very limited until you reach the outlook ledge near the summit. The last section of this route uses the easier Old Mast Rd., as Kelley Trail is more difficult to descend.

Kelley Trail leaves from the east end of the parking area at a gate and coincides with Old Mast Rd. at easy grades to a junction at 0.3 mi. where Kelley Trail leaves the road on the right. It ascends easily and turns right onto an old logging road at 0.5 mi., which it follows for 0.1 mi., then turns left back into the woods. The trail continues to climb moderately alongside Cold Brook to enter a secluded, beautiful box canyon through which the brook flows. This is perhaps one of the most beautiful and wild sections of trail in the White Mountains. The trail ascends through the narrow canyon, crossing the brook a few times. In its upper section, the trail passes small gorges formed during the last ice age when the canyon was the outlet of a glacial lake, then reaches the bowl-shaped amphitheatre known as "Pleistocene Plunge Pool" at 1.9 mi. The trail makes a steep climb out of the canyon along the left side, then ascends a rough and rocky section as it squeezes through a cut at the top. Above here, grades ease and the trail ascends gradually to Paugus Pass at 2.3 mi., where Kelley, Oliverian Brook, Lawrence and Walden Trails meet.

Turning right, Lawrence Trail ascends at mostly easy grades to pass a junction with Cabin Trail on the right at 2.6 mi. (this trail can be used as an easier alternative descent route, combined with a walk back along NH 113A to the parking area). The trail then makes a descent to the base of The Overhang, a 2,615 ft. eastern knob of Mt. Paugus, then continues ahead on a relocated section which bypasses the former very steep and rough route which has been closed. This relocation, as well as others further ahead, feature much easier grades and smoother footing. The trail passes under a wooded cliff then makes an easy traverse and swings left at a series of switchbacks. Above this section, Lawrence Trail turns right to rejoin the former route, crosses two small streams, then enters a second relocated section on switchbacks. The trail swings right and ascends easily, dips to cross a small brook, then climbs gradually to reach Paugus' South Peak at 3.8 mi., a large area of open ledge surrounded by trees.

To reach the southwest view, turn right past broken boulders perched on a ledge, then follow a short side path through a band of scrub to emerge on expansive sloping ledges.

For the return trip, double back to Paugus Pass, but continue straight on Lawrence Trail instead of turning left onto Kelley Trail. Follow Lawrence Trail for 0.3 mi. to a junction with Old Mast Rd., then turn left for an easy 2.0 mi. descent back to Ferncroft.

VIEW HIGHLIGHTS

Some hikers arrive at the south summit of Mt. Paugus and are disappointed. Where are the sweeping views? Following the side path described above, you emerge on large open ledges with an expansive vista east and southeast. Most striking is the massive Mt. Passaconaway, a short 3 mi. away, with Square Ledge lying far below; Paugus offers a unique perspective on this remote backcountry cliff. Also visible are the wooded cliffs of The Overhang, which Lawrence Trail passes under on its way to Mt. Paugus. To the left of Passaconaway lies Mt. Whiteface (with Sandwich Dome popping up behind it), the unassuming summit bump of ex-52WAV peak Hibbard Mountain, and rounded Mt. Wonalancet.

Seen over Wonalancet and in the distance is Mt. Cardigan, with Mt. Israel further left and closer in. Young Mountain is seen in the foreground below Israel. Further left from Israel, Mt. Kearsarge rises prominently on the horizon with Lovewell and Ragged Mountains to the right of it. To the south/southeast, the long ridge of Red Hill in Moultonborough is visible with the Wapack Range and Mt. Monadnock far beyond in the distance.

ADDITIONAL ROUTE
Cabin Trail, Big Rock Cave Trail, Old Paugus Trail, Lawrence Trail
8.2 mi. counter-clockwise loop with 3,000 ft. elevation gain

This rougher loop option, beautiful during fall foliage season, starts and ends on NH 113A in Wonalancet. It involves some very steep and rugged climbing along Old Paugus Trail, which takes care to follow in places. This route also allows for a visit to Big Rock Cave, an impressive boulder cave large enough to walk through. To reach the trailhead follow the directions above for the Ferncroft parking area, but continue on NH 113A 0.5 mi. further to a small parking area on the right.

WINTER

Mt. Paugus is seldom hiked in winter due to its rugged terrain and remote location within a wilderness area, which can make route-finding along sparsely marked trails difficult. Winter hikers should expect strenuous trail breaking. Crampons may be required on the sloping southwest ledges near the summit if icy. The deep, shaded box canyon along Kelley Trail is potentially tricky in icy conditions. The parking area at Ferncroft is plowed.

If approaching via Cabin Trail, the small parking area on NH 113A is usually plowed enough for a few cars. The easy grades of Cabin Trail make for good snowshoeing, but Old Paugus Trail can be very difficult in unbroken snow. The steep gully scramble part of the way up can be dangerous if filled in with ice. Route-finding may also be difficult.

Mt. Roberts

Elevation: 2,584 ft.
Location: Town of Moultonborough
Map: LRCT Castle in the Clouds map
Locator map: 29

Located within the remnants of the ancient ring-dike volcano that is today's Ossipee Range, Mt. Roberts is one of the most popular hikes in the Lakes Region, offering spectacular views over Lake Winnipesaukee from its open south ridge, which Mt. Roberts Trail traverses. A side path on the ascent leads to a good viewpoint west and an outlook near the summit provides views north to the White Mountains. Mt. Roberts is a part of Lakes Region Conservation Trust's Castle in the Clouds Conservation Area.

Shoe magnate Thomas Gustave Plant began the effort for conservation of this land in the early 1900s when he began buying up old farms and lots in the Ossipee Range for his Lucknow Estate, where he later built his Castle in the Clouds in 1913-14. After Plant's death in 1941, the property passed through the hands of several parties until LRCT purchased it in 2002.

The name of the peak comes from the Roberts family, early settlers who moved to the area following the Revolutionary War. Isaac and Nancy Roberts built a home here in the early 1800s along what is today's Cold Spring Trail in the Ossipee Range, the cellar hole of which is still present. The farm stayed in the Roberts family until 1911, when two of the Roberts' seven children, Lydia and Jane, sold 100 acres to Alfred H. Handley, who was the personal secretary of Thomas Plant. Working with Plant's brother William, he aided in acquiring the various properties that would make up the Lucknow estate, known today as the Castle in the Clouds.

In 2010, Mt. Roberts was added to the 52WAV list to replace the diminishing views on Mt. Wolf.

Looking out over the Lakes Region from Mt. Roberts' open south ridge.

GETTING THERE

Parking is available in a dedicated hiker lot at the top of Ossipee Park Rd. in Moultonborough. From NH 25, take NH 109 south for 2.1 mi., continuing straight onto NH 171 where NH 109 diverges right. In 0.5 mi. turn left onto Ossipee Park Rd. and continue 1.3 mi. to the parking area and kiosk.

RECOMMENDED ROUTE
Mt. Roberts Trail
5.2 mi. round-trip with 1,400 ft. elevation gain

This orange-blazed trail offers a direct, moderate ascent to the summit of Mt. Roberts with excellent views along the mountain's open south ridge. Footing is generally good with a few rougher sections.

From the parking area, continue along the paved road, turning left at the first intersection onto another road. Continue straight onto a gravel driveway where the paved road diverges right as Cold Spring Rd. Where the driveway turns left toward the stables, bear right across a pasture to the start of the trail (sign) along the right edge of the woods at 0.2 mi.

Mt. Roberts Trail begins along an old woods road and at 0.4 mi. from the parking area, bears left at a fork to almost double back on itself, ascending easily to the top edge of the pasture which was crossed earlier. At the far side of the pasture, the trail swings right and begins climbing moderately at first, then at alternating easy to moderate grades. At 1.2 mi., a short side path on the left (sign) leads to a large open ledge with expansive views west. The main trail resumes a moderate ascent with rocky footing at times, reaching another outlook at 1.6 mi. Views now increase as the trail gains the south ridge and ascends through areas of ledge and unusual scrub oak forest. Follow cairns and paint blazes carefully in open areas and keep to the trail to avoid trampling sensitive vegetation.

Above the highest ledge at 2.3 mi., the trail heads back into the woods through a narrow spruce corridor and continues a moderate climb to the junction with High Ridge Trail. Follow this trail to the right (the two trails briefly overlap here) to reach the northern viewpoint, summit sign, and cairn at 2.6 mi. The actual high point of Mt. Roberts is located just off the trail within the short loop that High Ridge Trail makes around the summit.

VIEW HIGHLIGHTS

Summit view: The near-summit outlook provides a distant view north toward the Sandwich Range. Mts. Whiteface and Passaconaway are the most prominent features with The Bowl, a wooded glacial cirque, between them. Mt. Carrigain pokes its head up over The Bowl. To the left of Whiteface, Mt. Tripyramid, Mt. Osceola, and the huge mass of Sandwich Dome can be seen. Rising up in front of that vista is trailless and appropriately named Black Snout, the northernmost of two peaks in the Ossipee Range which bear this name. To the right of Black Snout, Mt. Washington can be seen on clearer days and further right, Mt. Chocorua peeks over the ridge. Close by is Mt. Roberts' neighbor Faraway Mountain with its communications antennas mixing in with the natural trees.

Red Hill outlook: The ledge viewpoint 1.2 mi. up the trail looks mainly southwest with the ridge of Red Hill rising nearby on the right.

South ridge: The best views along Mt. Roberts Trail are from the open south ridge. The scene stretches from Mt. Shaw and the southern Black Snout all the way across Lake Winnipesaukee, accentuated by the Belknap Range on the far side. On extremely clear winter days, a very distant Mt. Monadnock can be seen with the prominent Mt. Kearsarge to its right. Swinging even further right, the view moves around to the long ridge of Red Hill followed by the Squam Range.

WINTER

Mt. Roberts is an excellent and popular snowshoe trek with moderate grades the whole way. Crampons may be needed along the walk up the south ridge and its open ledges but only in very icy conditions. These ledges are also exposed to the wind. The parking area atop Ossipee Park Rd. is plowed.

Mt. Shaw

Elevation: 2,990 ft.
Location: Town of Moultonborough
Map: LRCT Castle in the Clouds map
Locator map: 30

Mt. Shaw, located within the 5,381-acre Castle in the Clouds Conservation Area, is the highest point in the Ossipee Range, and offers an expansive vista north to the White Mountains from a near-summit outlook. The true summit is on the southern end of the loop which High Ridge Trail makes around the top of the mountain. Mt. Shaw also bore a fire tower from 1916 to 1922.

The peak is named for Benjamin Shaw of Lowell, MA, the first owner of the CITC property back when it was a private summer estate in the late 1800s. Shaw was the inventor of the Shaw-Knit Machine, a device which manufactured stockings. Many of today's hiking trails in this area follow the original carriage roads built as part of his estate.

Originally, the name of the mountain was Black Snout, but that was later moved to a southern subpeak after the townspeople of Moultonborough voted for the name change during an 1882 town meeting. Unfortunately, this has at times caused confusion among Ossipee Range hikers, as another (trailless) peak north of Mt. Roberts is also named Black Snout.

GETTING THERE

Parking is available in a dedicated hiker lot at the top of Ossipee Park Rd. in Moultonborough. From NH 25, turn onto NH 109 south for 2.1 mi., continuing straight onto NH 171 where NH 109 diverges right. In 0.5 mi., turn left onto Ossipee Park Rd. and continue 1.3 mi. to the parking area and kiosk on the right.

Looking north toward the White Mountains from Mt. Shaw.

RECOMMENDED ROUTE

Cold Spring Rd., Cold Spring Trail, Faraway Mountain Connector, Faraway Mountain Trail, Oak Ridge Cutoff, High Ridge Trail
8.0 mi. round-trip with 1,740 ft. elevation gain
From the parking area, follow paved Ossipee Park Rd. and turn left at the first junction at 0.1 mi., quickly bearing right onto red-blazed Cold Spring Rd., part gravel and part pavement. The ascent is gentle, passing junctions with Pond Trail (orange blazes) on the right at 0.2 mi., and Whitten Trail (blue blazes) on the left at 0.5 mi. At 0.8 mi. at a four-way junction, turn right onto red-blazed Cold Spring Trail, which follows an old woods road past the

Roberts family cellar hole. At 0.9 mi. bear right onto Faraway Mountain Connector, blazed in both red and orange. This trail climbs moderately to a junction with orange-blazed Faraway Mountain Trail at 1.2 mi. Turn left here and at 1.3 mi., bear right at a fork onto Oak Ridge Cutoff, blazed in white. Following an old woods road, this trail climbs at easy to moderate grades with some rocky footing in places, passing a junction on the right with Upper Bridle Path (green blazes) at 1.8 mi. ,to a branched junction with blue-blazed High Ridge Trail at 2.3 mi.

Turn right onto High Ridge Trail, a former carriage road, for an easy ramble along the highest ridge in the Ossipee Range, where the trail doesn't dip below 2,300 ft. At 3.0 mi., High Ridge Trail turns left at a junction where yellow-blazed Turtleback Mountain Trail diverges right and ascends easily at first then moderately. It bears right at a fork at 3.5 mi. where an unmarked snowmobile trail comes in on the left (in reverse, bear left here), and at 3.6 mi., after a junction on the right with white-blazed Black Snout trail, High Ridge Trail makes the final easy ascent to the summit at 4.0 mi. and loops around it.

VIEW HIGHLIGHTS

The vista from Mt. Shaw is a wide panorama generally northwest to northeast and you have to move around a bit along the carriage road which loops over the summit to get the whole view.

Starting in the northwest, the highest ridge of the Ossipee Range heads off toward Mt. Roberts. Red Hill can be seen low and to the left of this ridge with Mt. Livermore behind it and Mt. Prospect in Holderness also behind it but to the right. The long ridge of the Squam Range is visible extending to the right from Prospect with Stinson Mountain beyond. To the right of Stinson and way in the back is the elongated crest of Carr Mountain. Further right, a cluster of peaks around Mt. Moosilauke come into view, including Chokecherry Hill, Mt. Cushman, and the huge mass of Moosilauke itself, followed by its subpeak, Mt. Blue.

Sandwich Dome's Black Mountain is seen under Blue before the ridge runs over the Dome itself. The northern Black Snout in the Ossipees lies under the summit of Sandwich. The horizon then moves right over Mt. Tecumseh, the Kinsmans, and the Osceolas before arriving at Franconia Ridge. The Tripyramids appear next on the right, followed by Mts. Whiteface and Passaconaway with the great wooded glacial cirque known as The Bowl between them. Mt. Wonalancet rises in front of The Bowl. Behind

Passaconaway is Mt. Carrigain and Vose Spur, separated by the neighboring Nancy Range by Carrigain Notch.

Mt. Tremont is seen to the right of the Nancy Range and closer in, then the view moves back to the long ridge of the southern Presidentials ascending to Mt. Washington, which is just about due north from this perspective. Mt. Chocorua stands in front of Washington. The Wildcats and Carters appear to the right of Washington, leading into the Moriahs, followed by the Baldfaces in Evans Notch. Kearsarge North pops up to the right of the Baldfaces, then the Green Hills of Conway appear closer in. Nearby and under that grouping is ledgy Bayle Mountain.

To the right of Bayle are the Nickerson Mountains in the northeast part of the Ossipees. Above them and in the background are numerous and distant peaks in western Maine, before the views moves around to the ridge of Pleasant Mountain in Bridgton, ME to the northwest.

ADDITIONAL ROUTE

The unofficial red-blazed Mt. Shaw Trail from NH 171 is a commonly-hiked route, and in combination with Black Snout Trail and High Ridge Trail, leads to the summit, but its lower section and parking area are located on private land. As such, it is not shown on official maps or described in this guide.

WINTER

The main route to Shaw is an excellent snowshoe trek with mostly easy grades. The old carriage roads which the trails follow are well packed down by snowmobiles and some of the trails within the CITC property are also groomed for cross-country skiing. The parking area atop Ossipee Park Rd. is reliably plowed.

Potash Mountain

Elevation: 2,691 ft.
Location: Town of Waterville Valley
Map: WODC map, AMC map - Crawford Notch/Sandwich Range
Locator map: 40

Steep-sided Potash Mountain, next door neighbor to fellow 52WAV peak Hedgehog Mountain, offers excellent views from its mostly open summit and from outlooks along Mt. Potash Trail. A portion of the mountain lies within the Sandwich Range Wilderness, whose boundary passes directly over the high point. An unusual feature of the summit area is a balanced boulder on the southeast side along the original route of the hiking trail. This was once easily rocked back and forth, but doesn't budge these days.

According to early local historian Charles Edward Beals, Jr., the mountain is named *"for its resemblance to an inverted potash kettle."* Potash, or potassium carbonate, is a substance extracted from wood ashes and was originally prepared in kettles. On current USGS maps, the name of the peak is labeled as Potash Mountain, although the hiking trail itself is called Mt. Potash Trail.

GETTING THERE

Parking is in a large lot (no longer a WMNF fee area) which provides access to UNH Trail, Downes Brook Trail and Mt. Potash Trail, and is located at the end of an access road (sign for all three trails) off NH 112 (Kancamagus Highway), 2.0 mi. west of Bear Notch Rd.

Potash Mountain's summit ledges.

ROUTE

Downes Brook Trail, Mt. Potash Trail

4.4 mi. round-trip with 1,450 ft. elevation gain

This sole route to Potash starts out relatively mellow but becomes quite a steep and rugged climb in its upper half, traveling through a variety of terrain. A rough, rocky traverse and steep ledges shortly below the summit provide a workout but also good views.

From the parking area, follow Downes Brook Trail straight ahead along an old road, quickly passing a junction on the left with UNH Trail for Hedgehog Mountain. Turn right at the top of a hill for an easy walk to the junction with yellow-blazed Mt. Potash Trail on the right at 0.3 mi. Turn right again for a level walk to the crossing of Downes Brook at 0.4 mi. At times of high water, this wide crossing can be difficult or even impassable. An alternative approach can be made by walking back out to NH 112 from the parking area and heading west for 0.6 mi. to gated WMNF Forest Rd. 511 on the south side of the road. Limited roadside parking is also available here; do not block the gate. Proceed south on this forest road for 0.7 mi. to where Mt. Potash Trail crosses, just after a clear cut area on the right. Turn right up a set of small rock steps to rejoin the trail.

On the far side of brook, Mt. Potash Trail swings left and climbs easily to meet the aforementioned forest road at 0.7 mi. The trail crosses the road and ascends easily through a hardwood forest and then deep hemlock woods. It turns sharply left and makes a twisting ascent where footing becomes more rough and rooty over ledges. At 1.5 mi., the trail turns left onto a relocated section and climbs to the first viewpoint at 1.6 mi., an open ledge on the northeast shoulder of the mountain.

Mt. Potash Trail turns right to traverse the ledge, dips back into the woods to run along a level stretch, then resumes a moderate, rocky climb to a left turn at 1.9 mi., where the trail diverges from its original steeper route. The trail now makes a very rough and rocky traverse across the east side of the summit cone where footing is awkward. At the end of the traverse, it climbs up one short steeper pitch to reach the open ledges at the base of the summit cone at 2.1 mi., where views are excellent to the south.

The trail turns right onto sloping ledges which are mossy in spots (use caution here if wet or icy) and ascends steeply up open granite slabs (follow markings carefully) through areas of scrub. Higher up, grades ease as the trail ends in the flat summit area at 2.2 mi. The high point is an uplifted ledge marked by a yellow painted X, which also denotes a corner of the Sandwich Range Wilderness boundary.

VIEW HIGHLIGHTS

Summit view: Looking south, Potash faces some of the Sandwich Range's highest peaks, with Mt. Passaconaway being the most dominant. The long scar of Downes Brook Slide, frequented by backcountry skiers, is clearly visible on its northern slopes. Extending right from Passaconaway is the long ridge which connects it to Mt. Whiteface, seen near the head of Downes Brook Valley. The summit of Potash offers a unique view up this valley with the high ridge of the rolling Sleepers and the triple-peaked Tripyramids stretching out to the right of Whiteface.

Swinging around to the northwest and north, Mt. Osceola comes into view, as does the huge combined mass of the Hancocks and Mt. Carrigain, as well as the Nancy Range. In front of Mts. Lowell, Anderson, and Nancy is the isolated Greens Cliff. From the summit of Potash, descend northeast over ledges and follow a short, well-beaten side path to a view toward Mt. Washington and the Presidential Range.

Southeast view ledge: This ledge offers a good view southeast, looking up at the huge Mt. Passaconaway and out to Hedgehog Mountain, the Moat Range, Swift River Valley, and Mt. Chocorua. The open ledges at 2.1 mi. just before the final climb to the summit provide a similar perspective.

WINTER

Potash is a good intermediate snowshoe route, although there are steeper sections along with some sidehilling which can be tiring on the ankles. Crampons may be needed on the final steep climb to the summit. If not snow bridged, the crossing of Downes Brook may be difficult and potentially dangerous. In such cases, the forest road bypass described above should be used. Depending on snowfall amounts, there may be room to park along the highway near the gate for the forest road. The main parking lot is accessible in winter but may not be plowed immediately after a storm. If it is not plowed, limited parking may be available at the end of the access road.

Sandwich Dome

Elevation: 3,992 ft.
Location: Town of Sandwich
Map: WODC map, WVAIA map, AMC map - Crawford Notch/Sandwich Range
Locator map: 42

Sandwich Dome is the highest of the 52WAV peaks — just shy of being a 4,000 footer — as well as one of the most sprawling, and offers good views from its small summit clearing and subsidiary peaks. It is also the westernmost high peak in the Sandwich Range. The immense mass of Sandwich Dome looms large over the towns of Sandwich and Waterville Valley and lies mostly within the Sandwich Range Wilderness. Since the 1850s, the mountain has been accessible by wild, remote and scenic trail approaches from several directions, all worthy of exploration. The peak's summit is actually somewhat flat-topped with two small knobs of similar elevation. Only the slightly higher southwest knob is accessible by a trail. Waterville Valley historian Nathaniel Goodrich spoke of *"the smooth beauty of the twin domes"* as he gazed upon the mountain from the village below.

In 1923, logging resulted in a 3,500-acre fire in the Flat Mountain Pond area to the northeast. This blaze took the life of one firefighter.

The peak was originally known as Black Mountain, one of many such-named mountains in the state, but was given its present name in 1860 and formalized by the USGS in 1910. Confusingly, the Black Mountain moniker was then moved to the southwest shoulder, and later to a peak at the end of that shoulder.

A wintry look at Sandwich Dome from Jennings Peak

GETTING THERE

Parking is available in a small lot for Sandwich Mountain Trail off NH 49 in Waterville Valley, 10 mi. east of Exit 28 off I-93.

RECOMMENDED ROUTE
Sandwich Mountain Trail, Drakes Brook Trail

Sandwich Dome only: 8.3 mi. counter-clockwise loop with 2,700 ft. elevation gain
Include side trip to Jennings Peak: 8.7 mi. counter-clockwise loop with 2,850 ft. elevation gain

This commonly-hiked route provides a steep ascent up to the ridge via Sandwich Mountain Trail, with a descent via the easier and more gradual Drakes Brook Trail.

From the parking area, yellow-blazed Sandwich Mountain Trail first descends steeply to cross Drakes Brook, which may be difficult at times of high water. To avoid this crossing, walk back out to the highway and head west, crossing the bridge over the brook. Just past the bridge, turn left onto a rough herd path on the opposite side of the brook and continue for 0.1 mi., then turn right back onto the trail. The entrance to this herd path was marked by flagging in 2018.

From the brook, the trail first ascends moderately, entering the Sandwich Range Wilderness at 0.6 mi., then very steeply with alternating easier sections, to the northern end of the ridge and view ledge on the left with a vista east and northeast toward the Osceolas, the Hancocks, the Tripyramids, and Mt. Carrigain. This is a good spot for a breather after the stiff climb. Past this outlook, the trail descends slightly, then climbs over Noon Peak (2,976 ft.), with another excellent view ledge on the left just past the summit. It then descends briefly and ascends gradually along the beautiful ridge, passing through an expansive ledgy area, to a junction with Drakes Brook Trail on the left at 2.7 mi., and then the junction with Jennings Peak Spur on the right. This short trail ascends steeply for 0.2 mi. to the ledgy summit of Jennings Peak (3,493 ft.) and is well worth the side trip. See the Jennings Peak section for details.

From the junction, Sandwich Mountain Trail swings left and runs nearly level along the beautiful wooded ridge through a high elevation forest to pass a junction with Smarts Brook Trail on the right at 3.3 mi. Climbing becomes more moderate as the trail passes junctions on the right with Algonquin Trail at 3.8 mi. and Bennett St. Trail at 3.9 mi., then quickly reaches the summit of Sandwich Dome (the high point is atop an uplifted ledge) a short distance beyond.

VIEW HIGHLIGHTS

The small summit clearing of Sandwich Dome offers views that mainly look north toward the high peaks of the White Mountains. In the 19th century, the summit was more open with views in all directions. Since then the trees have grown up so the vistas are best seen by standing atop the uplifted summit ledge. From this ledge, 35 4,000 footers are visible.

Beginning in the far left through the trees is Mt. Kineo with Vermont's Breadloaf Range seen far beyond. Further right and nearby are Welch and Dickey Mountains, followed by Mt. Moosilauke back in the distance again. Next to the right is sharp Jennings Peak, followed by the Kinsmans and then back in to Mt. Tecumseh. Cannon Mountain and Northeast Cannonball are visible over the right slope of Tecumseh, with Scar Ridge further right and closer in. Franconia Ridge is seen next, along with rugged Mt. Osceola just across Waterville Valley. To the right of Osceola's East Peak is Mad River Notch through which South Twin, the Bonds, and Zealand Mountain can be seen. Close by and under the notch is Noon Peak.

To the right of Mad River Notch, the Hancocks are visible over Mt. Kancamagus, followed up by Mt. Field, the enormous Mt. Carrigain, and the Nancy Range. Above the Nancy Range, the peaks of the southern Presidential Range ascend beyond Mt. Washington, which rises high above Oakes Gulf with Boott Spur to the right. The upper Montalban Ridge and Mt. Isolation are inline with Boott Spur. Nearby and lower in this direction is the long ridge of Snows Mountain in Waterville Valley.

Next up on the right are the triple summits of the Tripyramids with the south slides visible below South Peak. The wavy Sleeper Ridge extends right from Tripyramid, with South Baldface, Sable Mountain, and the Doubleheads seen through the col between the two Sleeper peaks. To the right of East Sleeper are Mts. Passaconaway and Whiteface; Kearsarge North pops over the left slope of Passaconaway. From Whiteface, the view moves over to Mt. Paugus, the Three Sisters ridge, and Mt. Chocorua.

ADDITIONAL ROUTES

Smarts Brook Trail, Sandwich Mountain Trail
11.4 mi. round-trip with 3,100 ft. elevation gain
This longer western approach from NH 49 in Thornton, 4.0 mi. east of NH 175, ascends at easy to moderate grades up the beautiful and secluded Smarts Brook Valley alongside glacial boulders and cascades to the ridge between Jennings Peak and Sandwich Dome. This is a quieter alternative to the busier

Sandwich Mountain Trail approach and is well worth the additional distance for hikers who love walking beside water.

Flat Mountain Pond Trail, Bennett St. Trail
9.0 mi. round-trip with 2,900 ft. elevation gain
This lesser-used approach from Bennett St. in Sandwich offers a quiet route to Sandwich Dome on mostly easy to moderate grades, passing by scenic Great Falls along the way. There are no views, but the trail ascends through a beautiful high elevation forest. To reach the trailhead from NH 113A, take Whiteface Intervale Rd. for 0.1 mi. then turn left onto Bennett Street. In 1.6 mi. at a fork, stay straight and continue up a narrow dirt road to the trailhead at a gate in another 0.5 mi. This road can be rough at times, especially the last 0.1 mi., but is generally fine for all vehicles with care.

Algonquin Trail, Sandwich Mountain Trail
9.0 mi. round-trip with 2,900 ft. elevation gain
This remote approach from Sandwich Notch Rd. offers a more difficult, rugged, and quiet wilderness experience with excellent views and steep, exposed scrambling. The trailhead, with limited parking, is located 3.5 mi. south of NH 49 in Campton. Sandwich Notch Rd. is intentionally maintained to a minimal degree to preserve its historic nature, so high-clearance is highly recommended.

WINTER
Sandwich can be a winter wonderland in good conditions. Sandwich Mountain Trail makes for more difficult snowshoeing than the easier Drakes Mountain Trail. The crossings of Drakes Brook on both trails may be difficult if not well frozen (for the Sandwich Mountain Trail crossing, the bypass route described above can be used). Deep snow improves views above the trees at the summit. The parking area is not always plowed reliably and space may be more limited; do not block access to the electrical substation.

Plowed parking is available at the Smarts Brook trailhead, which is accessed mainly for local ski trails, but the hiking trail itself is lesser-used in winter and may require long, strenuous trail breaking.

For the approach from Bennett St., the last 0.5 mi. to the trailhead is not plowed but space for two cars is available at this point at the fork just before the bridge over Pond Brook, 1.7 mi. From NH 113A.

Sandwich Notch Rd. is closed in winter, rendering the Algonquin Trail inaccessible by vehicle.

The village of Waterville Valley and beyond as seen from Sandwich Dome.

Welch Mountain/Dickey Mountain

Elevations: 2,598 ft. / 2,722 ft.
Location: Town of Waterville Valley
Map: WVAIA map, AMC Map - Moosilauke/Kinsman Ridge
Locator map: 52

Note: While these mountains are indicated as two separate peaks on maps and can be climbed individually, they are combined into and count as one hike for the purposes of the 52WAV list.

Welch and Dickey Mountains are a pair of low but very scenic peaks located at the end of a southwest ridge extending from their 4,000 footer neighbor Mt. Tecumseh. Their extensive bare ledges, scorched by fire during the early 1800s, followed by an intense rainstorm several years later, were stripped of soil and trees to reveal panoramic views. The spectacular vistas make this one of the best "bang for your buck" short hikes in the White Mountains. Along with Carter Ledge on Mt. Chocorua and Mt. Webster, Welch Mountain is one of only a handful of locations in the White Mountains where the fire-dependent jack pine can be found.

The origin of the Welch name is uncertain, but it was applied to the peak by the 1850s. Dickey Mountain was originally considered a northern peak of Welch and was sometimes referred to as "Big Welch". The Dickey name first appeared on AMC maps during the 1930s and is thought to have been derived from two possible origins. The first being a young farm laborer named Martin Dickey who lived in Waterville Valley during the 1860s and the second being area guide Monroe Dickey, born in Thornton in 1838.

Hikers descend Dickey Mountain's great southwest slab.

GETTING THERE

The trailhead and parking area (WMNF fee area) are off Orris Rd. in Thornton. On summer weekends it is recommended to arrive as early as possible as this hike is popular and the lot fills up quickly. An alternative to begin your hike later in the day or visit during the week if possible. To reach the trailhead from I-93, take Exit 28 and follow NH 49 east for 5.5 mi. Turn left onto Upper Mad River Rd. for 0.7 mi., then turn right onto Orris Rd. and continue 0.6 mi. to the trailhead. Restrooms are available.

ROUTE

Welch-Dickey Loop Trail

Welch Mountain only: 3.8 mi. round-trip with 1,550 ft. elevation gain
Dickey Mountain only: 4.2 mi. round-trip with 1,650 ft. elevation gain
Complete counter-clockwise loop over both: 4.4 mi. with 1,800 ft. elevation gain
While either peak can be climbed individually, they are most commonly combined into the loop which is described below. This loop can be done in either direction, but it is generally easier to ascend the steeper ledges on

Welch and descend via Dickey. Footing is generally good throughout the loop. The open ledges are grippy when dry, but use caution if wet. The ascent up Welch involves some moderately challenging scrambles.

From the top of the parking area, yellow-blazed Welch-Dickey Loop Trail starts at a fork, turns sharply right to cross a small brook, then swings left and ascends moderately alongside it. The trail then makes two right turns away from the brook and climbs at easy grades. At 1.2 mi. the trail swings left up inclined ledges, then right, to reach a ledgy area and the first outlook on the open shoulder of Welch. Follow blazing carefully in this stretch and keep off fragile vegetation which has been ringed by small stones. The trail reaches a large granite slab at 1.3 mi. which provides excellent views over Mad River Valley to Sandwich Dome, Jennings Peak, and the Tripyramids. This spot also allows for a good view of Welch Mountain's summit ahead.

The trail turns left here and runs nearly level then begins climbing through areas of scrub and ledge to ascend a huge, exposed, steeply-sloping slab with an excellent view at top. Above this slab, the trail swings left and winds up through more slabs and patches of woods, then scrambles up ledge steps through a large split rock and crosses another sloping slab. It bends left past a rock wall, then ascends over open ledges to the summit at 1.9 mi. The highest point is atop an uplifted ledge on the left.

From the summit, the trail descends quite steeply over ledge steps (use caution if wet), with a high dropoff on the right, to the saddle between the peaks, which is marked by a large cairn. The trail re-enters the woods for a short easy walk, then curves left to begin a steep and more rugged climb with several scrambles toward Dickey, swinging right to traverse the top of an exposed sloping ledge, then turning left through a belt of scrub to emerge on more slabs.

On the right at this belt of scrub, an unmarked and obscure side path leads 0.2 mi. to an enormous open slab (visible from the main trail) on the northern shoulder of Dickey. This is perhaps the best spot on the mountain with wide views to neighboring Fisher Mountain, Hogsback Mountain, Green Mountain, Foss Peak, Mt. Tecumseh and the Mad River Valley. It is easy to stray off this path, but since the target ledge can be clearly seen the route can be navigated visually. Use care to walk on ledge only and do not trample the fragile vegetation in this area.

The main trail continues ascending over open ledges with views to reach Dickey's flat summit at 2.4 mi., where views are more limited than on Welch. The trail runs across the wooded crest, swings left to begin the descent over open ledges, then swings right to traverse a huge angled slab which is sometimes wet. This slab is best negotiated along the right (top) edge. The trail dips back into the woods at the bottom right of this slab, then turns left at a cairn and climbs up another ledge. Descend along this broad slab, turn left at the bottom, then make a brief climb to emerge on Dickey's great lower slab, with the deep valley between the peaks far below. Use caution here if wet and keep children and pets close as the dropoff on the left is straight down. Views are excellent here with Welch looming high on the left. In foliage season this is a prime viewing area.

Walk easily down this massive slab to soak in the views before dropping back into the woods at 3.2 mi. Descend a minor scramble, traverse another ledge, then hop down at left turn, as the trail follows a ledge wall on the left which often has impressive ice formations in winter. The trail descends a steep section on rock steps, then meanders moderately down the south ridge of Dickey; grades ease lower down. At 4.3 mi., the trail reaches a junction with Brown Ash Swamp Trail (a mountain bike route formerly known as Dickey Notch Trail), which turns right for Dickey Notch. Welch-Dickey Loop Trail turns left here for an easy 0.1 mi. descent back to the trailhead and parking area.

VIEW HIGHLIGHTS

Welch Mountain summit: Welch's uplifted summit ledge affords excellent views in all directions. Its nearest neighbor to the southwest is Dickey Mountain. To the right at the end of a ridge extending northeast from Dickey is Mt. Tecumseh, followed by Green Mountain and the unofficially-named Foss Peak. Next up to the right are Scaur Peak and the Tripyramids, the rolling ridge of the Sleepers, with the low ridge of Snows Mountain below and in front of those peaks.

Across the Mad River Valley to the east is the massive Sandwich Dome, with the sharp Jennings Peak on the left and Sachem Peak below. Looking further right to the southeast across Sandwich Notch, Dinsmore Mountain and the Squam Range can be seen along with Red Hill. Mt. Major is seen beyond Red Hill, as is the Belknap Range. Close by to the south is the Campton Range with Hersey Mountain appearing over the right end of it.

Continuing to the right, a distant Mt. Kearsarge appears over Bridgewater Mountain, with Plymouth closer in and to the right of Bridgewater. Lovewell Mountain is over the left end of Plymouth, while Mt. Sunapee is seen over the right end. Mt. Cardigan is visible after Plymouth, followed by Stinson

Mountain. Closer in under Stinson is the ledgy Cone Mountain across Dickey Notch, then the long ridge of Carr Mountain comes into view behind Cone. On extremely clear days Killington Peak can be seen behind Carr. Further right is an excellent look across the wooded ravine between Welch and Dickey with the latter peak's great southwest ridge and slab on full display. Beyond the slab the view moves out to Mt. Kineo and Mt. Moosilauke.

Dickey Mountain summit: Dickey is less open at the top than Welch, but several open ledge viewpoints provide outlooks in various directions, largely similar to the ones on Welch. They include a ledge just east of the summit which provides a view north, a nearby ledge which offers a view south, and a short distance east is a vast area of open ledge which offers wide views from the northwest to the south. Dickey's open southwest ridge features excellent views to the south and southeast, as well as back up to Welch.

Dickey Mountain's northern slab: Perhaps the best view on the mountain, and certainly the most open, is the great slab located at the end of the side path 0.2 mi. north of Dickey's summit. This massive expanse of granite provides an even closer look up the ridge to Mt. Tecumseh. An additional view seen here is a look north to the Kinsmans and Franconia Ridge. This vantage point cannot be seen from Welch as Dickey itself blocks the view.

WINTER

The loop over Welch-Dickey is a wonderful winter trek in the right conditions. Plenty of snow is needed to cover the steep ledges which are potentially dangerous if icy; full crampons may be required in such conditions. Where the trail drops off the lower Dickey slabs and into the woods can also collect a lot of ice. As most blazing will be hidden by snow, the trail must be followed carefully on the open ledges. Some protection from the wind is offered in wooded sections but other areas are very exposed. The large parking area is plowed but the bathrooms are not available.

Alternatively, the first open ledges on the Welch side of the loop (2.6 mi. round-trip with 850 ft. elevation gain) and the great lower slab on the Dickey side (2.4 mi. round-trip with 1,150 ft. elevation gain) make for excellent shorter objectives. Both offer excellent views. Use caution on the Dickey slab in winter as it is something you definitely don't want to slide off.

Western New Hampshire

Black Mountain (Benton)

Elevation: 2,829 ft.
Location: Town of Benton
Map: AMC Map - Moosilauke/Kinsman Ridge
Locator map: 01

Taking a break on the ledges along the upper Chippewa Trail on Black Mountain.

Black Mountain is not the highest peak in the Benton Range, a series of ledgy mountains in western New Hampshire, but it is certainly the most scenic. Its open, swirling quartzite ledges provide expansive views in multiple directions. Moses Sweetser wrote of Black Mountain in his 1876 White Mountains guidebook: *"From several of the Connecticut Valley hamlets this fine peak is seen, boldly relieved against the sky, and forming the most conspicuous element in the landscape."*

A series of fire towers were in operation at the summit from 1911 to 1964, with the most recent being removed in 1978; a few relics are still present.

Tilton resident Maude Bickford, along with her small dog Fritz, was one of the early staffers for the tower, part of a group of women recruited by USFS to serve as fire lookouts. This group was known as the WOOFs, or Women Observers of the Forest.

On the southwest side of the mountain are two historic lime kilns constructed in 1838 and 1842, which can be visited via a side path off Chippewa Trail. The kilns were an important part of 19th century industry in this area, heating mined limestone into powdered lime for use in agriculture and other products. The kilns operated for about 50 years and the site is currently maintained for public access. More information is available at haverhill-nh.com.

As is the case with many other Black Mountains around the state, this Black Mountain probably received its name from the dark conifer growth on its upper reaches.

GETTING THERE

A small parking area with room for a few cars is located along Lime Kiln Rd. in Haverhill. From NH 25 in East Haverhill, take Lime Kiln Rd. northeast, paved at first and then dirt, for 3.1 mi. to the trailhead and a small parking area (the trail sign is not always visible from the road) on the right.

RECOMMENDED ROUTE

Chippewa Trail

3.6 mi. round-trip with 1,600 ft. elevation gain

Yellow-blazed Chippewa Trail, once known as Southwest Trail, offers a steeper but also more scenic approach to Black Mountain than the more gradual and viewless Black Mountain Trail, especially in its upper half, as the trail climbs over open ledges with expansive views. Also watch markings on these ledges carefully as they are somewhat faded.

From the parking area, Chippewa Trail descends moderately at first over log steps through a logged area to cross several small brooks (the third of which may be flooded by beaver activity), then climbs to a T-junction with a old woods road at 0.2 mi. (turn left here and follow signs for the short side trip to the lime kilns).

Chippewa Trail turns right onto the road, then left off it at the second of two left forks (yellow blaze), and soon enters the Forest Society's Kingsbury Timber - Chippewa Trail Lot. At times this section of Chippewa Trail may be closed or disrupted by logging operations. The trail ascends moderately at first along another road, passes an old cellar hole on the right at the edge of a recent clear-cut area, then soon becomes steeper as it makes its way up the southwest ridge.

The trail turns sharply left at 1.0 mi. and then again at 1.1 mi., where a short side path diverges right to an outlook ledge with views south and west. Above this point, spectacular views in various directions increase, accessed by short side paths, as the trail breaks out into the open to reach large ledges with expansive views southeast, south and west. The cliffs here warrant exploration, but use caution as the dropoff is precipitous. Just ahead is a look up to the rocky summit of Black Mountain. The trail descends slightly back into the woods, then climbs gradually to a junction with Black Mountain Trail at 1.8 mi.

Turn right at the junction and make a short climb through a wooded gateway to emerge on the narrow ridgecrest and site of the former fire tower, where iron relics are still embedded in the quartzite ledges. From this spot, the best western viewpoint is 100 ft. to the right, while the best eastern views are found by turning left. The high point is the fire tower site. Also on the northeast end of the ridge, about 0.1 mi. from the summit, is Tipping Rock, a large glacial boulder perched on a flat, open ledge.

VIEW HIGHLIGHTS

South outlook: Fine views south are instantly available as soon as you step out of the woods and onto Black's ledgy ridgecrest. The most dominant feature is Mt. Moosilauke, just 6 mi. away to the southeast — one of the finest views anywhere of this gentle giant. Benton Ravine is well seen below the rounded summit. Moosilauke's South Peak is at the right end of the mountain, with Mt. Clough lower and closer. Moosilauke's lower spurs Hurricane Mountain and Chokecherry Hill are visible to the right of Clough. Across the valley of Titus Brook to the south are Black's neighbors in the Benton Range, starting with Jeffers Mountain, and the backside of the Hogsback ridge extending over to the abrupt cone of officially-trailless Sugarloaf Mountain. Blueberry Mountain can also be seen beyond Jeffers. Seen in the distance over the ridge between Jeffers and Sugarloaf are Forbes and Ragged Mountains, Tinkham Hill, Mt. Kearsarge, and Mt. Cardigan, and a far away Mt. Sunapee is visible over Sugarloaf. Further right are Smarts Mountain, Mt. Cube, and Piermont Mountain all lined up in a row, followed by Mt. Ascutney in Vermont.

West outlook: From the western end of the summit ridge, expansive views open up across the Connecticut River Valley and deep into Vermont. Continuing to the right of Ascutney, many other far off Vermont peaks are visible including Mt. Snow, Stratton, Bromley and Okemo Mountains, and Peru Peak. Looking southwest and down are the rocky crags which Chippewa Trail traverses, and on the horizon in this direction, the entire ridge of the Green Mountains takes rise, continuing many miles north to Mt. Mansfield and Jay Peak, Mts. Hor and Pisgah, and Bald Mountain near Lake Willoughby in Vermont's Northeast Kingdom. On the far right looking north are Burke and Umpire Mountains, East Haven Mountain, and East Mountain. Seen in the valley below are the towns of Bath, Woodsville, North Haverhill and Haverhill Corner, NH, and Wells River, Newbury and Bradford, VT.

East outlook: The vista here requires a short walk down to the eastern end of the summit ridge taking care to not trample and vegetation. Short connecting paths make passage easy to an enormous open ledge 0.1 mi. east of the summit. This is also where Tipping Rock is located.

Mt. Moosilauke dominates the southeast view as described earlier. To the left of Moosilauke East Osceola and Scar Ridge are seen, followed by ex-52WAV peak Mt. Wolf. Mts. Liberty and Flume are left of Wolf with the Kinsmans next in line. Mt. Lincoln is just left of South Kinsman, and behind North Kinsman is Mt. Lafayette. Close by and under the Kinsmans is the wooded and very ferny Howe Hill, which was once accessible by trail but is now a relatively easy bushwhack. Further left from the Kinsmans is Cannon Mountain, and Big Bickford and Scarface Mountains can be seen over the left ridge of Cannon.

The view moves around to Cherry Mountain and Mts. Starr King and Waumbek, with Mts. Agassiz and Cleveland in Bethlehem in front and closer in. Further left is Mt. Cabot, rising over Cooley and Cole Hills after which the Pilot Range comes into view. On the far left the Nash Stream Valley peaks appear — Long Mountain, the Percy Peaks, Mt. Muise, Sugarloaf, Bunnell Mountain, and Savage and Goback Mountains.

ADDITIONAL ROUTES

Black Mountain Trail

4.8 mi. round-trip with 1,300 ft. elevation gain

This longer and lesser-used approach from Howe Hill Rd. in Benton is easier and more gradual, following old logging roads and the eroded former fire warden's road with no views until the top. From NH 116 in Benton, follow

Howe Hill Rd. for 0.8 mi. to a parking area in front of a fence on the left (hiker sign), taking care to not block the adjacent private driveway. High-clearance vehicles can drive 0.2 mi. further up the unmaintained portion of the road to another parking area at the official start of the trail.

Black Mountain Traverse
3.9 mi. traverse with 1,600 ft. elevation gain
This route traverses the entire Black Mountain ridge from southwest to northeast starting on Lime Kiln Rd. and uses the steeper Chippewa Trail for the ascent and the more gradual Black Mountain Trail for the descent. This hike requires a somewhat lengthy car spot. Add 0.2 mi. if parking at the maintained end of Howe Hill Rd. for Black Mountain Trail.

WINTER
Views on Black Mountain are spectacular in the clear winter air. The steep climb up Chippewa Trail can be challenging if not broken out and crampons may be required on the upper open ledges if conditions are crusty or icy. Open areas may be an issue if windy but these stretches are short-lived. Lime Kiln Rd. is plowed in winter as is the parking area.

If approaching via Black Mountain Trail, Howe Hill Rd. is plowed up to the last house at the end of the road, with parking by the fence. The remaining 0.2 mile to the actual trailhead is not plowed. The moderate grades of Black Mountain Trail make for good snowshoeing and part of the route is sometimes packed down by snowmobiles. Deep snow greatly improves the normally eroded footing. This route is also wooded the whole way, offering good protection from the wind.

Blueberry Mountain

Elevation: 2,663 ft.
Location: Town of Benton
Map: AMC Map - Moosilauke/Kinsman Ridge
Locator map: 02

Blueberry Mountain is situated at the southern end of the Benton Range, a series of ledgy mountains which include fellow 52WAV peak Black Mountain. Once fully open, Blueberry still offers excellent views, especially toward its larger neighbor Mt. Moosilauke, from various bare ledges along Blueberry Mountain Trail, the sole hiking trail on the peak. A side path leads to the actual summit which is a short distance off the main trail.

Moses Sweetser wrote highly of Blueberry in his 1876 guidebook: *"For about 1 M. from the summit the mountain is free from trees and is covered with alternate bands of carpet-like moss and granite ledges moderately inclined. The work of ascent and exploration is thus rendered easy and pleasant."* He also described the view as being that *"of great extent and beauty"*.

In the 1930s, Dartmouth Outing Club constructed a shelter just 50 yds. from the summit, but it was removed only a decade later.

No surprise here as to how the mountain received its name. In the 1800s when the upper slopes were mostly treeless, blueberry bushes were abundant.

A grand view of Mt. Moosilauke from Blueberry Mountain Trail.

GETTING THERE

As of late 2019, the southeast trailhead for Blueberry Mountain Trail remains inaccessible by vehicle due to Long Pond Rd. (WMNF Forest Rd. 19) being repaired from damage caused by a 2017 storm. Active logging was also underway here. At times, the road may be posted against foot traffic while heavy equipment is in the area. See fs.usda.gov for updates. If the road is accessible by foot, hikers should park at the junction of Long Pond Rd. and High St., 1.0 mi. north of NH 25, where there is room along the road. Please do not block the end of the road or the gate. If Long Pond Rd. is open for driving, the formal trailhead and a small parking area are 0.7 mi. up the road on the left.

RECOMMENDED ROUTE
Blueberry Mountain Trail (southeast approach)
Summit only: 4.8 mi. round-trip with 1,310 ft. elevation gain
Northwest ledges: 5.4 mi. round-trip with 1,410 ft. elevation gain

> **A note on access via Long Pond Rd.:** The distance and elevation gain noted above include the walk from High St. If the road is open to the trailhead, subtract 1.4 mi. round-trip and 210 ft. from the totals.

Yellow-blazed Blueberry Mountain Trail traverses the peak from southeast to northwest, and this southeast approach is the shorter and more traveled of the two ascents. Footing is generally good and grades are easy to moderate the whole way. Logging operations have disrupted both ends of Blueberry Mountain Trail in recent years; follow signs and markings carefully.

From the parking on High St., pass through the gate and ascend easily on Long Pond Rd. to the trailhead on the left at 0.7 mi. (sign). Blueberry Mountain Trail ascends easily along a wide logging road, turning right off it at a small cairn and a boulder with a yellow blaze at 0.9 mi. The trail then climbs moderately along an older woods road, recrosses the original logging road at 1.1 mi. (a short distance right is an excellent view up to Mt. Moosilauke from the top of a clear-cut area), then continues a gentle climb through formerly logged woods which very abruptly change to dark conifer forest at 1.5 mi. It reaches the first ledges at 1.8 mi., where looks back provide views to Mts. Moosilauke and Clough.

At 2.0 mi. the trail swings right in an area of ledges. At this turn, the former Owls Head Trail, now fully reclaimed by nature, departed left and descended moderately for 0.8 mi. to the high cliff known as Owls Head, frequented by rock climbers and prominently seen rising over man-made Oliverian Pond from NH 25.

Blueberry Mountain Trail winds its way up the ridge over ledges with a few minor scrambles, to a junction with a short side path on the right at 2.3 mi. which leads to a large open ledge and an excellent view of Mt. Moosilauke; this is perhaps one of the finest perspectives on this giant. The main trail continues climbing easily to the height-of-land at 2.4 mi., just shy of the summit. Here, an unmarked side path on the right leads to the actual summit, across from a large boulder on the left side of the trail. There is also an old double yellow blaze on a tree to the right but it is very faded and hard to see. In late 2019, this junction was also marked with two small cairns. This side path zig zags 90 yds. up through a narrow ledge cut with one minor scramble to Blueberry's high point at 2.5 mi., marked by a small cairn. Old iron pins and trace of a triangle etched into the summit ledge can still be seen from when Blueberry was a U.S. Coastal Survey station in the late 1800s.

For additional views to the northwest toward Vermont, backtrack to the side path junction and turn right onto the northwestern section of Blueberry Mountain Trail. The trail descends easily on a winding route with one minor scramble for 0.3 mi. to reach a large open area of ledges with expansive views. Visiting this outlook requires a 100 ft. ascent on the return trip.

VIEW HIGHLIGHTS

Many years ago, the summit and upper reaches of Blueberry were completely open with unobstructed views all around. Decades of the tree growth have reduced the panoramas, but several excellent viewpoints still exist from various open ledges.

South outlook: This open ledge just 20 ft. off trail, 2.2 mi. up from High St., provides the best views in this direction. The view, best if standing, begins on the far left with Mt. Kineo, connected by a ridge to Whitcher Hill, and then onto the extended ridge of Carr Mountain. A portion of the village of Glencliff is visible below Carr. Extending right from Carr is one of its subpeaks Ames Mountain, with Oregon and Mowglis Mountains, Firescrew, and Mt. Cardigan further back. On clear days, Mt. Kearsarge can be seen to the left of Cardigan. Closer in to the right of Cardigan is Wyatt Hill, and Mt. Sunapee can sometimes be spotted on the horizon. Further right, Smarts Mountain rises in the distance, and Mt. Mist with a slice of Wachipauka Pond is visible below. Mt. Cube appears next in line, and on the far right is a partial view of Piermont Mountain with Vermont's Glebe and Stratton Mountains visible on clear days.

East outlook: An open ledge 2.3 mi. up from High St. provides an excellent view east toward Blueberry's largest neighbor Mt. Moosilauke. From this vantage point is a unique look directly into the ravine of Slide Brook between the main summit and South Peak, surrounded by gravelly slides.

Northwest outlook: This open ledgy area along the northwestern section of Blueberry Mountain Trail provides good views out over the Connecticut River Valley toward Vermont, as well as looks to other peaks in the Benton Range. The full vista can be seen by moving around a bit.

Starting on the far left is Mt. Cube, Mt. Ascutney, Stonehouse Mountain, Stratton Mountain, and Cube's neighbor Piermont Mountain, with parts of the village of Haverhill visible in the valley below. On very clear days the extended ridge of the Green Mountains can be seen along the distant horizon. Looking southwest are the sharp Killington and Pico Peaks, Mt. Carmel, Bloodroot Mountain, Farr Peak, Cape Lookoff Mountain, Philadelphia Peak, Monastery Mountain, and Worth Mountain appearing between Sherburne Pass and Middlebury Gap. Further right are the peaks in Vermont's Presidential Range: Bread Loaf Mountain, Mt. Wilson, and Mt. Grant among others. Two more of Vermont's 4,000 footers, Mts. Abraham and Ellen, appear to the right of the Presidentials followed by the Signal Mountain range, Mt. Mansfield's long ridgecrest, and the sharper peaks of the Sterling Range. The twin rounded summits of Marshfield and Burnt Mountains are visible next in line, with the Woodbury Mountains further right and more distant. The view then moves around further northwest to the very distant northern Green Mountain peaks of Big Jay and Jay Peak, both only really visible on extremely clear days. Moving back in closer to the north-northwest, the view comes back to New Hampshire with a look out to Blueberry's neighbors in the Benton Range: Sugarloaf Mountain, Black Mountain, and the rugged cliffs of The Hogsback, which connects Sugarloaf to Jeffers Mountain, the next peak up the range from Blueberry.

Blueberry Mountain summit: Views from the high point of Blueberry are mostly restricted by tree growth, but wandering around the summit area provides looks to Mt. Moosilauke, Carr Mountain, Ragged Mountain, Mts. Cardigan and Cube and Piermont Mountain.

ADDITIONAL ROUTES
Blueberry Mountain Trail (northwest approach)
5.8 mi. round-trip with 1,500 ft. elevation gain

This longer and lesser-used approach from Blueberry Mountain Rd. (WMNF Forest Rd. 107) offers a quieter and more gradual climb, mostly along old logging roads. From East Haverhill, take Lime Kiln Rd. for 1.4 mi., then bear right onto Page Rd. In 0.8 mi., turn left onto Blueberry Mountain Rd. and continue to a gate in 0.1 mi., where there is limited parking.

Blueberry Mountain Trail Traverse
4.5 mi. traverse with 1,500 ft. elevation gain

This route, which requires a car spot, traverses the entire Blueberry Mountain Trail from northwest to southeast, starting at the gate on Blueberry Mountain Rd. If Long Pond Rd. on the southeast end of the trail is still inaccessible at the time of the hike, add 0.7 mi. to the distance.

OVERNIGHT OPTIONS

Jeffers Brook Shelter is located at the base of Blueberry Mountain just off Town Line Trail, 0.2 mi. south of Long Pond Rd. The shelter is first come, first served, and water is available from Jeffers Brook. There is a privy. Town Line Trail is a section of the Appalachian Trail, so this shelter is fairly busy in the summer months. More information is available at fs.usda.gov.

WINTER

Blueberry Mountain is an excellent winter hike with easy to moderate grades for snowshoeing and fairly good protection from the elements. Crampons may be required on the open ledges in crusty or icy conditions. Parking is usually available along High St. but may not be possible depending on snowfall amounts. Alternate plowed parking is available 0.3 mi. further up High St. at the lot for Glencliff Trail, although it is small and tends to fill up quickly on weekends by hikers bound for Mt. Moosilauke.

If attempting to ascend from the northwest, Page Rd. is plowed out to the last house, but the short stretch of Blueberry Mountain Rd. before that point to the trailhead is not plowed. As there is no room to park along Page Rd., this approach to Blueberry is less feasible in winter unless snowfall is light.

Mt. Cardigan

Elevation: 3,149 ft.
Location: Town of Orange
Map: NHDP map, AMC Southern New Hampshire Guide map
Locator map: 13

Mt. Cardigan is one of the finest peaks in west-central New Hampshire, offering unrivaled vistas in all directions from its completely open summit, which also has an active fire tower. Ironically, Cardigan became bare due to an 1855 fire which swept over the ridge. Excellent views can also be found on

Cardigan's South Peak (2,862 ft.), as well as its northern subpeak Firescrew (3,063 ft.), and neighboring Orange Mountain (2,684 ft.) to the south.

The origin of the Cardigan name is uncertain but it may be of English descent like many New England locations. According to a 1941 issue of Appalachia, the peak was named after the original township in which most of it lies, which was granted in 1769 as Cardigan. In 1790, the town was incorporated as Orange, but the mountain retained its original name. Local residents once referred to the mountain as Old Baldy, an obvious reference to Cardigan's bare ledges. Firescrew gets its unusual name from the swirls of smoke and flame which rose from the mountain during the 1855 blaze. An 1898 issue of Granite State Monthly refers to Mt. Cardigan as Cardigan Dome, Firescrew as North Peak, and Grotto Cave as Cardigan Cave.

Approaching the summit of Mt. Cardigan in winter.

GETTING THERE

Parking is available at AMC Cardigan Lodge at the end of Shem Valley Rd. in Alexandria. From NH 3A in Bristol, 2.0 mi. north of NH 104, take West Shore Rd. northwest for 1.7 mi., continuing straight onto Cardigan Mountain Rd. (signs pointing the way to the lodge begin here) which turns into Fowler River Rd. once it crosses into Alexandria. In 1.1 mi., bear left onto North Rd. and continue to Alexandria Village in 0.9 mi. Here, turn right onto Washburn Rd. for 0.1 mi., then bear right onto Mt. Cardigan Rd. for 3.6 mi. to a junction where Brook Rd. diverges sharply right at a hairpin turn. Continue straight onto Shem Valley Rd. to reach the lodge in 1.4 mi. Shem Valley Rd. is usually passable for any vehicle but can be muddy and rutted in the spring.

RECOMMENDED ROUTE
Manning Trail, Mowglis Trail, Clark Trail, Holt-Clark Cutoff, Holt Trail

6.0 mi. counter-clockwise loop with 1,920 ft. elevation gain

This very scenic loop over Mt. Cardigan and its northern subpeak Firescrew offers a little under two miles of open ledge walking with expansive views. Grades are generally moderate except for some steep scrambling up to the Firescrew ridge and the steep slabs on Cardigan's summit cone. Footing is also generally good with some rougher sections. The route is described here in the counter-clockwise direction as the scrambles along Manning Trail are easier to ascend.

From the far end of the parking area at Cardigan Lodge, Manning Trail, blazed in yellow, heads west along a wide road, quickly passing a junction on the right with Back 80 Trail, then heads through an area of campsites to reach a forked junction with Holt Trail which diverges left. Manning Trail bears right onto an old woods road, ascends easily, then turns right off the road (signs) at 0.6 mi. The trail climbs moderately and crosses Allieway Ski Trail, one of several backcountry ski trails on this side of the mountain, then ascends more steeply with rougher footing and one minor scramble to a ledge with a view toward Mt. Cardigan. The trail then re-enters the woods and descends to a small brook with several giant boulders on the left, which it follows for a short distance and then crosses. After a brief ascent away from the brook, the trail emerges on the lower ledges of Firescrew at the eastern end of the ridge. Views open up as the trail ascends over open slabs. At the top of this section, the trail dips back into the woods and scrambles up a steep and rough section which is often wet. A well-beaten bypass on the right provides an alternative route. Above this point, a few more scrambles lead to the open ridge as grades ease. The trail winds up the open ridge from this point through many twists and turns (watch blazes and cairns carefully), with excellent views with Mt. Cardigan visible ahead. Walking becomes easy as the trail reaches a junction with Mowglis Trail at 2.6 mi., close to the Firescrew summit. The high point is an uplifted ledge on the right.

Turning left at this junction, white-blazed Mowglis Trail descends easily southwest through alternating areas of ledge and scrub to a broad saddle. Here, an obscure 0.2 mi. side path leaves on the left and descends very steeply down tricky slabs to Grotto Cave; this path was illegally blazed in blue in 2016. The main trail then begins the final ascent to Mt. Cardigan, easily at first, then steeply up the cone over open slabs with expansive views, reaching the bare summit and fire tower at 3.2 mi.

After a long breather to soak in the views, descend southeast for a very short distance on white-blazed Clark Trail over vast ledges to a junction with West Ridge Trail, blazed in orange, which continues ahead. Clark Trail turns left here and descends along the summit ledges, easily at first, then steeply to a junction with South Ridge Trail and the fire warden's cabin on the right at 3.4 mi. Clark Trail's blazing color changes to yellow as it turns left and descends moderately through a mix of ledge and scrub to cross a small brook, reaching the junction with Hurricane Gap Trail on the left (this trail may be relocated in the future). Continuing a moderate descent, the trail passes the P.J. Ledge viewpoint on the left and a junction with Alexandria Ski Trail, then reaches a junction at 4.1 mi. with Holt-Clark Cutoff on the left.

Holt-Clark Cutoff descends moderately through switchbacks to a junction with Vistamont Trail on the right (this trail leads to the ledgy Orange Mountain, an excellent destination with wonderful views), then soon ends at Grand Junction at 4.8 mi., an area where several hiking and ski trails meet. Turn right onto Holt Trail and then bear right onto Manning Trail for a 1.2 mi. walk back to the lodge.

VIEW HIGHLIGHTS

Cardigan's 360-degree views are mostly distant but extend in all directions from the completely bare summit. On clear winter days, the Adirondack Mountains in New York can be seen.

Close by to the north is Cardigan's ledgy subpeak Firescrew, a wonderful destination in itself. Beyond Firescrew is a jumble of peaks and ridges which make up the bulk of the White Mountains, stretching from the Benton Range on the left to Mt. Moosilauke, the Kinsmans, Franconia Ridge, the Presidentials, and the Sandwich Range on the right.

Looking west is closer Plymouth Mountain with the Ossipee Range beyond. To the right of the Ossipees is the Belknap Range, then the landscape flattens out with dozens of small hills in eastern and southeastern New Hampshire punctuating the horizon, before Mt. Kearsarge pops up beyond Cardigan's southern ridge. This ridge extends out from the mountain's South Peak across Orange Mountain, Crane Mountain, Grafton

Knob, and Brown and Church Mountains. The Skyland Trail from Alexandria Four Corners traverses this ridge.

Just about due south, a very distant Mt. Monadnock can be seen on extremely clear days, followed by peaks in the New London, Grantham and Croydon areas, including the bare summit of privately-owned Croydon Peak. To the right of Croydon is the prominent Mt. Ascutney in Vermont, before the view shifts around to the west to the distant long ridge of the Green Mountains, with Killington and Pico Peaks being the most visible.

Closer in and only 20 mi. away to the northwest is Smarts Mountain, which was once connected to Cardigan via a long-distance trail. Mt. Cube is seen to the right of Smarts, followed by Piermont Mountain, before the view arrives back at the Benton Range.

The views from Firescrew are largely the same as those on Cardigan, except with a wider vista to the north. Looks back to the south are partially obscured by Cardigan itself.

ADDITIONAL ROUTES

West Ridge Trail
3.0 mi. round-trip with 1,250 ft. elevation gain
This direct route from Cardigan Mountain State Park in Orange is the easiest and shortest approach to the summit. As such it is also very popular and heavily-traveled, but is an excellent route for both children and beginner hikers. From US 4 in Canaan, follow NH 118 north for 0.5 mi. then turn right onto Cardigan Mountain Rd. and follow signs to the state park in 4.0 mi.

Holt Trail, Clark Trail, Holt-Clark Cutoff
4.8 mi. counter-clockwise loop with 1,750 ft. elevation gain
Holt Trail from AMC Cardigan Lodge provides the most difficult route to the summit, with very steep ledges, great exposure and two very difficult scrambles in its upper half. While not located in the White Mountains, Holt Trail is considered to be one of the most difficult routes in New Hampshire.

> **Warning:** The upper section of Holt Trail should not be attempted if it is wet or icy, and should definitely not be used for descent. This route is best suited for experienced hikers only.

Knowles Hill Rd., Church Hill Rd., Skyland Trail, South Ridge Trail, Clark Trail, Woodland Trail

10.6 mi. clockwise loop with 2,810 ft. elevation gain

This long, remote and scenic trek from Alexandria Four Corners in Alexandria provides a quieter approach from the south. This route is lightly traveled and you will encounter few other hikers. Skyland Trail is a ridgecrest route with numerous ledgy viewpoints, passing over Brown Mountain, Church Mountain, Grafton Knob, Crane Mountain, and Orange Mountain on the way to Mt. Cardigan, before the route loops back to Church Mountain via the lesser-used Woodland Trail (requires some care to follow) from Cardigan Lodge. To reach Alexandria Four Corners from Alexandria Village, follow the directions above for AMC Cardigan Lodge but stay on Washburn Rd., bearing right at a fork 0.6 mi. from the village, and continue to the crossroads at 3.8 mi. Limited roadside parking is available anywhere at this intersection but use care to not block residential access.

Elwell Trail, Mowglis Trail, Clark Trail, Holt-Clark Cutoff, Holt Trail, Manning Trail

15.2 mi. traverse with 4,760 ft. elevation gain

This long traverse starting near Wellington State Park in Bristol and ending at AMC Cardigan Lodge makes a very remote approach through the wild country north of Mt. Cardigan. Portions of the lightly used Elwell Trail may be difficult to follow west of Bear Mountain, but the trail has been seeing improved maintenance in recent years. Hikers should be aware that Elwell Trail is frequently disrupted by logging, which can make it difficult to follow. This route requires a car spot. To reach the trailhead, follow the directions above for AMC Cardigan Lodge but turn right at 1.7 mi. from NH 3A to stay on West Shore Rd. and continue 1.2 mi. to the parking area for Elwell Trail (sign) on the left.

OVERNIGHT OPTIONS

AMC Cardigan Lodge is a full-service, year-round facility at the eastern base of the mountain, offering private and bunk rooms. In addition, designated camping sites are located nearby off Holt and Back 80 Trails.

AMC High Cabin, off Hurricane Gap Trail about a half mile below the summit, features bunk beds, a wood stove and a composting toilet.

A designated backcountry group camping site with five tent platforms is located off Woodland Trail, 1.0 mi. from Cardigan Lodge.

Reservations are required for the above two options. More information is available at outdoors.org.

Crag Camp, originally built in the 1920s and maintained by staff from Camp Mowglis, is a remote, primitive shelter located along Mowglis Trail, 0.5 mi. north of Firescrew. A nearby brook provides an unreliable water source. It is available for use on a first come, first served basis. This shelter has "character" and isn't the most luxurious, but is perfectly fine for an overnight stay.

WINTER

Mt. Cardigan is a beautiful winter hike in good conditions, offering relief from the summer crowds. Crampons are often needed on the open ledge sections, especially when ascending or descending the steep summit cone. Route-finding along the open Firescrew ridge and Mowglis Trail may be difficult in unbroken snow (blazing along Mowglis Trail is also white) and the scrambles along Manning Trail can be tricky if icy. If necessary, these can be bypassed off to the side. Cardigan's completely open summit makes it vulnerable to severe weather conditions usually experienced on much higher peaks. The base of the fire tower offers some protection from the wind, but be mindful of falling rime ice. When descending off the summit, follow signs and cairns carefully, as several trails leave in different directions. The parking area at Cardigan Lodge is plowed as is Shem Valley Rd., which can become quite narrow due to snowbanks.

The upper Holt Trail is not recommended in winter except for those with ice climbing experience. Crampons, ice axe and rope are mandatory. This route is potentially very dangerous if icy.

Cardigan Mountain State Park is gated in winter so a 0.7 mi. one-way road walk is required to reach the West Ridge trailhead. Plowed parking for several vehicles is available outside the gate at the junction of Cardigan Mountain Rd. and Burnt Hill Rd. in Orange. From this point, the hike is 4.4 mi. round-trip with 1,490 ft. elevation gain.

The southern approach via Skyland Trail may not be possible in winter due to lack of parking at Alexandria Four Corners. This trail is also seldom hiked in winter so route-finding and trail breaking will likely be challenging.

The east slopes of Cardigan are also very popular with backcountry skiers and snowboarders who use a network of ski trails originally cut by the Civilian Conservation Corps and AMC in the 1930s. These ski trails are not maintained for summer use and hikers are requested to not use them.

Mt. Cube (South Peak)

Elevation: 2,916 ft.
Location: Town of Orford
Map: AT map, NG White Mountains map
Locator map: 16

Winter on Mt. Cube's South Peak.

Located within the Middle Connecticut River Mountains in western New Hampshire, scenic Mt. Cube also lies along the Appalachian Trail, which passes over the open South Peak. Mt. Cube is also the eastern terminus and highest point along the Cross Rivendell Trail, a long-distance hiking route stretching 36 miles westward to Flagpole Hill in Vershire, VT. Mt. Cube offers excellent views from both its North and South Peaks, which are separated by a shallow col. South Peak is required for the 52WAV list but North Peak (2,890 ft.) is also well worth the visit.

While the mountain does appear flat-topped and somewhat square from some vantage points, its name is derived from a local legend regarding a hunting dog named Cuba who was attacked by a bear on the mountain during the 19th century. The Cuba name was also given to a remote waterfall (once accessible by trail) along Brackett Brook on the northeast slope of the mountain. A different tale states the Cuba name originated from a West Indian sailor living in the area, presumably after the Caribbean island. The 1932 Dartmouth Outing Club Handbook mentions this name was in use as early as 1805.

GETTING THERE

Parking for several vehicles is available in the turnaround at the end of Baker Rd. in Orford, 0.1 mi. north of the trailhead. From NH 25A, 8.2 mi. west of NH 25 in Wentworth, take Baker Rd. south for 0.8 mi. to parking on the right at the turnaround. Be careful to not block the adjacent private driveway.

RECOMMENDED ROUTE

Cross Rivendell Trail

To South Peak only: 4.2 mi. round-trip with 1,600 ft. elevation gain
To South and North Peaks via Mt. Cube Trail and North Peak Side Trail: 5.0 mi. round-trip with 1,600 ft. elevation gain

Of the three approaches to Mt. Cube, Cross Rivendell Trail is the shortest and one of the most accessible. The trail passes two good viewpoints along the way. There are a few short, steep pitches, including the final ascent to the summit, but grades are generally moderate and footing is mostly good. This section of the CRT is located mostly on private land. Please stay on the marked route.

From the parking at the end of Baker Rd., walk up the unmaintained section of the road for 0.1 mi. to where the blue-blazed trail turns left and enters the woods (sign). The trail ascends easily at first, and then moderately through several switchbacks, jumping on and off its original route several times, all part of a large relocation project undertaken in 2001 to 2003. It continues a moderate ascent up the western slope of the mountain where footing becomes rougher, reaching a hairpin turn to the left. Shortly above this turn the trail passes Spruce Outlook on the left, a cleared viewpoint with a look over to the pyramid-shaped Sunday Mountain, also located along Cross Rivendell Trail. Past the outlook the trail continues to climb moderately with a few short twists and turns to an open ledge at 1.5 mi. with views to the west. The trail turns left here and descends easily to cross a small brook, then resumes a moderate ascent and swings left and right to arrive at the base of the final scramble to the summit. Ascend steeply over the open ledges (use caution if wet) to the partly bare summit of South Peak at 2.1 mi., where Kodak Trail leaves right, and Mt. Cube Trail continues ahead. During the 1870s, Cube's South Peak was the site of a triangulation station for the U.S. Coastal Survey, overseen by Professor E.T. Quimby of Dartmouth College. An old iron bolt and etched triangle can still be seen in the summit ledge.

To visit North Peak, continue straight ahead on the white-blazed Mt. Cube Trail along a ledgy ridge and bear left to drop down a small step (use caution if wet or icy). Turn left (look for an ancient metal trail blaze nailed to a tree here) and descend moderately over ledges to a junction at 2.2 mi., where Mt. Cube Trail/AT diverge right and North Peak Side Trail (sign) continues straight ahead.

This short side trail, a former section of the AT, is mostly easy to navigate, but follow old orange/yellow blazes and cairns on the open ledges carefully. From the junction, North Peak Side Trail descends easily over ledge steps to traverse a broad quartzite ledge, followed by several twists and turns to reach high, open ledges at 2.5 mi., a short distance from the true summit of North Peak. This path has no clear ending on the ledges, it just sort of fades out when it gets there. Hikers may need to make their own route for the last several yards to the cliffs, being careful to not step on any vegetation.

VIEW HIGHLIGHTS

Mt. Cube is graced with two summits which both offer excellent views in different directions. South Peak generally looks south and west while the ledges on North Peak look northeast.

South Peak: Looking south, the dominant feature is the huge mass of Smarts Mountain just 4 mi. away. The backside of the Eastman Ledges, over which the Kodak Trail ascends, can be seen in the foreground under Smarts. Mt. Cardigan is in view to the left of Smarts, with a distant Mt. Kearsarge to its right. Further left is nearby Black Hill, with many central New Hampshire hills beyond. Hersey Mountain is to the left of Black Hill, followed by Mt. Crosby and Tenney and Plymouth Mountains, with the Belknap Range visible over Tenney's long ridge.

To the right of Smarts, off-limits-to-the-public Grantham Mountain and Croydon Peak are visible in the distance over two humps along Smarts' Lambert Ridge. Further right is Moose Mountain in Hanover, which the AT traverses, with Holts Ledge and the Dartmouth Skiway closer in. To the right of these is a distant look to Mt. Ascutney in Vermont, while close by to the southwest are several lower satellites of Smarts — Mousley, Moody,

Stonehouse, and Bundy Mountains. On clear days Stratton Mountain can be seen over Mousley. Okemo Mountain is to the right of Moody, as are Peru Peak and Bromley Mountain. Further to the right is the Shrewsbury-Killington-Pico Range in Vermont's Green Mountains.

Descending back down a few yards along Cross Rivendell Trail opens up a wide view west, with just about the entire spread of the Green Mountains on full display on the horizon, beyond waves of rolling ridges leading out from Cube. The view here stretches from Stratton Mountain on the left to Jay Peak on the right.

North Peak: Over on Mt. Cube's North Peak, roomy quartzite ledges offer a dramatic view down to the Baker River Valley and out to the White Mountains. On the far left is a distant look toward the Northeast Kingdom of Vermont, and close by to the right of that is Piermont Mountain and the Benton Range behind it — Black Mountain, Sugarloaf, The Hogsback, Jeffers Mountain, and Blueberry Mountain. Portions of Lakes Tarleton and Armington lie under Jeffers.

Looking northeast, the view swings around to Mt. Moosilauke, which dominates the scene; this point of view also affords a look directly into Slide Brook Ravine. Mt. Clough is shown to the left of Moosilauke, and the Kinsmans appear beyond Tunnel Brook Notch, the gap between Moosilauke and Clough. The long Blue Ridge drops off from the right of Moosilauke before ascending to Mt. Cushman. The Hancocks can be seen through this saddle along with Mt. Carrigain. East Scar Ridge peeks over the right of Cushman, followed by Mt. Osceola, nearer Mt. Kineo and distant Mt. Tecumseh and the Tripyramids. The Sleepers are visible to the right of those peaks, with Mt. Whiteface even further right.

Looking east is the long, wavy crest of ex-52WAV peak Carr Mountain, with Stinson Mountain peering over the middle of Carr's south ridge. The view then extends out to Rattlesnake Mountain in Rumney, onto the Belknap Range, Tenney, Crosby and Hersey Mountains, and ending at the ledgy dome of Mt. Cardigan.

ADDITIONAL ROUTES

Mt. Cube Trail

7.4 mi. round-trip with 2,300 ft. elevation gain

This route from NH 25A, a section of the Appalachian Trail, provides an easier but longer ascent up the eastern slope of the mountain with one potentially difficult crossing of Brackett Brook, and is viewless until the summit is reached. Roadside parking is available in a pull-off next to the trailhead, 4.5 mi. west of NH 25 in Wentworth.

Kodak Trail
7.8 mi. round-trip with 2,100 ft. elevation gain
Kodak Trail is also a section of the Appalachian Trail and is reached from Quinttown Rd. in Orford. This route provides a longer but more scenic approach from the southwest, climbing over the Eastman Ledges along the way. From NH 25A, 10.5 mi. west of NH 25 in Wentworth, turn left onto Quinttown Rd. In 1.7 mi. stay straight onto Jacobs Brook Rd. where Mousley Brook Rd. turns right, and continue 1.2 mi. to a parking area on the left before a gate. The last 0.1 mi. of this road is rougher.

OVERNIGHT OPTIONS
Mt. Cube has had a plethora of various shelters and cabins over the years but today only one remains. Dartmouth Outing Club's Hexacuba Shelter, a unique six-sided structure, is located on a short spur path off Kodak Trail. The shelter sleeps eight, is free to use, and is first come, first served with no reservations. There are also two tent sites just beyond the shelter, and a unique "penta-privy" nearby. The water source here is not reliable. In mid to late summer expect to share the shelter with AT thru-hikers. More information is available at fs.usda.gov.

WINTER
Cross Rivendell Trail makes for an excellent snowshoeing route with no sustained steep sections aside from the final pitch to the summit, which can be difficult in crusty or icy conditions. If visiting the ledges on North Peak, use caution if icy as the dropoff is significant. Baker Rd. is plowed and parking is available in the turnaround at the end.

For Mt. Cube Trail, the parking pull-off along NH 25A is plowed with room for several cars. The easy to moderate grades along this route make for excellent snowshoeing.

The regular parking area for Kodak Trail is usually not accessible in winter. In early 2020, Quinttown Rd. was getting plowed to a point 2.1 mi. from NH 25A at a house where limited parking was available. Starting here adds a 0.7 mi. walk each way. Alternate roadside parking is also available at the junction of Quinttown Rd. and Mousley Brook Rd., 1.1 mi. from the summer trailhead.

Smarts Mountain

Elevation: 3,238 ft.
Location: Town of Lyme
Map: AT map, NG White Mountains map
Locator map: 44

Along Lambert Ridge Trail, the most scenic route to Smarts Mountain.

Smarts Mountain is the highest and largest of the Middle Connecticut River Mountains, a chain of peaks running northeast to southwest in western New Hampshire. The Appalachian Trail runs over the western summit knob (the highest point of the mountain) and for northbound AT hikers Smarts is the first 3,000 ft. mountain they encounter in New Hampshire. Smarts also has an old 40 ft. fire tower which features panoramic views. The slightly lower eastern summit knob once had a fire tower in the early 1900s. Otherwise, the summit of Smarts is heavily wooded.

There have been two plane crashes on Smarts. In 1971, a twin-engine Piper Apache bound for Lebanon from Portland, ME slammed into the mountain during thick fog. On Christmas Eve 1996, a Learjet on its way from Bridgeport, CT to Lebanon crashed into the northeastern side of one of Smarts' foothills. The cause of this crash was determined to be human error and led to the longest missing aircraft search in the state's history, as the wreckage remained undiscovered until 1999.

The origin of the peak's name is not quite clear, but in Moses Sweetser's 1876 guidebook to the White Mountains, he included Smarts as one of many mountains named for local settlers. It was also once known as Maskoma Mountain, a reference to a nearby lake and river of the same name. Opened in 1937 and abandoned in the late 20th century due to light use and maintenance, the 20 mi. Maskoma Trail once connected Smarts with Mt. Cardigan to the southeast. Lambert Ridge was named in honor of a family who settled in Lyme during the 19th century.

GETTING THERE

A small parking area for both Lambert Ridge and Ranger Trails is located along Dorchester Rd. in Lyme. From NH 10 in Lyme Center, take Dorchester Rd. for 3.2 mi. to a fork where Grafton Turnpike bears right for Dartmouth Skiway. Bear left to stay on Dorchester Rd., now dirt, and continue 1.9 mi. to the trailhead and parking area (kiosk) on the left.

RECOMMENDED ROUTE
Lambert Ridge Trail (Appalachian Trail)
7.8 mi. round-trip with 2,700 ft. elevation gain
Out of the four approaches to Smarts, this is the most scenic, with several open quartzite ledges in the lower half providing excellent views. As a section of the Appalachian Trail, it is blazed in white and well-maintained.

From the parking area, Lambert Ridge Trail ascends from near the road (sign), climbing moderately through switchbacks, then more steeply with rougher footing after a brief level section. At 0.7 mi., the trail reaches its first outlook via a short side path which leads right to a ledge with a view to Holts Ledge, Dartmouth Skiway, and the top of Moose Mountain's North Peak. The trail continues on a steep ascent to reach an open cliff at 0.8 mi. with wide views east toward Mt. Cardigan. At the top of the cliff, the trail turns left to climb a steep section, then ascends at easy to moderate grades along the ridge with a few steeper pitches and several ledge outlooks along the way. The trail continues along the ridge through a mix of forest and ledge to reach an outlook on the right at 1.8 mi. to the bulk of Smarts Mountain ahead, descends steeply, then at 1.9 mi. emerges on large open ledges with views to the southeast.

Above these ledges the trail scrambles steeply over a ledge which is the high point of Lambert Ridge, makes a steep and rough descent off the narrow ridge to cross a small brook, then ascends gradually through a beautiful, broad hardwood plateau. It makes a steep climb to a junction with Smarts Ranger Trail at 3.4 mi., which comes in on the right (in the reverse direction, turn right at this junction if not using Smarts Ranger Trail for descent), and from this point forward, both trails run together to the summit.

    Lambert Ridge Trail turns left, hops up a ledge shelf, and begins a rougher and steeper ascent to reach a large rock slab covered in mossy slime which is often wet. Wooden steps and iron rungs (more suitable for small feet) have been installed here to aid in climbing. If this pitch is too slippery, it can be bypassed in the woods on the left. Above this slab, the steep climbing continues via switchbacks, then grades ease as the trails gain the ridge at 3.8 mi., passing a side path on the right (sign) which leads to Smarts Mountain Tentsite and a viewpoint to the south. The trails continue easily to reach a short side path on the left at 3.9 mi., which ascends to the high point and base of the fire tower (in mid-2020, the tower was temporarily closed due to the COVID-19 pandemic). To reach the old fire warden's cabin, J Trail and Daniel Doan Trail, continue ahead on the main route for 100 ft.

VIEW HIGHLIGHTS

A steep ascent up the 55 steps of the fire tower brings you above the trees where there are panoramic views in all directions. The tower is not staffed and to reach the cab you will need to push open the fairly heavy trap door. It may not seem like it will open at first but it will. Views are best enjoyed from the tower on a clear day as they are mostly distant.

    Looking north, nearby Mt. Cube can be seen 4 mi. away, with Piermont Mountain poking up behind it. Further right Mt. Moosilauke comes into view, with Mt. Washington in the far distance beyond, before moving over to the long ridge of Carr Mountain, distant Sandwich Dome and closer Stinson Mountain. To the east are the Squam, Ossipee, and Belknap Ranges in the Lakes Region, with the prominent Mts. Cardigan and Kearsarge in the distance to the southeast.

    Several peaks in southern Vermont are seen to the south and southwest including Mt. Ascutney, Dorset Mountain, Stratton Mountain, Ludlow Mountain, and Killington and Pico Peaks. Further to the west more peaks in the Green Mountains become visible such as Mts. Abraham and Ellen, Camel's Hump, and Mt. Mansfield's Chin, before gazing into Vermont's Northeast Kingdom.

    The broad open ledge along Lambert Ridge Trail, 1.8 mi. from the trailhead, offers a commanding view up to Smarts Mountain itself with the fire tower and south-facing slide/fire scar clearly visible. 20 mi. to the southeast is the bare Mt. Cardigan and its subpeak Firescrew. To the south-southeast is a look out to distant Mt. Kearsarge.

A cleared outlook at Smarts Mountain Tentsite offers a view out to Reservoir Pond, Mt. Kearsarge, Mt. Cardigan, Mt. Sunapee, Croydon Peak, and Mt. Ascutney in Vermont.

ADDITIONAL ROUTES
Smarts Ranger Trail
7.2 mi. round-trip with 2,100 ft. elevation gain
This route, the former fire warden's Jeep road, offers what is probably the most gentle approach to the summit (aside from the steep final half mile), but is in generally poor condition and receives little maintenance. Hikers should expect few blue blazes, numerous blowdowns and wet/muddy footing. The upper section above Grant Brook (this crossing can be difficult in high water) is also very eroded with some slippery ledges. Smarts Ranger Trail also begins at the Lambert Ridge trailhead and can be used with that trail to form a 7.8 mi. loop hike.

Daniel Doan Trail (formerly Mousley Brook Trail)
6.4 mi. round-trip with 1,900 ft. elevation gain
This blue-blazed, lesser-used approach from the northwest, a former section of the Appalachian Trail, starts on remote Mousley Brook Rd. in Orford. It is the shortest route to Smarts but footing is often wet and muddy and the trail is sometimes difficult to follow in its lower section. From NH25A, 10.5 mi. west of NH 25 in Wentworth, turn left onto Quinttown Rd. In 1.7 mi., turn right onto Mousley Brook Rd., bearing right to stay on it at 1.8 mi. Continue to the maintained end of the road at 2.5 mi. from NH 25A, where parking is available on the left at an orange DOC sign. Beyond this point, the road becomes private and vehicle traffic is prohibited but hikers are welcome.

J Trail (Appalachian Trail)
8.6 mi. round-trip with 2,100 ft. elevation gain
This white-blazed approach from the north starts on Jacobs Brook Rd. in Orford (directly opposite Kodak Trail for Mt. Cube) and follows a current section of the Appalachian Trail along the gradual north ridge of Smarts. See the Mt. Cube (South Peak) section (Kodak Trail approach) for driving directions and parking information.

OVERNIGHT OPTIONS

The former fire warden's cabin near the summit along Daniel Doan Trail, constructed in 1939, is now a shelter for hikers on a first come, first served basis and is very busy during AT thru-hiker season. A privy is a short distance west and water may be available from Mike Murphy Spring (sign), a short distance east, although the source is unreliable and often unappetizing; hikers are encouraged to carry in their own water. Smarts Mountain Tentsite, site of a former Dartmouth Outing Club shelter, is located at the end of a spur trail (sign) just off the combined Ranger/Lambert Ridge Trails, a short distance west of the summit. Fires are permitted in designated areas only.

WINTER

Lambert Ridge Trail is a spectacular trip in good winter conditions with mostly moderate grades for snowshoeing, although steeper sections could present more of a challenge. Crampons may be needed on the open ledges along the ridge if icy. The final half mile where Lambert Ridge and Smarts Ranger Trails coincide can be tricky if icy due to the steep grades and ledgy terrain, again possibly warranting full crampon use. The steep slab with the iron rungs can be bypassed in the woods if necessary. The fire tower may not be accessible if encrusted in ice; also be alert for falling chunks. The climb to the tower also presents exposure to the wind, but the cabin just beyond the summit provides excellent shelter from the elements. The parking area on Dorchester Rd. is usually plowed, but may not be right after a storm.

Smarts Ranger Trail becomes a somewhat more attractive route with deep snow as its eroded and wet footing are buried, although blowdowns will still likely have to be negotiated. However, the mostly easy grades of this route make for good snowshoeing. Unless well frozen, the crossing of Grant Brook could be problematic. This trail is also not blazed beyond the brook in the ascending direction.

The parking area for Daniel Doan Trail at the end of the maintained section of Mousley Brook Rd. is plowed.

The regular parking area for J Trail is usually not accessible in winter. In early 2020, Quinttown Rd. was getting plowed to a point 2.1 mi. from NH 25A at a house where limited parking was available. Starting here adds a 0.7 mi. walk each way. Alternate roadside parking is also available at the junction of Quinttown Rd. and Mousley Brook Rd., 1.1 mi. from the summer parking area.

Stinson Mountain

Elevation: 2,890 ft.
Location: Town of Rumney
Map: AMC Map - Moosilauke/Kinsman Ridge
Locator map: 49

The footings from the former fire tower on Stinson Mountain.

The partly open summit of Stinson Mountain was home to a fire tower from 1911 to around 1967, the concrete footings of which are still in place today. From this ledgy summit, there are good views south, and a somewhat overgrown and hard to spot side path just off the summit leads to a restricted view northwest. Stinson is a broad, sprawling peak prominently visible from many locations around the Baker River Valley. Drivers along I-93 also get a good look at Stinson as they approach Plymouth from the north or south.

The mountain's name originates from a violent incident which occurred during colonial days. Noted hunter and trapper David Stinson frequently visited the region in the mid 1700s, and after collecting a large quantity of pelts during a hunting excursion, he and his companions were ambushed by hostile Indian warriors. According to legend, the attack occurred at nearby Stinson Lake, where Stinson was shot and killed. The name first appeared as "Stinson's Mountain" on Philip Carrigain's 1816 White Mountains map.

GETTING THERE

A small parking area is located on Lower Doetown Rd. in Rumney. From NH 25 near Rumney Village, take Main St., which becomes Stinson Lake Rd., north for 5.0 mi. Turn right onto Cross Rd. for 0.8 mi., then turn right again onto Lower Doetown Rd. and continue 0.3 mi. to the trailhead (sign: "Stinson Mountain Trail") on the left at a fork where WMNF Forest Rd. 413 bears left and the remainder of Lower Doetown Rd. becomes private on the right. This road is passable to the trailhead in summer, but can be muddy in spring. Alternate roadside parking is available for a few cars at its junction with Cross Rd. (sign: "Stinson Mountain Trail").

ROUTE

Stinson Mountain Trail

3.8 mi. round-trip with 1,400 ft. elevation gain

The sole hiking trail on Stinson Mountain offers a mostly easy approach to the summit, especially in the lower half. Footing is generally good with some rocky sections above the junction with the snowmobile trail. The hiking trail is marked with infrequent and faded yellow blazes.

From the parking area, Stinson Mountain Trail enters the woods and proceeds southeast along an old farm road at easy grades in an area criss-crossed by old stone walls, crossing a snowmobile trail at 0.4 mi. The ascent continues easily as the trail meets the old tractor road for the former fire tower, now part of the same snowmobile trail crossed earlier. The trail turns left onto this road at 0.9 mi. and follows it to a fork at 1.1 mi., where Stinson Mountain Trail bears right and the snowmobile trail continues straight ahead (this section of the snowmobile trail can be used in conjunction with the hiking trail to make a loop over Stinson, but its use is not generally recommended outside of winter as it can be wet and muddy. In 2019, new bridges and other efforts were underway to improve this section of the snowmobile trail).

From the junction, which in early 2020 was marked by an orange sign, Stinson Mountain Trail ascends moderately southeast through a short series of switchbacks with generally rocky footing to rejoin the snowmobile trail just below the summit at 1.8 mi. Hikers have an option here, as the route splits to make a loop. Turning right, ascend easily and watch for an easy to miss brushy side path on the right to the northwest viewpoint, just before the two branches of the loop rejoin. Just beyond, the main trail makes a short climb to reach the ledgy summit and fire tower footings at 1.9 mi.

VIEW HIGHLIGHTS

Although the fire tower on Stinson's summit has been gone for many years now, there is still a wide 120-degree view to the south. Trees have grown up to obscure views in the other directions. The main focus of the view from Stinson's summit is south over the Baker River Valley between the towns of Plymouth and Rumney, some 2,000 ft. below.

Summit view: On the opposite side of the valley are Plymouth Mountain on the left and Tenney Mountain and its wind farm on the right. Mt. Kearsarge is seen far beyond Tenney, just behind Ragged Mountain. To the right of Tenney are Mt. Crosby and Fletcher Mountain (also marked by wind turbines) with Tinkham Hill and Forbes Mountain visible through the gap between Tenney and Crosby. On exceptionally clear winter days, a very distant Mt. Monadnock can be seen beyond Tinkham. The bald dome of Mt. Cardigan is to the right of Fletcher, and Lovewell Mountain and Mt. Sunapee are to the left of Cardigan. To the far right, looking southwest, are Croydon Peak and Vermont's Mt. Ascutney, with Stratton Mountain sometimes visible to the left of it. Further right in the far distance Bromley Mountain can be seen with Equinox Mountain in back, along with Okemo and Dorset Mountains. Stepping down the front ledges a bit, the village of Rumney and Rattlesnake Mountain on the south end of the long Carr Mountain ridge come into view.

Back at Plymouth Mountain, Hersey Mountain, the high point of Sanbornton, is seen to the left, and in the distance, the Belknap Range appears further left with a section of I-93 winding under Belknap Mountain; Piper Mountain is to the right of that peak. The Belknaps' most well-known peak, Mt. Major, is seen at the far left of that range. Further left but closer in is Mt. Prospect in Holderness, with the ridgeline of Mt. Webster to Prospect's left and Red Hill behind that. On the far left is the Ossipee Range, with Mts. Morgan and Percival in the Squam Range next in line.

Southwest outlook: This stand-up view from the end of the obscure side path which leaves the summit begins with a look over Stinson Lake into the Three Ponds area, with Black Hill seen directly above the right end of Stinson Lake. Whitcher Hill rises behind Black. To the right, the great bulk of Mt. Moosilauke stands in the background with its various subpeaks on full display. To the left of Moosilauke is Mt. Clough, followed by three peaks in the Benton Range — Blueberry, Jeffers and Black Mountains.

WINTER

Stinson is an excellent winter hike with easy to moderate grades for snowshoeing and good protection from the weather. Hikers will often encounter backcountry skiers along the way. Keep alert for snowmobiles where the hiking trail coincides with their route as well as on Lower Doetown Rd. near the trailhead. The road has been getting plowed in recent years by a local landowner, but the trailhead parking area is usually not plowed. Sometimes it is packed down by vehicles, but in general it is recommended that winter hikers park at the plowed junction of Lower Doetown and Cross Rds., where there is room for a few vehicles. The walk in from here adds 0.3 mi. each way, bringing the total round-trip distance to 4.4 mi. with no change in elevation gain.

Stinson Mountain's summit ledges.

Central White Mountains/Crawford Notch

Middle Sugarloaf

Elevation: 2,538 ft.
Location: Town of Bethlehem
Map: AMC map - Franconia/Pemigewasset
Locator map: 11

Boulders deposited by a glacier sit on the Middle Sugarloaf summit ledges.

Middle Sugarloaf, along with its neighbors North Sugarloaf (2,310 ft.) and trailless South Sugarloaf (3,024 ft.), lie at the northern end of the Little River Mountains, a chain of low peaks extending north from Zealand Ridge over Mt. Hale. Middle Sugarloaf's bare summit ledges offer panoramic views in nearly all directions. These ledges, as well as those on neighboring North Sugarloaf, are the result of forest fires which ripped through Zealand Valley in 1886 and 1903, fueled in part by logging slash.

    The southeast cliffs of Middle Sugarloaf are also well known to rock climbers. A notable feature of North Sugarloaf is a small pit along Sugarloaf Trail, where the mining of smoky quartz is allowed with hand tools only. In season, both peaks offer abundant blueberries.

As is the case with numerous other mountains around New Hampshire with the same name, these Sugarloaves were so named because their shapes resemble the cone-shaped "loaves" in which sugar was once sold. Middle and North Sugarloaf were also once known as the "Baby Twins," a reference to their much higher neighbors South and North Twin Mountains. This name was also given to a former hiking trail.

GETTING THERE
Parking for several vehicles is available in a small lot along Zealand Rd. (WMNF Forest Rd. 16) in Bethlehem, 1.0 mi. south of US 302.

ROUTE
Sugarloaf Trail
Middle Sugarloaf only: 2.8 mi. round-trip with 900 ft. elevation gain
Middle and North Sugarloaf: 3.4 mi. round-trip with 1,100 ft. elevation gain
While short, Sugarloaf Trail is quite rugged in places, and provides a moderately steep ascent to the col between North and Middle Sugarloaf, ending with a steep and rugged climb up to Middle, with an optional short side trip to North.

Yellow-blazed Sugarloaf Trail leaves the far end of the parking area and runs nearly level along the edge of Zealand River to a junction with Trestle Trail at 0.2 mi., which continues straight ahead. Sugarloaf Trail bears left here and ascends to cross an old logging road, then climbs more moderately through a section of massive glacial boulders; the trail itself passes through one which is split. The trail then steepens and ascends through a series of switchbacks over rock steps to a T-junction at 0.9 mi., where branch trails split off to each peak (turning right here ascends 0.5 mi. to the summit of North Sugarloaf).

Turning left toward Middle Sugarloaf, the trail ascends at easy grades along the ridge, passes over a ledgy bump, ascends briefly, then eases to reach a right turn. The trail then makes the final climb to the summit up a steep and rocky section with a wooden ladder at the top (use caution here with children and pets or if wet). Above the ladder, the trail emerges onto open ledges near the summit at 1.4 mi. The high point, a short distance on the right within the scrub, can be accessed by a beaten path.

VIEW HIGHLIGHTS

Middle Sugarloaf: Views atop Middle Sugarloaf are expansive but require some wandering around the summit ledges to get the complete picture. The most prominent feature seen from Middle Sugarloaf is the north peak of Mt. Hale, with trailless South Sugarloaf below. Hale's east peak extends out to the left. From the north peak, a long ridge extends right over which North and South Twin Mountains can be seen, along with Peak Above The Nubble, or "3813". Further right is the tiny bump of Haystack Mountain, also known as The Nubble, with distant peaks in Vermont far beyond, and Mts. Cleveland and Agassiz in Bethlehem closer in.

Nearby to the northwest is Beech Hill with the Jay Peaks above, looking far into Vermont. This distant vista continues around to Mt. Prospect in Lancaster and its stone fire tower, then arrives at Middle Sugarloaf's neighbor North Sugarloaf. Cherry Mountain rises across the Ammonoosuc River Valley. To the northeast, the Crescent Range in Randolph comes into view, as do Mts. Deception and Dartmouth.

The dramatic Presidential Range then appears: Mts. Adams, Jefferson, Clay, and Washington, followed by Mts. Monroe, Franklin, and Eisenhower. Just across Zealand Valley, ledgy Mt. Oscar is spotted to the right of Washington, with Wildlife Pond and a section of the Zealand River below Oscar. The Rosebrook Range, home to the Bretton Woods ski area on the other side, extends right from Oscar over Mts. Rosebrook, Stickney and Echo. At the far end of Zealand Valley are Mts. Tom and Field in the Willey Range.

North Sugarloaf: If making the side trip to North Sugarloaf, views from its open summit are largely the same as those back on Middle, though slightly lower. The view from the high east cliffs where the hiking trail makes a sharp right for the summit should also not be missed; these cliffs provide an excellent outlook down into and up the Zealand Valley.

OVERNIGHT OPTIONS

Zealand Campground, located at the junction of US 302 and Zealand Rd., offers first come, first served campsites (daily fee; no reservations accepted) along the Ammonoosuc River. Handicap accessible sites are also available. The campground features toilets, hand pump water, and a picnic area. More information is available at fs.usda.gov.

Also along Zealand Rd. are the two Sugarloaf Campgrounds, offering wooded campsites by reservation near the Zealand River. They also offer handicap accessible toilets and hand pump water. More information is available at recreation.gov.

WINTER

Middle Sugarloaf becomes a longer trek in winter as Zealand Rd. is gated, which requires an additional 1.3 mi. walk in from the winter parking area to the trailhead. This parking area is located along US 302, 0.3 mi. east of Zealand Rd. It is recommended that hikers arrive as early as they can, as the lot is also heavily used by snowmobilers and tends to fill up quickly with trailers. Total distance for the hike from this point is 5.4 mi. round-trip with 1,050 ft. elevation gain. Sugarloaf Trail is popular in the winter and is usually broken out fairly quickly after a storm. Zealand Rd. is usually well packed down by snowmobiles and skiers. Crampons may be needed on the ladder up to the Middle Sugarloaf summit ledges and on the ledges themselves if icy.

Mt. Avalon

Elevation: 3,461 ft.
Location: Town of Bethlehem
Map: AMC map - Crawford Notch/Sandwich Range
Locator map: 12

Mt. Avalon is sometimes bypassed by many hikers who are visiting its higher 4,000 foot neighbors in the Willey Range, but it makes for an excellent destination in itself, with commanding views of the Presidential Range and Crawford Notch as the reward for a stiff climb. A rocky spur of Mt. Field, Avalon's summit is actually composed of two bumps of similar size, with the high point being on the slightly higher eastern bump.

Mt. Avalon was named in 1876 by early White Mountains guidebook author Moses Sweetser, who likened the peak to the hills of Avalon in southeastern Newfoundland.

GETTING THERE

Parking is available near Macomber Family Information Center, located in the historic Crawford Depot train station on US 302 in Crawford Notch, adjacent to the AMC Highland Center, 8.5 mi. east of the junction with US 3 in Twin Mountain. Parking is prohibited at the Highland Center lot.

Looking south through Crawford Notch from Mt. Avalon.

ROUTE

Avalon Trail, Mt. Avalon Spur
3.6 mi. round-trip with 1,540 ft. elevation gain

The short ascent to Mt. Avalon starts out deceptively easy with good footing, but soon becomes quite steep and rough in its upper half.

From Macomber Family Information Center, cross the active tracks of the Conway Scenic Railroad (use caution) and enter the woods onto the combined yellow-blazed Avalon and Mt. Willard Trails. In 0.1 mi., Mt. Willard Trail leaves left at a kiosk, while Avalon Trail continues straight ahead, ascending easily to the first crossing of Crawford Brook (may be difficult in high water).

Beyond the brook, the trail passes both junctions on the left for a short loop trail leading to Beecher and Pearl Cascades (worth the side trip on the way up or down), then climbs more moderately and dips to the second crossing of the brook at 0.8 mi.

At 1.3 mi., Avalon Trail bears left where A-Z Trail continues ahead for Mt. Tom, and begins a long, very steep ascent with rugged footing to a junction with a signed spur trail on the left at 1.8 mi. This 100 yd. spur climbs steeply with one ledgy and potentially difficult scramble near the top to emerge on the open summit ledges. Use caution when ascending and descending this section if wet.

VIEW HIGHLIGHTS

Mt. Avalon's summit ledges offer a 180-degree view stretching from the north to south. The western vista is blocked by the Willey Range.

Starting on the far left is the highest peak in that range, Mt. Tom. Further right and in the distance are several peaks in the Northeast Kingdom of Vermont, including Burke Mountain and Mt. Pisgah, before the view comes back to the closer Mt. Martha/Owl's Head, Mt. Waumbek, the Weeks, and Mt. Dartmouth. The Presidential Range then starts rising to the northeast, starting at Mt. Jefferson and moving to the right over Mts. Clay, Washington, Eisenhower and Pierce. The ridge moves closer across Mt. Jackson to end at Mt. Webster, which forms the eastern wall of Crawford Notch opposite Avalon. Seen between Jackson and Webster and 600 ft. below is Mt. Willard. To the right of Webster, the view looks straight down Crawford Notch, where Stairs Mountain, Mt. Resolution, Mt. Parker, North Moat Mountain, and Bear Mountain are visible, before getting lost behind 4,000 Footers Mt. Willey and Mt. Field.

WINTER

The initial easy grades of Avalon Trail make for good snowshoeing, but the steep section as well as the scramble to the summit can be tricky in icy or crusty conditions. The section up to A-Z Trail is usually heavily traveled and broken out quickly after a storm. Deep snow opens up more views at the summit. The two crossings of Crawford Brook could be difficult if not well frozen. The parking area is not plowed, but limited roadside parking is available along the highway.

Mt. Crawford

Elevation: 3,128 ft.
Location: Township of Hadley's Purchase
Map: AMC map - Crawford Notch/Sandwich Range
Locator map: 15

Mt. Crawford's bare summit, which affords views in all directions, is one of the premier perches in the Crawford Notch area, offering expansive vistas into the notch itself, the Presidential Range, and nearby 52WAV peaks Mt. Resolution and Stairs Mountain. In his 1876 guidebook, Moses Sweetser wrote of Mt. Crawford, "*The peak is high and steep, especially on the E., where it is nearly precipitous, though by no means so phenomenally beetling as the picture in 'The White Hills' [authored by Thomas Starr King, 1859] would indicate.*"

The peak is named after the Crawford family who settled in this area during the late 1700s, establishing several inns within the Notch. In particular, the name was given in honor of Abel Crawford and his son Ethan Allen Crawford. Abel and Ethan Allen would gain fame by building the first footpath to Mt. Washington, starting at Crawford Notch. Their Crawford Path remains the oldest continually used hiking trail in the United States, having been originally laid out in 1819. Several other peaks and natural features in this area also bear the names of Crawford family members.

It was Boston dentist Samuel Bemis who coined the peak "Mt. Crawford" in the mid-1800s. Bemis built a stone house south of the Notch which is today known as Notchland Inn.

The summit cliffs of Mt. Crawford as seen from Davis Path.

GETTING THERE

A large parking area is located on the east side of US 302 along the Saco River, opposite Notchland Inn, 8.4 mi. southeast of AMC Highland Center.

ROUTE

Davis Path, Mt. Crawford Spur

5.0 mi. round-trip with 2,100 ft. elevation gain

The climb up Crawford doesn't come easy. The ascent up the ridge, after an initial easy stretch, becomes quite steep and rugged with rough, rocky footing in places. Scenic ledges in the upper section of this route and an open summit provide excellent views for the effort. Davis Path begins on private land; hikers should obey all posted signage and stay on the trail.

From the parking area, walk north along a gravel road (there is no public parking here) to cross the Saco River on Bemis Bridge and continue to a sign detailing the history of Davis Path. The yellow-blazed trail passes through a brushy stretch, then crosses a wet area (sometimes flooded) on a sketchy bog bridge, then swings right for an easy ascent to the Presidential Range-Dry River Wilderness boundary (sign) at 0.4 mi. The trail dips to cross a dry, rocky brook and continues an easy ascent, crossing another small brook, then passing a side path to a WMNF tent site on the right at 0.8 mi. In several areas along this stretch, climbing has been made easier with the addition of rock steps placed by AMC trail crews. The trail turns sharply right and ascends steeply, alternating between zig zags and longer steady stretches with fairly rough footing. Grades ease for a bit, then the trail makes a short scramble up to the first open view ledge, with a look back to Mt. Carrigain, the Nancy Range, North Moat Mountain, Mt. Chocorua, Mt. Tremont, and portions of the Sandwich, Twin, and Willey Ranges. Davis Path swings right here and ascends moderately with several small scrambles. Follow markings on ledges (old white blazes) carefully through here. At 2.2 mi., it reaches a junction with Mt. Crawford Spur (small sign on tree at left), which continues ahead as Davis Path turns right for points north.

Continue straight on this spur trail, at first up a large open slab marked by small cairns with excellent views at the top, then bear left through patches of woods mixed with ledges, to reach Crawford's open summit, where open ledges surround patches of scrub. Use caution on the northeast side of the summit which sits atop a precipitous cliff.

VIEW HIGHLIGHTS

While open and lofty, there isn't one location on Mt. Crawford's summit which offers a complete 360-degree panorama, but you can easily piece it together by roaming around the summit ledges. The views of the valley below are especially stunning during the foliage season.

Looking down the northwest ridge of Crawford is a look straight into Crawford Notch, in-between the Willey Range on the ledges and Mt. Webster on the right. The Frankenstein Cliffs can be seen below Willey. To the right of Webster, the long southern ridge of the Presidential Range ascends to Mt.

Washington with the glacial cirques under Eisenhower, Franklin, and Monroe fully in view.

The closer locomotive-shaped ridge of Stairs Mountain and its two Giant Stairs is in front of the Presidentials, and Wildcat Mountain's "D" Peak pops up through Stairs Col, as the view turns further right to the massive Mt. Resolution and its gravelly slides, with rounded Crawford Dome down in front. A long ridge extends right from Resolution and descends to Mt. Parker, with Kearsarge North popping up beyond this ridge. To the right of Parker, the Saddleback Hills, Douglas Mountain, and the Burnt Meadow Mountains can be seen in Maine.

Beyond the nearby rounded Crawford Dome and to the right of Parker, the Moat-Attitash Range comes into view, before swinging over to Mt. Chocorua and the Three Sisters, Bartlett Haystack, and Mt. Tremont, with officially trailless Mt. Hope between them and closer in. To the right of Hope, Mts. Passaconaway and Whiteface appear beyond Tremont. Further right, the Tripyramids are visible above Greens Cliff, followed by Mt. Carrigain and the Nancy Range.

Due west is a look out to Mts. Liberty and Flume as well as two of the Bond peaks — Bondcliff and Mt. Bond — with Mt. Guyot and North and South Twin Mountains to the right, before the view returns to the Willey Range.

OVERNIGHT OPTIONS

A primitive tent site is available at the end of a short side path (tent sign) off Davis Path on the right, 0.8 mi. from the trailhead. This area is typically very dry so backpackers should carry in all the water they will need. Please follow the WMNF backcountry camping rules if staying overnight in this area. More information is available at fs.usda.gov.

WINTER

Mt. Crawford offers spectacular views in winter air from its high summit but also biting winds on the exposed ledges. The stiff climb up the ridge can make for a difficult snowshoe trek if not broken out, and the route may be hard to follow in its upper section. However with good snow cover, the ascent is easier footing-wise. Crampons may be required on the upper ledges in icy or crusty conditions. The parking area on US 302 is plowed.

Mt. Parker

Elevation: 3,013 ft.
Location: Town of Bartlett
Map: AMC map - Crawford Notch/Sandwich Range
Locator map: 25

Mt. Parker's summit ledges with Mt. Washington in the distance.

Overlooked by many hikers, Mt. Parker offers excellent views from its partly open summit, offering solitude away from the busier trails within the Presidential Range-Dry River Wilderness. It is the southernmost 3,000 ft. peak on the main branch of Montalban Ridge, the longest southern spur off Mt. Washington.

The origin of the peak's name is uncertain but it may have been in honor of the Parker family who were residents of the village of Bartlett in the late 1800s. It first appeared on Professor Charles H. Hitchcock's 1876 map created for the New Hampshire Geological Survey.

GETTING THERE

Parking for a few vehicles is available in a small lot (sign) for Mt. Langdon Trail in Bartlett. From US 302 in Bartlett Village, take River St. north for 0.4

mi. Cross the bridge over the Saco River, then turn left onto Cobb Farm Rd. to the trailhead immediately on the right.

RECOMMENDED ROUTE
Mt. Langdon Trail, Mt. Parker Trail
7.8 mi. round-trip with 2,800 ft. elevation gain
This route provides a direct ascent to the summit of Mt. Parker with mostly moderate grades and generally good footing the whole way. Mt. Parker Trail climbs over Oak Ridge (2,125 ft.) in both directions so hikers should be prepared for some elevation gain on the return trip. Mt. Langdon Trail begins on private property; please stay on the trail.

From the parking area, Mt. Langdon Trail passes a gravesite on the right, then ascends easily up an old logging road, soon passing a side trail to Cave Mountain (sign) on the left at 0.3 mi. Bear left at a fork where an alternate loop diverges right to rejoin the trail. At 1.0 mi., Mt. Langdon Trail enters the WMNF and then enters the Presidential Range-Dry River Wilderness (sign). The trail crosses two small brooks and begins the ascent up Oak Ridge, reaching the wooded summit at 2.2 mi. It then descends moderately to the col between Oak Ridge and Parker, leaves the wilderness area, and reaches a junction with Mt. Parker Trail at 2.5 mi., which continues straight ahead (Mt. Langdon Trail turns right here for Mt. Langdon Shelter).

Continuing straight, Mt. Parker Trail crosses a broad col where the route may be difficult to follow in places, then swings left and begins a moderate winding climb up the southern slopes of Parker, with brief level sections allowing for rest breaks. The trail continues a meandering ascent through conifer forest with areas of blowdown, and at 3.8 mi. makes a short but steep climb to emerge on the summit with its stunning vista toward the Presidential Range.

Additional views to the west and southwest over Razor Brook Valley are available from an off-trail ledge. From the summit cairn, bushwhack about 100 yds. slightly down the west side of the summit through somewhat dense growth, crossing a wooded ledge with an old cairn along the way.

VIEW HIGHLIGHTS
Main summit: The most impressive view from Parker's partly open summit is the look up the remote Rocky Branch Valley to Mt. Washington, 10 mi. away. To the right of Washington is Boott Spur and on the left, Mts. Monroe, Franklin, and Eisenhower begin their run down the southern ridge. The

upper Montalban Ridge forms the left edge of the valley, with Mts. Davis and Isolation seen extending from Boott Spur.

Close by under Eisenhower is the broad mass of Resolution, connected to Parker via a bumpy ridge. Mt. Webster is visible over the saddle to the left of Resolution. Further left is the ledgy Crawford Dome, with the Willey Range rising beyond. Mt. Crawford is next to the left, then the view moves over to the Twin Range, Mt. Guyot and Mt. Bond. To the left of Bond is the Nancy Range, Vose Spur, and Mt. Carrigain, with a northern spur of Mt. Hancock poking up between Vose Spur and Mt. Lowell.

Back over at Mt. Washington, there is much to see to the right of the mountain as well. The Wildcats and Carter Dome can be seen with the latter's long shoulder, Rainbow Ridge, extending right toward Perkins Notch. To the right of the Notch, Jackson's Black Mountain leads to a more distant view of the Baldfaces, Sable and Chandler Mountains, Caribou Mountain, and Eastman Mountain, all in the Evans Notch area. Next to the right and closer in are the recognizable Doubleheads, with low Iron Mountain in front with its south cliffs on the right end. Thorn Mountain is visible above Iron's cliffs, with the northern Mt. Shaw and the northern Twins beyond. Further right, just shy of due east, is Kearsarge North.

West outlook: This open ledge, reached by a short bushwhack described above, offers a panoramic view west, sweeping around from the Sandwich Range on the left to Mt. Resolution on the right. Especially interesting is the look down into the remote valley of Razor Brook which is walled in by various ridges extending from Mts. Resolution, Crawford, Hope and Hart's Ledge. Higher peaks seen from this perspective include the Willey Range, Mt. Carrigain, the Osceolas, Mt. Tremont, the Tripyramids, and Mts. Whiteface, Passaconaway, Paugus, and Chocorua.

ADDITIONAL ROUTE
Davis Path, Mt. Crawford Spur, Stairs Mountain Spur, Mt. Parker Trail, Mt. Resolution South Peak Spur, Mt. Langdon Trail
13.1 mi. traverse with 3,800 ft. elevation gain

For backpackers or strong day hikers who can arrange a car spot, this traverse starting on US 302 offers a grand tour of the Presidential Range-Dry River region through spectacular scenery, passing over Mt. Resolution and Mt. Parker, with side trips to Mt. Crawford, Stairs Mountain, and Resolution's seldom-visited South Peak. See the Mt. Crawford section of this guide for parking information.

OVERNIGHT OPTIONS

Mt. Langdon Shelter is located near the junction of Mt. Langdon and Mt. Stanton Trails. The shelter has a fire ring and pit toilet and water is available in a nearby brook. In 2016, this shelter was proposed for removal by USFS due to light use and deteriorating conditions, but remains sound enough and was still in use as of 2019.

A primitive tent site is available at the end of a short side path (tent sign) off Davis Path on the right, 0.8 mi. from US 302. Another is located just behind the summit ledges on Stairs Mountain. This area is typically very dry, so backpackers should carry in all the water they will need. Please follow the WMNF backcountry camping rules if staying overnight in this area. More information on these locations is available at fs.usda.gov.

WINTER

Mt. Parker is an excellent but not heavily-traveled winter hike, with easy to moderate grades making for good snowshoeing. Mt. Parker Trail may be difficult to follow if unbroken, especially inside the wilderness boundary where blazing is light or non-existent. The regular parking area may not be plowed, but plowed parking is usually available diagonally across from the trailhead at the junction of River St. and Yates Farm Rd.

If approaching via Davis Path, the parking area on US 302 is plowed. Davis Path is usually well broken out as far as Mt. Crawford, but less so after that. Route-finding could be challenging along the open ledges of Mt. Resolution, and the section of Mt. Parker Trail between Resolution and Parker is rarely hiked in winter so trail breaking will be very likely.

Mt. Pemigewasset

Elevation: 2,552 ft.
Location: Town of Lincoln
Map: AMC map - Franconia/Pemigewasset
Locator map: 27

Mt. Pemigewasset is a very popular hike in the Franconia Notch region, and for good reason. Its near-summit ledges offer excellent views which are especially impressive during foliage season. Located on the mountain's southern cliffs is Indian Head, a natural rock profile seen prominently from

US 3. This profile was originally hidden by trees but was revealed by a fire around 1901, and quickly became a popular tourist attraction in the early 20th century.

The name Pemigewasset comes from the Abenaki word "bemijijoasek", which roughly translates to "swift current and where the side (entering) current is." This name is also applied to the 70 mi. Pemigewasset River and the 45,000-acre federally-designated Pemigewasset Wilderness, the state's largest wilderness area.

A sea of forest extends from the near-summit ledges on Mt. Pemigewasset.

GETTING THERE
Parking is available at the Flume Visitor Center parking lot off US 3 in Lincoln, accessed by Exit 34A off Franconia Notch Parkway. Hikers should park at the northern end of the lot near the entrance to the Franconia Notch Recreation Path, a popular walking and cycling route.

RECOMMENDED ROUTE
Mt. Pemigewasset Trail
3.8 mi. round-trip with 1,250 ft. elevation gain
Of the two routes to Mt. Pemigewasset, this is the most traveled. Blazed in

blue, grades are moderate and footing is good thanks to volunteer reconstruction efforts in recent years.

From the parking area, walk north along the recreation path for 150 yds., then turn left (sign; mileage indicated here is off slightly) onto the trail. It descends to pass under US 3 via a pedestrian tunnel, turns left to cross a brook on a footbridge, descends again, and then swings right to pass under both lanes of Franconia Notch Parkway via tunnels. The trail enters the woods at 0.4 mi. and begins a steady, moderate climb through a hardwood forest, making several easy brook crossings in its lower section. It passes a large glacial boulder on the right at 1.5 mi., and at 1.7 mi., the trail swings left to gain the ridgecrest as the forest transitions to conifers. At a junction with Indian Head Trail on the right at 1.8 mi., Mt. Pemigewasset Trail bears left (this junction can be potentially confusing for new hikers as both trails are blazed in blue and signage only points toward Indian Head Trail). Walking is now easy along the ridgecrest with one short dip and a hop up a ledge leading to the abrupt open ledges atop the summit cliffs at 1.9 mi. Use caution with pets and children here or if wet or icy as the drop-off in front is significant.

From the ledges, continue to follow blue blazes on the ground (avoid yellow blazes which used to mark a now-abandoned route) for 90 yds. around to the left to reach the mostly wooded high point.

VIEW HIGHLIGHTS

The views from Mt. Pemigewasset have been revered for generations. Frank O. Carpenter's 1898 *"Guide Book to the Franconia Notch and the Pemigewasset Valley"* describes that *"a striking view is obtained of the Notch, and the rugged shoulders of Lafayette, and to the south the pleasant hills and farms of the Pemigewasset Valley"*. Much of this scenery is still visible today although tree growth now blocks the view to Mt. Lafayette and Franconia Notch.

From the main ledges, high up on the right is the massive southeast shoulder of South Kinsman. Far across the valley is the long ridge of ex-52WAV peak Mt. Wolf and its unofficially-named subpeak "Wolf Cub", with Mt. Moosilauke seen through the Notch between them. Moosilauke's subpeaks Mt. Jim and Mt. Waternomee extend left from the main peak, followed by Mt. Cushman and Green Mountain in Landaff. Looking directly south, I-93 snakes its way out toward Grandview Mountain, Plymouth Mountain, Hersey Mountain, Mt. Prospect in Holderness, and Dickey Mountain. Further left, Mt. Tecumseh, Mt. Osceola and the jagged Scar Ridge are visible before the view becomes obscured by trees.

From the true summit of Pemigewasset, there is a restricted view through the trees to Mts. Liberty and Flume, with Flume's slide-scarred western face fully visible.

ADDITIONAL ROUTE
Indian Head Trail
3.8 mi. round-trip with 1,550 ft. elevation gain
This yellow-blazed and lesser-used route, fairly rough and steep in its upper half, improved through excellent trail work in recent years, ascends Mt. Pemigewasset from a parking area at the end of a short side road (sign: "Trailhead Parking") off US 3, 0.2 mi. south of Indian Head Resort.

WINTER
Mt. Pemigewasset is an excellent and very popular winter hike with moderate grades for good snowshoeing and no major water crossings. Mt. Pemigewasset Trail is also sheltered from the elements until reaching the top. Use caution on the sloping summit ledges in icy or crusty conditions. In deep snow the views to Franconia Ridge from the true summit are improved. The parking area at Flume Visitor Center is usually well-plowed.

Indian Head Trail is less frequently used in winter, as the short access road to it is not plowed. Despite this, vehicles sometimes still drive the road and pack it down, although plowing along US 3 can leave a bank at the entrance. High clearance is recommended to reach the trailhead. Drivers should also be alert for snowmobiles who cross right at the start of the side road. Depending on the snow banks, limited parking may be available alongside US 3. Parking by permission may also be available at nearby Indian Head Resort.

Mt. Resolution

Elevation: 3,426 ft.
Location: Township of Sargent's Purchase
Map: AMC map - Crawford Notch/Sandwich Range
Locator map: 28

Mt. Resolution is a remote, massive, flat-topped peak within the Presidential Range-Dry River Wilderness and offers excellent views from its near-summit ledges. Bare rock slabs and gravelly slides scar the west side of the mountain, but this wouldn't be the only damage the mountain would receive. Few details are available, but sometime between 1815 and 1855, a devastating forest fire swept through the Mt. Resolution area. In a trail description for Mt. Crawford, Moses Sweetser's 1876 guidebook states that *"the mountain was burnt over about the year 1815, and even the soil was destroyed"*.

Resolution's summit ridge has two small knobs of just about equal height. Mt. Parker Trail passes over open ledges near the high point of the southwest knob (these ledges are the destination needed for the 52WAV list). The true summit of the mountain is on the northeast knob, reached only by a 0.2 mi. bushwhack. While the distance is indeed short, the vegetation and tree growth between the two knobs is very dense, making for tough going. Resolution's ridgecrest is also very broad and fairly flat which can make it confusing to navigate, but for hearty bushwhackers willing to put up a little fight, the true summit offers excellent views to the north as a reward.

The name of the peak comes from the strong determination of an early businessman and trail builder. In 1844, Crawford Notch innkeeper Nathaniel T.P. Davis began the monumental task of constructing Davis Path, a 15 mi. bridle path stretching from the Notch to Mt. Washington. After the initial section was completed to just beyond Mt. Crawford, the difficulties involved caused Davis to lament that the entire route may not be feasible and he temporarily abandoned the project. But determined to finish the trail, he soon returned to work, reaching Mt. Washington in 1845. In honor of Davis' resolve, it was Boston dentist and Crawford Notch resident Samuel Bemis who bestowed the name "Resolution" upon the mountain where work on the trail had resumed.

GETTING THERE

A large parking area is located on the east side of US 302 along the Saco River, opposite Notchland Inn, 8.4 mi. southeast of AMC Highland Center.

RECOMMENDED ROUTE

Davis Path, Mt. Parker Trail

Main Mt. Resolution ledges only: 8.4 mi. round-trip with 2,800 ft. elevation gain
Include side trip to South Peak: 9.8 mi. round-trip with 3,050 ft. elevation gain

The ascent to Resolution involves a steep and rough grind up the ridge to just below the summit of Mt. Crawford, then an easy ramble followed by another steep ledgy climb up to ledges near Resolution's southwest summit. Open ledges along Davis Path past Mt. Crawford provide excellent views along the way. Follow blazes and cairns along these ledges carefully. Davis Path begins on private land; hikers should obey all posted signage and stay on the trail. The short section of Mt. Parker Trail is poorly marked on the open ledges; follow faded blazes and small cairns carefully.

    From the parking area, walk north along a gravel road (there is no public parking here) to cross the Saco River on Bemis Bridge and continue to a sign detailing the history of Davis Path. The yellow-blazed trail passes through a brushy stretch, crosses a wet area (sometimes flooded) on a sketchy bog bridge, then swings right for an easy ascent to the Presidential Range-Dry River Wilderness boundary (sign) at 0.4 mi. The trail dips to cross a dry, rocky brook and continues an easy ascent, crossing another small brook, then passing a side path to a WMNF tent site on the right at 0.8 mi. In several areas along this stretch, climbing has been made easier with the addition of rock steps placed by AMC trail crews. The trail turns sharply right and ascends steeply, alternating between zig zags and longer steady stretches with fairly rough footing. Grades ease for a bit, then the trail makes a short scramble up to the first open view ledge with a look back to Mt. Carrigain, the Nancy Range, North Moat Mountain, Mt. Chocorua, Mt. Tremont, and portions of the Sandwich, Twin, and Willey Ranges. Davis Path swings right here and ascends moderately with several small scrambles. Follow markings on ledges carefully through here. At 2.2 mi., it reaches the junction with Mt. Crawford Spur (small sign on tree at left) which continues ahead.

    Davis Path turns right here and descends easily, then climbs gradually to open ledges with excellent views north and back to the cliffs on Mt. Crawford. The trail continues at easy grades with minor ascents and descents, skirting to the southeast of a minor bump known as Crawford Dome. No trails reach Crawford Dome, but capable bushwhackers will enjoy expansive views from numerous open ledges near its summit. From here, Davis Path stays fairly close to the 3,200 ft. contour as it makes its way around the west side of Mt. Resolution, descending slightly to a four-way junction in a small clearing at 3.7 mi. Mt. Parker Trail, which leads to Mts. Resolution and Parker, turns sharply right. Bearing left, an abandoned spur trail descends to the site of the former Resolution Shelter (camping is prohibited here) and bearing right, Davis Path continues ahead to Stairs Mountain and points north.

    Mt. Parker Trail first makes a steep and rough ascent up an eroded pitch to emerge on large steeply-sloping ledges and the first views to the west. These ledges are often wet so use caution with footing; working around the top edge is the best route. At a ledgy knob, the trail bears left and ascends moderately through a mix of ledge and scrub, then descends to cross a small stream which drains a secluded bog below the true summit of the mountain. Mt. Parker Trail then ascends easily to its height-of-land on the open ledges of the southwest summit knob.

For hikers who still have energy and haven't had enough of the views, a visit to Resolution's South Peak is worth the short side trip. This seldom-visited rocky knob commands views in all directions from its flat top, which is reached by an overgrown and hard to spot side path, the remainder of a loop trail that was built over it in 1935. Note that this side trip involves 200 ft. of climbing on the way back.

From the main ledges on Resolution, continue south along Mt. Parker Trail over ledges, soon descending back into the forest. Grades are easy with minor ascents and descents. The trail levels out for a stretch and at 0.6 mi., where the trail turns left just before it starts to dip again, keep an eye out for the entrance to an obscure path on the right. There is no sign here but the entrance looks like a water bar and is easy to miss. The path descends slightly, pushing through brushy growth, ascends to the base of the south knob, and scrambles up a ledge. It turns left, runs through low shrubs, then turns right up a ledge step to the flat summit.

A glacial boulder on Mt. Resolution's ledges.

VIEW HIGHLIGHTS

Main ledges: The expansive ledges near the southwest summit Knob provide 180-degree views west toward layer after layer of mountains and ridges in the Pemigewasset, Sandwich, and Presidential Range-Dry River Wilderness areas. First up on the far left are the highest peaks in the Sandwich Range: Mts. Passaconaway, Whiteface, and Tripyramid, with Mt. Tremont and Greens Cliff seen below. Looking southwest is Mt. Crawford and its ledgy sibling Crawford Dome. Far in the distance beyond Crawford are Mt. Tecumseh and the Osceolas. Further right is the grand Mt. Carrigain, the Hancocks, and the Nancy Range. Directly west are the Bonds and Twins, with Mt. Guyot in between. Directly across lower Crawford Notch are the Frankenstein Cliffs, and from this vantage point, one of the only spots where you can get a direct overhead view of Arethusa Falls, which appears as a small light strip amongst the forest. Looking northwest, the high peaks of the Willey Range come into view, as do Mts. Webster and Jackson on the opposite side of the Notch proper. Extending up the ridge from Jackson, Mts. Pierce and Eisenhower peek over the long profile of nearby Stairs Mountain. Beyond the Upper Stair are Mts. Franklin and Monroe with Mt. Washington rising above Oakes Gulf. To Washington's right, Boott Spur and Slide Peak can be seen as scrub on Resolution begins to infringe upon glimpses to the Wildcats and Carters.

South Peak: Mt. Resolution's South Peak is a hidden gem, opening up views you don't get from the main peak. It takes some wandering about to get the whole panorama. The most dominant feature is the main mass of Resolution, seen closeby to the north northwest. Looking to the south are Bartlett Haystack and Bear Mountain, with Mt. Paugus seen between them. The sharp point of Mt. Chocorua can be seen over Bear. Moving left, Table Mountain and the long Attitash Ridge can be seen with Mt. Parker, just 1.5 mi. away, close by in the foreground. Rising behind Parker is North Moat Mountain. Below the Attitash Ski Area and further left, the peaks of the lower Montalban Ridge descend in succession: Mt. Langdon, The Crippies, and Mts. Pickering and Stanton. Distant Conway Lake is seen between Langdon and The Crippies, with views out to mountain ranges in western Maine beyond. Next to the left is Black Cap and the Green Hills of Conway followed by Kearsarge North, with Iron Mountain seen below. Further left are the Doubleheads, the Baldfaces, Sable and Chandler Mts. and Jackson's Black Mountain. Moving further left are the Wildcats and Carters, followed by Slide Peak, Boott Spur, Mt. Washington, and Mt. Monroe.

ADDITIONAL ROUTE
Rocky Branch Trail, Stairs Col Trail, Davis Path, Mt. Parker Trail
9.2 mi. round-trip with 2,350 ft. elevation gain

This more gradual approach from the end of Jericho Rd. (WMNF Forest Rd. 27) in Bartlett, which begins 1.0 west of NH 16 in Glen, is far easier and less rugged than coming in from US 302, with two miles of easy walking along an old railroad grade, before a moderate climb up and over Stairs Col below the peak. As of early 2020, the end of Jericho Rd. was still closed and the bridge over Rocky Branch at the start of the trail was damaged, both due to a 2017 storm. Roadside parking is available at a gate 1.75 mi. before the end of the road. From this point, the round-trip distance is 12.7 mi. with no change in elevation gain. See fs.usda.gov for updates regarding the road.

OVERNIGHT OPTIONS

A primitive tent site is available at the end of a short side path (tent sign) off Davis Path on the right, 0.8 mi. from the trailhead. Another is located just behind the summit ledges on nearby Stairs Mountain. This area is typically very dry, so backpackers should carry in all the water they will need. Please follow the WMNF backcountry camping rules if staying overnight in this area. More information is available at fs.usda.gov.

The former Resolution Shelter was located off a side path at the junction of Davis Path and Mt. Parker Trail. Due to its age (ca. 1916) and steadily deteriorating conditions, the shelter was removed by USFS in 2012. The side path is officially closed and camping is not permitted at the former shelter site. An interesting tale in the shelter's history happened during the great hurricane of 1938. A hiking party who was hunkered down there were so protected by the surrounding terrain that they were oblivious to the storm until the next day.

For hikers approaching via Rocky Branch and Stairs Col Trails, Rocky Branch Shelter #1 and Tentsite is located near the junction of these trails, 2.0 mi. north of Jericho Rd. More information is available at fs.usda.gov. See the Getting there section above for details regarding the closure of Jericho Rd.

WINTER

While Davis Path is almost always well-traveled toward Mt. Crawford, it is less so beyond there toward Resolution. Hikers proceeding to Resolution may encounter strenuous trail breaking and route-finding along the open, ledgy sections of the ridge. The first sloping ledges along Mt. Parker Trail are potentially dangerous if icy, and full crampons may be required. The ledges along Mt. Parker Trail and near the summit of Mt. Resolution are fully exposed to the wind. The parking area on US 302 is eventually plowed but may not be immediately after a storm.

The approach via Rocky Branch Trail is still possible even with the partial closure of Jericho Rd. Rocky Branch Trail is usually well-broken out by snowshoers to the shelter but the remainder of the route may be less so.

Mt. Tremont

Elevation: 3,384 ft.
Location: Town of Bartlett
Map: AMC map - Crawford Notch/Sandwich Range
Locator map: 33

Mt. Tremont's summit provides a wide view of the Sandwich Range high peaks.

Mt. Tremont is a steep-sided and rugged peak located near the southern end of the Crawford Notch region. Its uplifted summit, the easternmost and highest of three bumps along the mountain's narrow ridgecrest, has a large open ledge with excellent views. Its French-origin name is derived from its triple summits. Tremont has a very sharp appearance when viewed from different vantage points, especially the southeast, but from other perspectives the ridgeline appears fairly flat.

Tremont's rough and tumble terrain and wilder trails give it a divided opinion among 52WAV peakbaggers — some enjoy its rugged character, while others are glad to check it off the list. For leaf peepers, Tremont is a worthy trip to enjoy the explosion of color far below in the valley surrounding Sawyer Pond.

GETTING THERE

Parking for several vehicles is available in a large pull-off on the northeast side of US 302, diagonal to the trailhead, 0.7 mi. southeast of Fourth Iron Campground and 0.5 mi. northwest of the WMNF Sawyer Rock Picnic Area.

RECOMMENDED ROUTE

Mt. Tremont Trail

5.6 mi. round-trip with 2,600 ft. elevation gain

Of the two approaches to Mt. Tremont, this is the shortest and by far the most traveled and accessible, but it is also far from easy. The initial portion of the trail follows a logging road as a warm-up, but then becomes quite steep and eroded in the second half, ascending the northeast slope of the mountain via more than 20 switchbacks. The trail is marked mostly with yellow blazes, but a few areas still display older blue blazes, while some sections have no blazing at all. However, the trail corridor is generally easy to follow. Footing is generally good down low but becomes rougher with many rocks and roots and you climb higher. The stats for this trail are a bit deceiving as most of the elevation gain is compressed into the second half. For many years Mt. Tremont Trail fell into a state of disrepair but over the last decade or so it has been greatly improved through regular volunteer maintenance.

From the parking pull-off, cross the highway and walk south a short distance to the start of the trail on the right (sign). The trail enters the woods and ascends easily along an old logging road, immediately crossing a small stream (often just a trickle). The trail soon joins alongside Stony Brook and continues an easy to moderate ascent. This is a very picturesque section of the hike with many cascades and one larger waterfall, especially impressive in times of high water. The trail continues to ascend, skirting a large washed out section around to the right, and after a minor brook crossing, climbs steeply to the top of a small ridge. Grades become easy as the trail crosses an overgrown logging road at 1.0 mi. to enter a flat and meandering stretch which is often wet. Follow blazing carefully in this area although recent maintenance has made the corridor better defined.

The trail swings left and then right to cross a small brook, then swings right again to ascend easily up a ridge with a few twists and turns. At the end of the ridge the trail descends moderately to cross a branch of Stony Brook (actually two small branches; may be difficult in high water) at 1.5 mi. This is a good place for a breather and a water or snack break to prepare for the climbing ahead.

On the far side of brook, the trail swings right and climbs more steeply up through switchbacks to make a long, moderate traverse up the northeast slope of the mountain. After a few more switchbacks the trail joins an old logging road, rough at times, turns left off it, and again begins ascending via switchbacks, steeply at times with rougher footing through blowdown-ridden woods. Evidence of past storm damage can be seen all around. As the trail gets closer to the summit, it ascends two very steep and eroded pitches. The first has plenty of roots to use as footholds. The second is a washed out section at a sharp left turn where the trail has been obliterated (this is due to be repaired in the future by USFS), which requires scrambling up the sides. There are trees to use as handholds here but use caution as they may be loose from erosion.

Above this pitch, the trail continues climbing steeply to a junction with a short side path which diverges to the right to a clifftop view looking west (use caution if wet), looping back in a short distance. The main trail bears left and hops up a ledge step to end at the summit and the junction with Brunel Trail (sign) at 2.8 mi., which descends very steeply down the other side of the mountain. The high point and a USGS benchmark are atop the uplifted ledge to the left.

VIEW HIGHLIGHTS

Mt. Tremont's summit ledges offer a sprawling panorama to the south, southwest and west. Recent illegal cutting of trees below the ledges has removed some obscuring growth.

Most prominent to the south is the eastern end of the Sandwich Range, with Mt. Chocorua partly obscured by trees, followed by Mt. Paugus, then fully out into the open to Mt. Passaconaway. Nearby under Passaconaway is Owl's Cliff, reached by Brunel Trail from Tremont. To the right of Passaconaway, nearly all of the Sandwich Range is on full display, from Mt. Whiteface to the Sleepers to Mt. Tripyramid. The view then swings over to

Mt. Tecumseh, the Osceolas, Scar Ridge, Mt. Huntington, the Hancocks, and Mt. Carrigain. Also from Tremont's summit ledges is a unique perspective straight down and far below to Greens Cliff, Sawyer Pond (with Sawyer Pond Shelter visible along the shore) and Little Sawyer Pond.

ADDITIONAL ROUTE
Rob Brook Rd. (WMNF Forest Rd. 35), Brunel Trail
11.0 mi. round-trip with 2,850 ft. elevation gain
This long and remote approach starting on Bear Notch Rd., 0.8 mi. north of NH 112 (Kancamagus Highway) is lightly used and maintained, very steep, and difficult to follow in places. Watch markings and signage carefully, especially in the saddle below Mt. Tremont. However, this route does provide access to the excellent Owl's Cliff viewpoint (2,940 ft.) via a short side trail.

OVERNIGHT OPTIONS
While there are no camping facilities on the mountain itself, car campers can utilize the walk-in primitive sites at Fourth Iron Campground off US 302, 0.7 mi. north of Mt. Tremont Trail. Located at the confluence of the Sawyer and Saco Rivers, Fourth Iron offers eight first come, first served sites which include bear boxes. The sites tend to fill up quickly on weekends and campers who are looking for quiet solitude may not find it here.

For backpackers, the nearest designated options are the campsites and shelter at Sawyer Pond, located 1.5 mi. from the end of Sawyer River Rd. This location offers one Adirondack-style shelter and six tent platforms. Two privys are also available. From the pond, a long, roundabout approach to Mt. Tremont of 11.2 mi. round-trip can be made using Sawyer Pond Trail, WMNF Forest Rd. 318, Rob Brook Rd. and Brunel Trail.

More information on both of these facilities is available at fs.usda.gov.

WINTER
Mt. Tremont is not frequently hiked in winter due to the parking pull-off not being reliably plowed, leaving little room for cars along the highway. In lean snow years, there may be enough room to park fully out of the travel lanes. The parking area at Fourth Iron Campground may be plowed, but there's no guarantee. As such, a winter trek up Tremont would likely involve steep and exhausting trail breaking, especially the relentless switchbacks in the upper half and the very steep pitches shortly below the summit. The summit ledge

may be icy and may require crampons. The branch crossing of Stony Brook is usually not too much of a problem in winter.

If considering the Brunel Trail approach, plowed parking is available at the start of Rob Brook Rd. As noted above, this route is rarely hiked in winter so long, difficult trail breaking and route-finding is likely along Brunel Trail. Rob Brook Rd. is frequently used by cross-country skiers.

Mt. Webster

Elevation: 3,910 ft.
Location: Township of Bean's Grant
Map: AMC map - Crawford Notch/Sandwich Range
Locator map: 34

A hiker relaxes on Mt. Webster's summit ledges.

Mt. Webster anchors the southern end of the Presidential Range and also forms the high eastern wall of Crawford Notch. It has an especially looming and massive presence when viewed from nearby Mt. Willard. Webster's western cliffs drop precipitously into the notch and are scarred by numerous slides and gullies which are well known to ice climbers. The compact summit is mostly open and provides excellent views.

It was originally called Notch Mountain due to its geographic location, but by 1848 the mountain had been renamed in honor of New Hampshire native Daniel Webster, who visited the White Mountains several times and made a famous ascent of Mt. Washington with Ethan Allen Crawford in 1831.

The steep western wall of Mt. Webster, along with Mt. Willey across the Notch, was carved out by the continental glacier as it squeezed through the narrow upper valley of the Saco River which gave the Notch its characteristic and dramatic U-shape.

GETTING THERE
Parking is in a large pull-off on the west side of US 302 near the height-of-land in Crawford Notch, 0.1 mi. south of AMC Highland Center.

RECOMMENDED ROUTE
Webster-Jackson Trail (Webster Branch), Webster Cliff Trail (Appalachian Trail)
5.0 mi. round-trip with 2,200 ft. elevation gain

This is the shortest ascent to Mt. Webster but not necessarily the easiest. It is fairly rough with rocky footing, especially up to the branch junction. The hike is mainly in the woods aside from the two viewpoints mentioned below. From the parking pull-off, cross the highway to the start of blue-blazed Webster-Jackson Trail, which ascends moderately to a junction with a side path on the right to Elephant Head, an open ledge with a view over Crawford Notch. This ledge is so named due to its appearance from the highway as a crouching elephant hiding within the trees.

The main trail continues climbing, then swings right through a section which alternates between easy traverses and steep, rocky pitches, reaching a junction with a side path to Bugle Cliff on the right at 0.6 mi. This short path climbs over a ledgy knoll and down to the top of Bugle Cliff which offers wide views west and northwest. Use caution here, especially if wet or icy, as there is a precipitous dropoff in front.

Webster-Jackson Trail crosses Flume Cascade Brook at 0.9 mi., then the grade is mostly easy to a fork at 1.4 mi., where the trail splits into two branches. The Webster Branch bears right here (the left fork leads to Mt. Jackson), and immediately makes a very steep and rough descent to cross Silver Cascade Brook below a cascade and deep pool. The trail climbs steeply up the other side, then makes a long, steady ascent where footing is rough and eroded, reaching the junction with white-blazed Webster Cliff Trail at

2.4 mi. Bear right for a short traverse followed by a brief climb to the open rocky summit at 2.5 mi. Look for an ancient wooden Appalachian Trail blaze on a tree in this final section.

VIEW HIGHLIGHTS

Wandering around the summit provides excellent views north, west and south. The best spot is at the northwest side of the summit, where there are views northeast to the Presidential Range, northwest towards Vermont, and from the front of the ledge, a dizzying view straight down a gully to the upper floor of Crawford Notch.

Directly across the Notch is its western wall formed by the Willey Range. Mt. Willey is scarred by dark talus slopes and the slab of the Willey Slide, visible high above the railroad. To the right of Mt. Tom at the northern end of the range are the craggy cliffs of Mt. Willard, some 1,000 ft. below. Looking northeast to the Presidential Range, it's pretty much a straight shot up the ridge, with Mt. Jackson, Mt. Pierce, Mt. Eisenhower and Mt. Monroe, leading up to Mt. Washington.

To the southeast is the prominent mass of Mt. Carrigain with Signal Ridge extending to the left. To the left of Carrigain is the nearer Nancy Range (Mt. Anderson, Mt. Lowell, Mt. Nancy, Mt. Bemis), with the Sandwich Range in the distance beyond.

Other 52WAV peaks visible from Mt. Webster include Mt. Starr King, Mt. Martha, Mt. Avalon, Smarts Mountain, Sandwich Dome, Mt. Tremont, Mt. Shaw, Mt. Paugus, Mt. Chocorua, North Moat Mountain, Mt. Crawford, and Mt. Resolution. On extremely clear winter days the distant Mt. Magalloway in Pittsburg can be seen to the northeast about 100 mi. away.

ADDITIONAL ROUTE

Webster Cliff Trail (Appalachian Trail), Webster-Jackson Trail (Webster Branch)

5.8 mi. traverse with 2,850 ft. elevation gain

With a short car spot, this south to north traverse provides spectacular scenery and steep, rugged climbing with a few difficult scrambles atop Webster's high cliffs. Parking for the northern end of Webster Cliff Trail is available at the junction of US 302 and Willey House Station Rd., 1.0 mi. south of the Willey House site.

OVERNIGHT OPTIONS

AMC Mizpah Spring Hut is available for backpackers heading north. Both are located along Webster Cliff Trail, 3.0 mi. north of Mt. Webster. The hut's self-service season is during the month of May, and full-service season is from Memorial Day weekend to October. Reservations are required. More information, reservations and exact dates are available at outdoors.org.

Next to the hut is Nauman Tentsite which offers first come, first served tent platforms, a composting outhouse, and bear boxes. Water is available from a nearby stream. A caretaker is on-site in season and a fee is charged. More information is available at fs.usda.gov.

WINTER

Webster can be a challenging winter hike depending on the conditions. The steep ascent up Webster-Jackson Trail may require crampons if crusty or icy, and the crossing of Silver Cascade Brook may be difficult if not well frozen. The steep drop to cross the brook may also be tricky. Webster's summit is exposed to the weather although only briefly. The parking area along US 302 is plowed.

If approaching from the south via Webster Cliff Trail, the parking area is plowed. This route is not frequently done in winter due to the steep terrain and exposure along the ridge. Strenuous trail breaking may be required and crampons may be necessary in icy conditions. Sections of this trail may be dangerous in winter.

Mt. Willard

Elevation: 2,850 ft.
Location: Township of Hart's Location
Map: AMC map - Crawford Notch/Sandwich Range
Locator map: 35

Mt. Willard anchors the northern end of Crawford Notch, and appears somewhat nondescript and gentle when driving south on US 302, but if approaching from the south, its towering, craggy cliffs of granite which are frequented by rock and ice climbers are a commanding presence. Willard is often recommended as a beginner 52WAV hike due to its short distance and mostly easy grades, with the reward being a huge payoff in the views department. It has been climbed since the mid-1800s and remains to this day one of the most popular half day hikes in the White Mountains.

A colorful character in Mt. Willard history was London-born John Alfred Vials, also known as "English Jack" and the "Hermit of Crawford Notch". Jack settled in the Notch after arriving to work on the Portland and Ogdensburg Railroad during the 1870s, the original precursor to today's Conway Scenic Railroad. Instead of moving on after the project was complete, he built a crude hut at the base of Mt. Willard just above the Gateway (the narrow cut where the highway, the railroad and The Saco River squeeze through). This hut was sometimes referred to as "The House that Jack Built" but he called it his "ship", likely a reference to his earlier seafaring days.

Jack became a well-known figure to tourists who visited the area as he regaled them with the tales of his past adventures while selling them his homemade beer. Some accounts claim he provided entertainment by eating frogs and other unusual creatures, but how much of that is truth and how much is legend is open to interpretation. An odd gentleman for sure, Jack was always well-mannered and good natured and stayed in the Notch until his death at age 85 in 1912.

Any description of Mt. Willard wouldn't be complete without mentioning the Evans family and the Mt. Willard section house, which was located at the base of the mountain's precipitous cliffs. This structure was built by the Maine Central Railroad to house the section foreman and crew who tended to the stretch of track below the cliffs, maintaining it through harsh blizzards and avalanches.

Section foreman Loring Evans and his wife Hattie resided in the house starting in 1903 along with four railroad crew members. Due to its precarious location along the tracks, the only way to reach the house was by train or via a steep trail. Hattie, in addition to assuming the domestic duties of the house, also gave birth to her and Loring's four children here. Each birth was attended by a doctor from Bartlett who was brought up the notch by train.

On a day that should have been full of celebration and gratitude, Loring was accidentally struck and killed by a locomotive while clearing ice from switches on Thanksgiving Day, 1913. Following this tragedy, Hattie made the decision to stay in the house to continue caring for the crew members and her four young children — Gordon, Mildred, Raymond and Enola — whose formative years were spent growing up beside the track.

Hattie remained in the house until 1942, and the structure was ultimately burned down by the Maine Central Railroad in 1972 after suffering many years of vandalism. Today all that remains of the section house is a portion of the foundation and a small memorial to the Evans family.

In addition to the old carriage road up the mountain originally constructed in the mid-1840s — part of which Mt. Willard Trail still uses today — Mt. Willard also was very briefly open to automobile traffic. An auto road was constructed to the summit by the Civilian Conservation Corps in 1937 but it was destroyed by the great hurricane of 1938.

Mt. Willard was originally named Mt. Tom after Thomas Crawford of the famed Crawford family and one of the first innkeepers in Crawford Notch. It was later renamed in honor of inn guest Joseph Willard, who was enamored with the view from its cliffs, and the Mt. Tom name was later moved to the nearby 4,000 footer. Hitchcock Flume, located on the east side of the mountain and formerly accessed by a steep side path, was discovered by New Hampshire state Geologist Charles H. Hitchcock in 1875 and was subsequently named in his honor.

The view of Mt. Webster towering over Crawford Notch from Mt. Willard.

GETTING THERE

Parking is available near Macomber Family Information Center, located in the historic Crawford Depot train station on US 302 in Crawford Notch adjacent to AMC Highland Center, 8.5 mi. east of the junction with US 3 in Twin Mountain. Parking is prohibited at the Highland Center lot as it is reserved for guests of the lodge.

ROUTE
Avalon Trail, Mount Willard Trail
3.2 mi. round-trip with 900 ft. elevation gain

The short trek to Mt. Willard follows sections of footpath and a former carriage road in its upper half, climbing the gentle northern slope of the mountain. Grades are easy to moderate with no sustained steep sections and footing is generally good except for the carriage road section which is rocky and eroded. There are no views along the trail until the expansive vista at the summit ledges. In 2019, trail reconstruction efforts were underway to mitigate some of the erosion caused by heavy hiker traffic.

The route begins by crossing the active tracks of the Conway Scenic Railroad (use caution), followed by an easy, level walk along the combined yellow-blazed Mt. Willard and Avalon Trails. At 0.1 mi., Mt. Willard Trail departs Avalon Trail on the left at a kiosk and continues easily to cross two small brooks (may be difficult at times of high water) at 0.2 mi., then swings right and ascends moderately to the picturesque Centennial Pool (a cascade) on the right at 0.5 mi. This makes for a great rest spot on the way up or down; a small rock staircase descends to the brook.

From the pool, Mt. Willard Trail swings left and climbs more steeply to a junction with the old carriage road at 0.7 mi. The trail bears right and climbs moderately along the wide, rocky, eroded road to reach the ridgecrest, where grades become easier and footing improves somewhat. At 1.5 mi., it passes the brushed-in abandoned side path to Hitchcock Flume on the left. Use caution if exploring this path as it is very steep, overgrown, and potentially dangerous, especially in winter. Mt. Willard Trail continues easily to a natural forest gateway, and abruptly breaks out onto the open ledges where the maintained trail ends. Use caution here with children and pets as the cliffs drop straight down.

From the main ledges, a beaten side path leads southwest over ledges to additional, more secluded clifftop viewpoints. Bushwhackers may be interested in visiting the actual high point of Mt. Willard which is rather broad, flat, and somewhat difficult to discern, located a short distance northwest of the ledges through open woods.

VIEW HIGHLIGHTS

Mt. Willard's ledges provide one of the most iconic and celebrated views in the White Mountains, looking south down the magnificent, glacially-carved, U-shaped Crawford Notch. The view here has often been compared to similar scenes in Europe.

On the left, the Mt. Webster towers about 1,000 ft. higher than Willard, forming the eastern wall of the Notch. To the left of Webster, the subtle summit of Mt. Jackson can be seen. For a view of Mts. Washington and Jefferson, carefully descend a short distance east along Mt. Willard's ledges.

Looking straight down Crawford Notch, Table Mountain is visible beyond the furthest edge of Mt. Webster, with Bear Mountain, Bartlett Haystack, Mt. Tremont, and Mt. Bemis further right. 700 ft. straight down, the highway, the Conway Scenic Railroad and the beginnings of the Saco River all snake their way along the floor of the Notch.

High on the right, forming the western wall of the Notch, are two of the three high peaks of the Willey Range: Mt. Willey and Mt. Field.

WINTER

Mt. Willard is a highly recommended peak for those just starting out with winter hiking or those looking for an easy snowshoe trek or winter gear shakedown. Grades are easy to moderate the entire way, the distance is short, and there is plenty of protection from the weather until the open summit ledges are reached. Both the short section of Avalon Trail and Mt. Willard Trail are heavily traveled in winter and are usually broken out rather quickly after a storm. In crusty or icy conditions, use caution on the summit ledges; crampons may be required. The parking area is not plowed in winter but limited parking is available along the highway.

Stairs Mountain

Elevation: 3,469 ft.
Location: Township of Sargent's Purchase
Map: AMC map - Crawford Notch/Sandwich Range
Locator map: 48

Resembling a long speeding locomotive from some vantage points, wild and rugged Stairs Mountain offers excellent views from high atop lofty cliffs located a short distance southeast of its wooded summit. Stairs' abrupt, stepped profile is a prominent feature when seen from the west. Located deeper into the Presidential Range-Dry River Wilderness than its more popular neighbor Mt. Crawford, Stairs' remoteness also adds to its appeal. Stairs can be hiked on its own but is also often combined with its neighbors Mts. Crawford and/or Resolution. Stairs' cliffs are also well known to backcountry rock climbers, and the mountain's East Peak is a frequent target for bushwhackers working on the New Hampshire 500 Highest list.

For reasons that should be obvious, the mountain was named for its recognizable shape. Moses Sweetser's early guidebooks referred to it as "Mt. Giant's Stairs" after *"two remarkable step-like terraces near its summit, which present the semblance of colossal stairs when seen from a distance"*. He went on to describe the steps as being *"cut with great regularity and sharpness of outline"*. The 1896 USGS topo map indicates the peak itself as Stairs Mountain and the cliffs separately as "Giants Stairs".

GETTING THERE

A large parking area is located on the east side of US 302 along the Saco River, opposite Notchland Inn, 8.4 mi. southeast of AMC Highland Center.

RECOMMENDED ROUTE

Davis Path, Stairs Mountain Spur
9.2 mi. round-trip with 2,700 ft. elevation gain
The ascent to Stairs involves a steep and rough grind up the ridge, then an easy ramble across it, followed by another steep and rugged climb up to the ledges. Open ledges along Davis Path past Mt. Crawford also provide excellent views for the effort. Follow blazes and cairns along these ledges carefully. Davis Path begins on private land; hikers should obey all posted signage and stay on the trail. The spur trail passes very close to the wooded high point of Stairs but does not cross over it.

From the parking area, walk north along a gravel road (there is no public parking here) to cross the Saco River on Bemis Bridge and continue to a sign detailing the history of Davis Path. The trail passes through a brushy stretch, crosses a wet area (sometimes flooded) on a sketchy bog bridge, then swings right for an easy ascent to the Presidential Range-Dry River Wilderness boundary (sign) at 0.4 mi. The trail dips to cross a dry, rocky brook and continues an easy ascent, crossing another small brook, then passing a side path to a WMNF tent site on the right at 0.8 mi. Climbing becomes steeper and footing becomes rougher as the trail ascends the west side of Bemis Ridge, alternating between shorter twists and turns and longer stretches. A short scramble leads to the first outlook ledge and view southwest toward Mt. Carrigain and 52WAV peaks North and South Moat Mountain, Mt. Chocorua, and Mt. Tremont. The trail swings right here and climbs moderately through a mix of ledge and scrub to the junction with Mt. Crawford Spur (sign) on the left at 2.2 mi.

Davis Path turns right here and descends easily then climbs gradually to open ledges with excellent views north and back to the cliffs on Mt. Crawford. The trail continues at easy grades with minor ascents and descents, skirting to the southeast of a minor bump known as Crawford Dome. No trails reach Crawford Dome, but capable bushwhackers will enjoy expansive views from open ledges near the summit. From here, Davis Path stays fairly close to the 3200 ft. contour as it makes its way around the west side of Mt. Resolution, descending slightly to a four-way junction in a small clearing at 3.7 mi. Mt. Parker Trail, which leads to Mts. Resolution and Parker, turns sharply right. Bearing left, an abandoned spur trail descends to the site of the former Resolution Shelter (camping is prohibited here).

Bearing right at the clearing, Davis Path descends easily with rough footing in places to Stairs Col at 4.0 mi., a ferny saddle between Stairs and Mt. Resolution, and a junction with Stairs Col Trail, which departs on the right. Davis Path bears left here, ascends moderately at first then easily, then becomes quite steep and rough with a few scrambles (potentially difficult if wet), to a junction with Stairs Mountain Spur on the right (sign) at 4.4 mi. This spur trail first ascends slightly, then descends easily for 0.2 mi., passing the wooded true summit of Stairs (just off trail on the left), then ends at the top of Giant Stairs and its magnificent 180-degree views. Use caution with children or pets or if wet as the drop is straight down.

VIEW HIGHLIGHTS

The main attraction from Stairs' sunny ledges is the massive bulk of Mt. Resolution directly across Stairs Col which blocks the view south. Highlights to the left of Stairs include the Doubleheads, Iron Mountain, Kearsarge North, Conway's Green Hills, and numerous peaks in western Maine. North Moat Mountain pops up just as the view disappears behind Resolution.

Re-emerging on the other side is Mt. Paugus, Hedgehog Mountain, and the rolling ridge of the Sandwich Range, including Mt. Passaconaway, the Sleepers, and the Tripyramids. To the right of North Tripyramid and closer to the foreground is Mt. Crawford. Further right, Mt. Tecumseh, the Osceolas, the Hancocks, the towering Mt. Carrigain, and the Nancy Range can be seen.

At the edge of Stairs Mountain's precipitous cliffs.

ADDITIONAL ROUTE

Rocky Branch Trail, Stairs Col Trail, Davis Path, Stairs Mountain Spur
8.8 mi. round-trip with 2,450 ft. elevation gain
This more gradual approach from the end of Jericho Rd. (WMNF Forest Rd. 27) in Bartlett, which begins 1.0 west of NH 16 in Glen, is far easier and less rugged than coming in from US 302, with two miles of easy walking along an old railroad grade before a moderate climb up and over Stairs Col below the peak. As of early 2020, the end of Jericho Rd. was still closed and the bridge over Rocky Branch at the start of the trail was damaged, both due to a 2017 storm. Roadside parking is available at a gate 1.75 mi. before the end of the road. From this point, the round-trip distance is 12.7 mi. with no change in elevation gain. See fs.usda.gov for updates.

OVERNIGHT OPTIONS

A primitive tent site is available at the end of a short side path (tent sign) off Davis Path on the right, 0.8 mi. from the trailhead. Another is located just behind the summit ledges on Stairs. There is also room up here for an additional tent. On clear mornings, the summit ledges make for stunning sunrises, and there is perhaps no finer location in this region to eat breakfast or sip your coffee. This area is typically very dry, so backpackers should carry in all the water they will need. Please follow the WMNF backcountry camping rules if staying overnight in this area. More information is available at fs.usda.gov.

The former Resolution Shelter was located off a side path at the junction of Davis Path and Mt. Parker Trail. Due to its age and steadily deteriorating conditions, the shelter was removed by USFS in 2012. The side path is officially closed and camping is not permitted at the former shelter site. For hikers approaching via Rocky Branch and Stairs Col Trails, Rocky Branch Shelter #1 and Tentsite is located near the junction of these trails, 2.0 mi. north of the end of Jericho Rd. More information is available at fs.usda.gov. See the Getting there section above for details regarding the closure of Jericho Rd.

WINTER

While Davis Path is almost always well-traveled toward Mt. Crawford, it is less so beyond there toward Stairs. Hikers proceeding on may encounter strenuous trail breaking and route-finding along the ridge. The steep section of Davis Path ascending to Stairs as well as the summit ledges may require crampons in crusty or icy conditions. Use caution as the drop off the cliff is straight down. The parking area on US 302 is plowed.

The approach via Rocky Branch Trail is still possible even with the partial closure of Jericho Rd. Rocky Branch Trail is usually well-broken out by snowshoers to the shelter but the remainder of the route may be less so.

The uppermost of Stairs Mountain's "Giant Stairs".

Eastern White Mountains

Eagle Crag

Elevation: 3,030 ft.
Location: Township of Bean's Purchase
Map: CTA map, AMC map - Carter Range/Evans Notch
Locator map: 03

Peering into western Maine from Eagle Crag.

Eagle Crag is a high perch along the open and very scenic Meader Ridge, which stretches north from the Baldfaces to Mt. Meader, southwest of Evans Notch. It is not a peak unto itself, but rather an open ledge on a bump along the ridge with excellent panoramic views in all directions.

On some online versions of the 52WAV list Eagle Crag is listed with Mt. Meader, which has caused some confusion for hikers. Mt. Meader is not on the list, but Eagle Crag is sometimes described with it to denote its location along Meader Ridge. While it is possible to hike Eagle Crag by itself, it is often included as a side trip as part of the scenic loop over the Baldfaces.

Like Eagle Cliff in Franconia Notch and other locations with eagle in their name, the Eagle Crag moniker is presumed to be derived from high, craggy cliff areas where eagles nest.

GETTING THERE
Parking is available at a large lot for Baldface Circle Trail on NH 113 in Chatham, just west of the Maine border, 25 mi. north of NH 16 in Conway and 12.7 mi. south of US 2 in Gilead, ME.

RECOMMENDED ROUTE
Baldface Circle Trail, Meader Ridge Trail, Bicknell Ridge Trail
8.1 mi. counter-clockwise loop with 2,550 ft. elevation gain
This route starts out fairly easy but becomes quite strenuous as you ascend. However, the tremendous views from Bicknell Ridge and Eagle Crag provide a reward for the hard work. Baldface Circle is very steep and rough near the ridge and includes a couple of difficult scrambles.

From the parking area, cross NH 113 and walk north a short distance to the start of yellow-blazed Baldface Circle Trail on the left. The trail climbs a short bank, then proceeds level or at easy grades with some rough footing to Circle Junction at 0.7 mi., where the trail splits.

Continue straight ahead to the crossing of Charles Brook (may be difficult at high water), then a branch of the same brook. The trail passes the junction with Bicknell Ridge Trail on the left at 1.4 mi., crosses another branch of Charles Brook, then passes the junction with Eagle Cascade Link on the left at 2.1 mi. It soon joins an old logging road as the ascent becomes more moderate, then very steep and rough as it scrambles up to the ridge to reach the junction with Meader Ridge Trail and Eagle Link at 3.7 mi. Turn right onto Meader Ridge Trail for an easy 0.1 mi. traverse over open ledges with spectacular views to reach Eagle Crag, a broad open ledge marked by a cairn.

Backtracking to the junction with Baldface Circle Trail, 3.9 mi. along this loop, continue straight (south) along that trail and ascend easily to the junction with Bicknell Ridge Trail on the left at 4.2 mi. This trail descends easily at first then more steeply over open ledges along the northern edge of Charles Ravine, offering excellent views south and east. At 5.3 mi., the trail passes a junction with Eagle Cascade Link on the left, then ruggedly descends back into the woods. Footing and grades improve as the trail crosses a branch of Charles Brook and continues to the junction with Baldface Circle Trail at 6.7 mi. The area around this junction was minimally impacted by logging in 2019. Turn right for a 1.4 mi. descent back to the trailhead and parking area.

VIEW HIGHLIGHTS

The wide vista from Eagle Crag stretches in nearly all directions, starting with a look down Meader Ridge toward Mt. Meader and West and East Royce Mountains. The view then swings around to peaks in the Caribou-Speckled Wilderness such as Speckled Mountain, Blueberry Mountain, Butters Mountain, Red Rock Mountain and Caribou Mountain. To the right of Caribou in the distance is Saddleback Mountain in the Rangeley Lake area of Maine. Moving more to the right is a vast flat expanse of southern Maine peppered with dozens of small peaks. Further right, the ridge of Pleasant Mountain rises from the landscape, followed by Green Mountain in Effingham and the Moose Mountains in Brookfield, before the view disappears behind Eastman Mountain, Kearsarge North and the Baldfaces. Emerging to the right of North Baldface is Black Mountain in Jackson, before moving over to the high ridges of the Carters and Moriahs seen across the expansive Wild River Valley. Just about due north is Mt. Success followed by the higher peaks of the Mahoosuc Range: Mt. Carlo, Goose Eye Mountain and Old Speck.

The descent along Bicknell Ridge Trail offers stunning views east and southeast into Maine. Especially striking is a look across Charles Ravine to South Baldface and its magnificent rocky northeast ridge.

ADDITIONAL ROUTE

NH 113, Mt. Meader Trail, Meader Ridge Trail, Baldface Circle Trail

9.3 mi. counter-clockwise loop with 2,850 ft. elevation gain
This longer loop option over Eagle Crag, also beginning and ending at the Baldface Circle trailhead, involves a rugged and very steep ascent and descent but also offers excellent views along Meader Ridge.

OVERNIGHT OPTIONS

For backpackers combining Eagle Crag with the Baldfaces, Baldface Shelter can be utilized. See the Baldfaces section for details.

While it's a bit out of the way, Blue Brook Tentsite is available for hikers approaching Eagle Crag from the north via Meader Ridge Trail. This former shelter site is located on a spur path off Black Angel Trail, 0.5 mi. west of Rim Junction, which is 1.4 mi. north of the junction of Mt. Meader and Basin

Rim Trails. There are three first come, first served tentsites, and water is available from an adjacent brook. Refer to the AMC WMNF Carter Range/Evans Notch or Chatham Trails Association maps for location.

WINTER
Eagle Crag is infrequently hiked in winter and crampons may be needed along open ledge areas and steep ascent to the ridge in crusty or icy conditions. The branch crossing of Charles Brook along Bicknell Ridge Trail may be difficult if not well frozen. The parking area is plowed. NH 113 is gated north of the trailhead and just south of US 2, so the only driving approach in winter is from the south.

Eastman Mountain

Elevation: 2,938 ft.
Location: Town of Chatham
Map: CTA map, AMC map - Carter Range/Evans Notch
Locator map: 04

The southwest view from Eastman Mountain.

Flanked to the north by its immediate 52WAV neighbors the Baldfaces, Eastman Mountain offers good views in most directions from its ledgy summit. While the scenery is somewhat obscured by trees, a 360-degree vista can be pieced together by wandering around the summit ledges. In season, blueberries are plentiful on these ledges. Eastman is sort of an outlier at the southern end of the Baldface-Royce Range, a chain of rugged and scenic peaks running along the west side of Evans Notch.

As with other similarly-named locations in this area, the peak gets its name from the Eastman family, early farmers who had settled in the small town of Chatham during the 1800s.

GETTING THERE

Parking is available at a large lot for Baldface Circle Trail on NH 113 in Chatham, just west of the Maine border, 25 mi. north of NH 16 in Conway and 12.7 mi. south of US 2 in Gilead, ME.

RECOMMENDED ROUTE

Baldface Circle Trail, Slippery Brook Trail (northern section), Eastman Mountain Trail

8.6 mi. round-trip with 2,650 ft. elevation gain
CTA map

This route offers a moderate ascent to Eastman, mostly along old logging roads with generally good footing. Eastman Mountain Trail has some minor scrambles approaching the summit.

From the parking area, cross NH 113 and walk north a short distance to the start of yellow-blazed Baldface Circle Trail on the left. The trail climbs a short bank, then proceeds level or at easy grades with some rough footing to Circle Junction at 0.7 mi. where the trail splits; the northern section continues ahead and the southern section bears left (on the right, a short side path (sign) leads to Emerald Pool, a popular swimming hole along Charles Brook). At Circle Junction, bear left to continue along Baldface Circle Trail, then turn left onto Slippery Brook Trail at 0.9 mi.

Slippery Brook Trail ascends briefly then descends to cross a branch of Chandler Brook, then merges onto an old logging road which it follows on a long, moderate ascent to the ridge and a four-way junction at 3.5 mi. in the col between Baldface Knob and Eastman. Slippery Brook Trail continues ahead toward Slippery Brook Rd., Baldface Knob Trail turns right and Eastman Mountain Trail turns left.

Eastman Mountain Trail heads southeast through a birch forest at easy grades then descends slightly to a small col. The trail climbs easily at first and then more moderately up the mountain's north ridge with a couple of minor scrambles to reach the ledgy summit at 4.3 mi.

VIEW HIGHLIGHTS

The most impressive view from Eastman is the look over to nearby South Baldface and its bare, ledgy cone. To the right of South Baldface, Shelburne Moriah pops up just over the horizon, followed by various Mahoosuc Range peaks such as Mt. Success, Goose Eye Mountain and Old Speck. Closer in, the double summits of West and East Royce can be seen. The view moves further right to Caribou, Ames and Speckled Mountains before arriving at a wide, mostly flat expanse of southern Maine which is dotted with small hills.

To the southeast, a small ridge extends from Eastman and runs over its south peak. The view then swings around to Kearsarge North, White Horse Ledge, North Moat Mountain, Big Attitash Mountain, the twin conical summits of the Doubleheads, and the nearby trailless Chandler and Sable Mountains. The top of Mt. Washington is just visible over Sable's ridge followed by Carter Dome, Mt. Hight and South Carter, before the vista disappears behind South Baldface.

ADDITIONAL ROUTE

Slippery Brook Trail (southern section), Eastman Mountain Trail
9.6 mi. round-trip with 1,520 ft. elevation gain
This lightly used alternative route from the end of Slippery Brook Rd. (WMNF Forest Rd. 17) in Chatham is longer, but grades are generally easy the whole way. This is probably the easiest route to Eastman and the Baldfaces, but the loop option over the latter isn't feasible from this side. Watch markings and signs carefully on the lower logging road section of Slippery Brook Trail. From NH 16 in Lower Bartlett, take Town Hall Rd. north for 2.5 mi. where it turns into Slippery Brook Rd. Bearing right at 5.9 mi., continue to the end of the road at 7.3 mi., where parking is next to a gate.

OVERNIGHT OPTIONS

For backpackers combining Eastman with the Baldfaces, Baldface Shelter can be utilized. See the Baldfaces section for details.

WINTER

The moderate grades along Slippery Brook and Eastman Mountain Trails make for good snowshoeing with no sustained steep sections or tricky ledges. This route is also wooded, offering protection from the weather until the summit. The parking area for Baldface Circle Trail is plowed. NH 113 is gated north of the trailhead and just south of US 2, so the only driving approach in winter is from the south.

Backcountry skiers may be interested in Slippery Brook Glade, an area of new ski trails which was opened in 2018, located on a ridge just to the north of Slippery Brook Trail. More information is available at granitebackcountryalliance.org.

The already long approach via Slippery Brook Trail from the south becomes even longer in winter as Slippery Brook Rd. is only plowed to a point 3.5 mi. from NH 16, stretching out the total round-trip distance to Eastman to an epic 17.2 mi. While this is indeed a trek, the mostly easy grades of this approach may be suitable for experienced skiers.

Imp Face

Elevation: 3,165 ft.
Location: Township of Bean's Purchase
Map: AMC map - Carter Range/Evans Notch
Locator map: 07

Imp Face (different from nearby Imp Mountain) is a high cliff on the western slope of North Carter Mountain near Pinkham Notch between NH 16 and the higher ridge of the Carter-Moriah Range. The cliff offers excellent views of the Presidential Range.

The cliff's name comes from the rocky human profile best seen from Dolly Copp Campground. Allegedly it was Dolly Copp herself, a charismatic character, farmer and innkeeper, who gave the cliff and Imp Mountain its name during the early 1800s. By a simple fluke of geography, the best spot to view the Imp Profile was from her property.

An 1887 guidebook refers to the Imp's human-like profile as *"a grotesque colossal sphinx which appears on one of the peaks of the Carter Range, the profile being formed by the upper crags of Mt. Imp, and having a weird resemblance to a distorted human face. This appearance is best observed in late afternoon, and from Copp's Farm, on the old road to Randolph."*

GETTING THERE
Roadside parking is available along NH 16, 5.5 mi. south of Gorham and 0.3 mi. north of the southern Imp trailhead. Both trailheads are signed but can be easy to miss if cruising along the road.

The top of the Imp Face cliff.

RECOMMENDED ROUTE
Imp Trail
4.4 mi. round-trip with 1,850 ft. elevation gain
Imp Trail is a loop starting and ending on NH 16 with a short road walk between the two trailheads. The route described here ascends from the northern trailhead to the clifftop viewpoint; see below for stats on the full loop. Grades are easy at first but become steeper closer to the cliff, and footing is generally good with a few rough spots.

From the highway, yellow-blazed Imp Trail ascends steadily alongside Imp Brook to eventually cross it (may be difficult at times of high water) at 0.8 mi. There is also an attractive cascade here. After the brook, the trail makes a steep ascent, runs mostly on the level, then steepens again to ascend along the north side of a ridge, climbing one short ladder. The ascent remains steady as the trail makes a sharp right turn at 1.8 mi., where footing becomes more ledgy. It swings left and ascends the northwest ridge, levels out again, and then breaks out onto the open ledges atop the cliff at 2.2 mi. Use caution if wet or with pets or children as the drop off is straight down for several hundred feet. If continuing along the complete loop, the trail turns left here; follow blazes carefully. For highpointers, the true wooded summit of the Imp Face bump is a short distance to the northeast of the main ledges and is accessible via a brief bushwhack off Imp Trail.

VIEW HIGHLIGHTS

Views from the Imp Face cliff are spectacular and somewhat dizzying, with the high ridge of the Carters towering on the left and the deep ravine which gives rise to Imp Brook far below.

Looking south to Pinkham Notch, the Wildcats pop up over a ridge of South Carter, then jumping across the Notch are the high peaks of the Presidential Range including Slide Peak, Boott Spur and Mts. Washington, Clay, Jefferson, Adams and Madison. Of particular note is the unique look straight into Great Gulf under Clay and Jefferson.

Moving right, the view turns to the Pliny and Pilot Range peaks of Mt. Waumbek, the Weeks, Mt. Cabot and The Horn, and almost directly north and in the foreground is the low Pine Mountain in Gorham, after which the view becomes obscured by trees.

ADDITIONAL ROUTE

Imp Trail complete loop

6.6 mi. clockwise loop with 2,050 ft. elevation gain

The entire loop over Imp Face is a rugged endeavor especially on the southern leg where footing is rocky and rough. A short walk north along NH 16 from the southern trailhead closes the loop.

OVERNIGHT OPTIONS

While located far above Imp Face off Carter-Moriah Trail, Imp Shelter and Tentsite is available for backpackers ascending to the ridge. A caretaker is on-site from Memorial Day to Columbus Day and a fee is charged in season. No fee is required outside of caretaker season. Water is available from a spring and there is a privy. More information is available at fs.usda.gov.

WINTER

Imp Face makes for an intermediate snowshoe hike with good protection from the weather until the top. Crampons may be required on the open clifftop ledges and on steeper parts of the trail. If continuing past Imp Face, deep snow greatly improves the rough, rocky footing on the southern end of the loop but due to lighter traffic, trail breaking may be required. The roadside parking areas are usually plowed wide enough for a few vehicles.

Mt. Kearsarge North

Elevation: 3,269 ft.
Location: Town of Chatham
Map: AMC map - Carter Range/Evans Notch
Locator map: 20

A hiker approaches the fire tower at the summit of Kearsarge North.

Mt. Kearsarge North, not to be confused with the similarly-named Mt. Kearsarge in southern New Hampshire (also a 52WAV peak), is a large, prominent mountain visible from many locations in the Mt. Washington Valley and western Maine. It's open, ledgy summit features panoramic views in most directions.

During a wave of mountaintop hotel construction in the mid to late 1800s, the summit of Kearsarge North was the site of a small hotel originally constructed around 1848 by four local men. The business stayed open for a few years but was ultimately abandoned. In 1869, the hotel was purchased by

Andrew Dinsmore, who reopened it until the structure blew down in an 1883 windstorm. Undeterred, Dinsmore rebuilt the hotel on a smaller scale but once again it was later abandoned. Pequawket Fire Lookout Tower was built in 1913 from the remnants of the destroyed 1883 structure and was added to the National Historic Lookout Register in 1991. As part of a group of women recruited by USFS to serve as fire lookouts known as the WOOFs, or Women Observers of the Forest, Dorothy Martin of Sandwich was one of the early observers on the tower, which remains today for first come, first served overnight stays.

During its hotel heyday, the grand vistas from the summit encouraged other plans to get tourists up there. In 1883, planning and engineering work was laid out for a short gauge railroad spanning 29 mi. from western Maine to North Conway and the base of the mountain. These plans also included a spiraling route around the mountain to the summit, and a spur line to Shingle Pond was proposed. While the Conway and Mt. Kearsarge Railroad was indeed officially incorporated, it never got out of the planning stage and no track was ever built.

Originally known as Pequawket Mountain, the name of the mountain was changed in 1957, immediately causing confusion with its southern sibling. Adding to that, the peak is sometimes called Mt. Kearsarge, Kearsarge North, or Kearsarge North Mountain. Like the southern Kearsarge, the current name is derived from "Carasarga", an Abenaki or Penacook term roughly translating to "notchpointed mountain of pines". The current spelling was adopted in 1816.

GETTING THERE

Parking for several vehicles is available in a small lot (sign) along Hurricane Mountain Rd., which skirts the Bartlett/Conway town line, 1.4 mi. east of NH 16. If the lot is full, as it often is, parking along Hurricane Mountain Rd. is prohibited; note all posted signs. Violators are subject to fines.

RECOMMENDED ROUTE

Mt. Kearsarge North Trail

6.2 mi. round-trip with 2,600 ft. elevation gain

This route starts out with an easy warm-up followed by a stiff climb up the south side of the mountain. While the distance to the summit is fairly short, the significant elevation gain compressed into that distance puts this climb on par with many higher peaks. Grades are generally moderate to steep with footing becoming increasingly rougher in the final third of the ascent.

From the parking area, yellow-blazed Mt. Kearsarge North Trail (note different name on signage) starts out level through a wet area, then ascends easily high above a brook, entering the WMNF at 0.7 mi. At 1.1 mi., footing begins to become rougher. The trail reaches a ledgy area at 1.8 mi. with restricted views southwest to Mt. Chocorua and the Moat Range, continues a moderate climb to cross over the ridge connecting Mt. Kearsarge North with its western subpeak Bartlett Mountain, then curves right. Climbing becomes steeper with rough, eroded footing in places as the trail ascends along the north side of the ridge. At 2.9 mi., the trail turns sharply right and makes its final ascent to the summit ledges, fire tower, and junction with Weeks Brook Trail which continues ahead.

VIEW HIGHLIGHTS

The summit ledges provide excellent views in most directions, but are restricted to the north somewhat by tree growth. You need to climb up to the fire tower deck to get the full panorama.

The view north looks into the Evans Notch area to the Baldfaces, Sable and Chandler Mountains, and the Royces. Between South Baldface and West Royce, Old Speck and Goose Eye Mountain in the Mahoosuc Range can be seen. Closer by to the northeast are Mt. Shaw and the Twins (different peaks from their counterparts further south), with a vast jumble of peaks in western Maine beyond.

This vista continues further right and becomes more flat until Pleasant Mountain rises from the surrounding terrain, which becomes more bumpy again before swinging around to nearby Hurricane Mountain and the Green Hills in Conway, including Black Cap and Middle and Peaked Mountains. Moving to the southwest, the Ossipee and Belknap Ranges come into view, before the Moat Range rises up with Mt. Chocorua and the Three Sisters in back. Below the Moats are White Horse and Cathedral Ledges. Over North Moat, the Sandwich Range stretches east toward Mt. Tecumseh.

Due west, mighty Mt. Carrigain comes into view along with the Nancy Range, with the lower peaks of Montalban Ridge, Mts. Stanton, Pickering and Langdon in the foreground below Carrigain. From Parker, the ridgeline continues right toward Mt. Resolution and Stairs Mountain, with Iron Mountain visible in the foreground beneath them. Beyond Stairs, Mts. Willey and Field can be seen before the Southern Presidentials come into view.

Looking northwest is the remote bump of Mt. Isolation, and close by under Isolation are Thorn, Middle and Tin Mountains in Jackson.

Mts. Franklin and Monroe appear on the horizon before Mt. Washington rises above it all, then the view descends to Mts. Adams and Madison, the Wildcats, and then the Carter-Moriah Range. Directly under the U-shaped Carter Notch, the twin summits of the Doubleheads can be seen.

ADDITIONAL ROUTE
Weeks Brook Trail
10.2 mi. round-trip with 2,700 ft. elevation gain
This longer and lightly used trail (recommended for more experienced hikers) from Hardwood Hill Rd. (WMNF Forest Rd. 317) in Chatham, difficult to follow in places, offers a quieter approach, passing by scenic Shingle Pond on the way. The lower section of the trail has been repeatedly disrupted by logging; follow blazes and other markings carefully. Parts of the trail between the pond and summit may also be overgrown. From the eastern end of Hurricane Mountain Rd. in Chatham, follow Green Hill Rd. north for 0.4 mi., then turn left onto Hardwood Hill Rd. (hiker symbol) and continue 0.1 mi. to a gate and limited parking.

OVERNIGHT OPTIONS
The fire tower is available on a first come, first served basis for overnight stays. A somewhat "primitive" privy is located just to the north of the summit on a side path (sign). There is no reliable water source, so hikers are urged to carry in what they need.

WINTER
Mt. Kearsarge North is a well-traveled peak located near a busy population center and as such the route is broken out fairly quickly after a storm. Mt. Kearsarge North Trail can collect a lot of ice, so crampons may be needed if snow cover is thin. The fire tower offers protection from the wind. Hurricane Mountain Rd. is gated in winter but the plowed trailhead parking is well before the gate. In winter, the amount of space in the lot can be reduced depending on snowfall amounts. Parking is not allowed along the road.

Weeks Brook Trail is seldom hiked in winter. Hardwood Hill Rd. is not plowed but depending on snowfall amounts there may be room along Green Hill Rd. to park fully out of the travel lanes; do not block plowing operations. This adds 0.2 mi. round-trip to the hike.

North Doublehead/South Doublehead

Elevations: 3,051 ft. / 2,939 ft.
Location: Town of Jackson
Map: AMC map - Carter Range/Evans Notch
Locator map: 36

Open ledges on South Doublehead provide an excellent vista toward the Presidential and Wildcat / Carter Ranges.

Note: While these mountains are indicated as two separate peaks on maps, they are counted as one hike for the purposes of the 52WAV list. Both peaks were combined for the list in 2020.

Adjacent to ex-52WAV neighbor Black Mountain (Jackson), the Doubleheads are a pair of prominent conical summits which drop off steeply in all directions. Both peaks are wooded at their true summits, but North Doublehead does offer a small directional view, while South Doublehead has a nearly 180-degree panoramic view from an off-trail ledge.

North Doublehead has been used by skiers since 1934 when the Doublehead Ski Trail was laid out by Gordon Langill of the Winnipesaukee Ski Club, and later cut by the Civilian Conservation Corps, who created many ski trails throughout New England. The lower part of the trail was relocated off private property in 2018.

Also in 1934, American composer Alan Hovhaness was inspired to write a composition for the piano entitled *"Fog on Mount Double Head"* after frequently climbing the White Mountains in his youth.

The Doublehead name is no doubt derived from the twin summits of the mountain, and it appeared on Jeremy Belknap's 1791 map of the White Mountains. This name is also applied to a mountain in the Lakes Region's Squam Range.

GETTING THERE

The former parking area on private Doublehead Drive in Jackson has been closed by the landowner, and a temporary parking area along Dundee Rd. adjacent to this is now posted no parking. Hikers should park in a new designated parking area which opened in 2018. From NH 16 in Jackson, take NH 16A at the covered bridge for 0.5 mi., bear right onto Black Mountain Rd. for 1.9 mi., passing Black Mountain Ski Area on the left, then turn right onto Dundee Rd. and continue 0.5 mi. to the parking area on the left. This new parking area may be closed at times by USFS during mud season.

RECOMMENDED ROUTE

Doublehead Ski Trail, Old Path

3.0 mi. clockwise loop with 1,530 ft. elevation gain

This route makes a steep loop over North Doublehead with an out-and-back side trip to the view ledges on South Doublehead. Footing is generally good along the ski trail although it is grassy so watch for ticks in summer. Old Path has some rough and rocky footing descending from the summit of North Doublehead.

From the parking area, ascend easily along a blue-blazed relocated section of Doublehead Ski Trail and bear right onto the former route at 0.3 mi. The wide ski trail ascends easily at first, then more moderately to a junction with Old Path on the right at 0.6 mi. The ski trail swings left and climbing becomes more steady as the grade steepens higher up. The trail slowly curves right and eases a bit along the ridge, then it ends at the wooded summit of North Doublehead and Doublehead Cabin at 1.8 mi. Behind the cabin to the right of the privy, a short side path descends slightly to an open ledge with a cleared view.

From the cabin, Old Path descends south, quickly making a steep and rough descent over broken ledge and rock, passing a short side path on the right which leads to a western outlook, to a junction with New Path at 2.1 mi., in the saddle between North and South Doublehead. To reach the South Doublehead outlook, continue straight on New Path for 0.2 mi. to a point where it turns left near the summit. At this turn, opposite the wooded high point just off the trail, a short side path descends a few yds. to the right to roomy open ledges.

From the junction with New Path, Old Path turns right and descends off the eastern side of the ridge fairly steeply most of the way, then more moderately, to the junction with Doublehead Ski Trail at 2.7 mi. Bear left onto the ski trail, then turn left to return to the parking area.

VIEW HIGHLIGHTS

North Doublehead outlook: The summit of North Doublehead is mostly wooded but the viewpoint behind the cabin provides a good look down to secluded Mountain Pond and the hills surrounding it including Walter Mountain, Mt. Shaw (not the one in the Ossipees), Slope Mountain and Round Mountain. Beyond Mountain Pond is a look into a broad expanse of western Maine where Kezar Lake is partly visible.

South Doublehead main outlook: The excellent view ledge on South Doublehead offers a wide birds-eye vista high above the village of Jackson, which extends from the Lakes Region and the Sandwich Range all the way around to the deep Carter Notch between the Wildcats and Carter Dome.

On the far left is a distant look out to the Lakes Region followed by the Moat-Attitash Range, with Thorn Mountain in Jackson lower and closer in. Tin Mountain can be seen to the right of Thorn. Back in the distance to the right of the Moats are the Sandwich Range peaks. Mt. Carrigain is just shy of due west, with Iron Mountain visible closer in. The long crest of Mt. Resolution and Stairs Mountain are seen to the right of Iron with Jackson's Eagle Mountain down in front of Stairs. Back in the distance and further right are a bit of South Twin Mountain and the Willey Range, before the view ascends over the southern ridge of the Presidential Range to Mt. Washington. To the right of Washington, the view jumps across Pinkham Notch to the Wildcats, drops to U-shaped Carter Notch, then runs over the high ridge of the Carters and Moriahs. Nearer and under this view is Black Mountain in Jackson with its ski slopes visible on the left end of the ridge.

South Doublehead view ledges: If approaching via New Path, a short spur trail splits off to the right at the ridge and leads 0.2 mi. to two ledgy bumps with restricted views. The most prominent feature seen here is a look over to darkly wooded North Doublehead and a patch of open ledge on its southern slope. Also visible from this perspective are the Baldfaces and other peaks in the Evans Notch area.

ADDITIONAL ROUTE
Dundee Rd., New Path, Old Path, Doublehead Ski Trail
4.1 mi. counter-clockwise loop with 1,770 ft. elevation gain
This route allows for a steep, rugged loop over South and North Doublehead, starting with a short walk along Dundee Rd. from the new parking area. In 2016, New Path was proposed to be closed by USFS due to severe erosion, but the proposal was deferred due to public opposition and the trail was still in use as of 2020. Use caution on this trail as it is very steep and footing is slippery and poor.

OVERNIGHT OPTIONS
Historic Doublehead Cabin is available for use by reservation. The cabin features bunks, a wood stove and a nearby outhouse. There is no water source at the summit; the nearest source is about halfway down Doublehead Ski Trail. More information is available at recreation.gov.

WINTER
This is another 52WAV hike with a ski trail, making it a popular winter destination. Hikers should stay to the side, yielding to fast moving skiers, and should wear snowshoes to preserve the trail. Crampons may be needed on the steep section of Old Path below the summit in icy conditions. Doublehead Cabin is kept locked when not in use and cannot be relied on for shelter in bad weather or in an emergency. Deep snow opens up views a bit from the outlook behind the cabin. The parking area off Dundee Rd. is plowed but space may be tight.

If approaching via New Path, additional roadside parking may be available at the trailhead depending on snow banks. Please do not block access for local residents. Crampons may be required on the steep sections of this trail. Deep snow improves the normally eroded and gravelly footing.

North Moat Mountain

Elevation: 3,203 ft.
Location: Town of Bartlett
Map: AMC map - Crawford Notch/Sandwich Range
Locator map: 37

Layers upon layers of ridges as seen from North Moat Mountain.

North Moat Mountain is the tallest and northernmost peak in the Moat Range, a high, five mile ridge most prominently seen from the town of Conway. This ridge forms the western wall of the Saco River Valley. North Moat offers excellent views in all directions from its open, rocky summit, which have been enjoyed by climbers since the mid-1800s.

Moat Mountain Trail traverses the entire range, providing stunning views along the way. These views are the result of a wind-driven 1854 fire which swept over the mountain, stripping the trees and soil down to bare rock. Parts of the Moat Range are composed of Moat Volcanics, one of only a handful of locations in the White Mountains where volcanic rock is prevalent.

The Moat Mountain name goes back to a 1771 map of the Town of Albany, where it was indicated as "Mote". This misspelling would also later appear on George P. Bond's 1853 map of the White Mountains and on Arnold Guyot's 1860 map. Jeremy Belknap's earlier 1791 map indicated it as "Moat Mountain". The name was assigned by local residents due to the many beaver ponds, or "moats", which lie along the eastern base of the mountain.

GETTING THERE

Parking is available in a large lot (WMNF fee area) for Diana's Baths on West Side Rd. in Conway, 2.4 mi. west of NH 16. This lot is very busy with tourists in the summer and fills up quickly. Hikers are urged to arrive as early as possible. Parking is prohibited along the roadway; violators will be fined.

RECOMMENDED ROUTE
Moat Mountain Trail, Red Ridge Trail
10.2 mi. clockwise loop with 2,900 ft. elevation gain
This scenic loop over North Moat climbs the spectacular open Red Ridge and descends via Moat Mountain Trail. Some sections are steep and rough, especially on the final approach to the summit and along Red Ridge Trail.

From the parking area, Moat Mountain Trail follows a wide tourist path for 0.6 mi. to the site of an old mill along Lucy Brook. The trail turns right onto an old road and passes Diana's Baths on the left, which consists of a series of ledgy cascades. The trail bears left, ascends easily, then crosses a small brook to reach a junction with Red Ridge Trail on the left at 1.2 mi. Continuing straight, Moat Mountain Trail dips to cross Lucy Brook (difficult at high water), meanders away from it and then back, reaching a junction with Attitash Trail at 2.4 mi.

Turn left here to stay on Moat Mountain Trail and begin a steady climb, mostly wooded at first, then mixing with areas of ledge and scrub with several limited viewpoints. The ascent remains steady to a large open ledge at 3.6 mi., which has a good view to the northeast at the top. The vista here includes Carter Dome, Black Mountain in Jackson, the Doubleheads, the Baldfaces, Eastman Mountain and Mt. Kearsarge North. The climb is steep to another outlook with views to the Green Hills in Conway. Above this outlook, the trail continues a steep ascent, then eases along a nearly level shoulder; the summit of North Moat can be seen ahead.

The trail now enters the final climb to the top, soon becoming very steep over ledge steps. The last stretch is fully out in the open, ascending over rough ledges to the gravelly summit at 4.3 mi. The highest point is slightly southeast of a USGS benchmark on the west side of the summit.

Moat Mountain Trail continues off the south side of the summit, descending steeply at first, then moderately with a few steeper sections including one chimney-like pitch which requires scrambling down. The trail dips to a wooded saddle then ascends to the unofficially named Red Ridge Peak (2,785 ft.) at 5.4 mi., where there are excellent views to the east. This peak was originally known as Middle Moat Mountain before that name was moved to the next summit to the south in 1979.

Here, Red Ridge Trail departs left and descends through a short section of scrub, then out into the open along red-tinted ledges which give the ridge its name. This stretch of beautiful ridge walking provides excellent views. The trail then drops down a steep, eroded trap dike and descends a gravelly section (use caution with footing here) with good views at the top. It continues steeply down through zig zags to cross Moat Brook at 7.0 mi., then turns right and sharply left. The trail crosses WMNF Forest Rd. 379 at 7.5 mi., and ascends easily to a junction with Red Ridge Link (for White Horse Ledge) on the right at 8.3 mi. It then crosses a snowmobile trail and continues an easy descent to cross Lucy Brook (difficult at high water), and ends at a junction with Moat Mountain Trail just beyond at 9.0 mi. Turn right for a 1.2 mi. walk back to the Diana's Baths parking area.

VIEW HIGHLIGHTS

North Moat's open summit offers some of the best vistas in the Whites with no higher peaks for miles around and is *"not encumbered by trees or bushes"*, according to early White Mountains guidebook author Moses Sweetser. 34 4,000 Footers and countless other peaks and natural features can be seen from this vantage point.

Highlights to the south and southeast include the lower peaks of the Moat Range, with the pointed peak of South Moat at the end of the ridge. Looking to the right reveals the Ossipee and Belknap Ranges. Perhaps the most striking view in this direction is the entire Sandwich Range on full display to the southwest, beginning with Mt. Chocorua and stretching all the way around to the Sleepers, followed by Mt. Tecumseh and the Osceolas. To the west are looks out to Mt. Moosilauke in the distance with Mt. Tremont, the Hancocks, Mt. Carrigain, Franconia Ridge, the Bonds, the Twins and the Willey Range and other peaks in the Crawford Notch area closer in.

Swinging more to the right, Stairs Mountain and Mts. Resolution and Parker come into view, as does the Presidential Range including Mts. Eisenhower, Franklin, Monroe and the mighty Mt. Washington. To the right of Washington are Mts. Adams and Madison with the craggy cliffs of Iron Mountain below.

Looking north, to the right of the Presidentials, are the Wildcats, Carter Dome and Mt. Hight. Black Mountain in Jackson with its ski trails can be seen, as can Shelburne Moriah and the Baldfaces, Royces, Doubleheads and

Eastman Mountain. Further distant in this direction are the higher peaks of the Mahoosuc Range, including Mt. Carlo, Goose Eye Mountain and Old Speck. Continuing to the right is a look into western Maine to peaks and hills within the Caribou-Speckled Mountain Wilderness Area.

To the east-northeast is Kearsarge North and a look across the Saco River Valley to the Green Hills: Black Cap, the ski slopes of Mt. Cranmore, Peaked and Middle Mountains, and the lesser summits of Rattlesnake Mountain and Redstone Ledge. Looking further east is a view to the prominent ridge of Pleasant Mountain in Maine, along with Sebago Lake and the Burnt Meadow Mountains. Seen in the foreground below Conway Lake is the Moat Range's magnificent bare Red Ridge, descending into the valley below.

ADDITIONAL ROUTES

Moat Mountain Trail
8.6 mi. round-trip with 2,650 ft. elevation gain
This alternative out-and-back route leads directly from the same trailhead as above to the bare North Moat summit, and skips the scenic ledge walking along Red Ridge. The upper section of this trail is very steep and rough.

Moat Mountain Traverse
9.7 mi. traverse with 3,350 ft. elevation gain
This complete north to south traverse of the range, starting at Diana's Baths in Conway and ending at Passaconaway Rd. in Albany (see South Moat Mountain section for driving directions), follows Moat Mountain Trail across all three Moat peaks (North, Middle and South), with stunning views most of the way. This is one of the most scenic ridge walks in the Whites. This hike requires a car spot.

WINTER

North Moat is a difficult hike in winter with potentially icy conditions on the steep upper sections of Moat Mountain and Red Ridge Trails. Full crampons may be required. The crossing of Lucy Brook may be difficult if not well frozen. Route-finding may also be difficult along the open, ledgy sections of both Moat Mountain and Red Ridge Trails. The summit of North Moat and the upper sections of both trails are greatly exposed to the wind and weather. If doing the traverse from the north, the parking area at Diana's Bath is plowed and the first 0.6 mi. to the cascades is usually well broken out. Parking is prohibited along West Side Rd.; violators will be fined. Route-finding along the open ridge, especially along the flat crest of Middle Moat Mountain, can be challenging, and exposure to the weather is great. At the southern end of the range, the trailhead on Passaconaway Rd. must be approached from the Conway side as the Kancamagus Highway side is gated. This trailhead is plowed.

Shelburne Moriah Mountain

Elevation: 3,743 ft.
Location: Town of Shelburne
Map: AMC map - Carter Range/Evans Notch
Locator map: 43

Deep within the Wild River Wilderness on the way to Shelburne Moriah.

One of the most remote 52WAV peaks to get to on foot, Shelburne Moriah is the crown jewel of the northern Carter-Moriah Range and offers stunning vistas in most directions from its summit and nearby ledges. Its sub-alpine environment provides hikers with a preview of terrain found further north in the Mahoosuc Range.

The Hebrew meaning for "provided by Jehovah", Shelburne Moriah was named after the hill in Jerusalem where Solomon built the Temple and was originally given to the 4,000 footer Mt. Moriah, presumably by an area settler. This name was also applied to Middle Moriah Mountain and first appeared on Philip Carrigain's 1816 map of New Hampshire. The Shelburne reference comes from the mountain's location near the Town of Shelburne. The peak was previously known as Bald Mountain due to its expansive areas of open ledge.

GETTING THERE
Parking is available in a small lot for Rattle River Trail (sign) along US 2, 3.5 mi. east of NH 16 in Gorham.

RECOMMENDED ROUTE
Rattle River Trail (Appalachian Trail), Kenduskeag Trail
11.2 mi. round-trip with 3,000 ft. elevation gain
A section of the Appalachian Trail and blazed in white, Rattle River Trail provides an easy walk in with good footing, before a relentless steep and rough climb up to the ridge. Kenduskeag Trail is lightly maintained and may require care to follow in places. It traverses the ridge over scenic ledges to the summit of Shelburne Moriah and can be muddy in late spring.

From the parking area, Rattle River Trail follows an old logging road at easy grades alongside its namesake river. At 0.3 mi., a snowmobile trail joins from the right, then leaves on the left at 0.6 mi. The hiking trail crosses a tributary stream and ascends easily to Rattle River Shelter at 1.7 mi.

The trail crosses Rattle River (difficult at times of high water), then crosses a branch of it. It continues ascending easily to cross another branch of the brook at 3.2 mi., then climbing becomes more moderate over a long stretch of rock steps. Grades become much steeper as the trail begins a relentless climb out of the valley, eventually easing to reach the junction with Kenduskeag Trail at 4.3 mi.

The route turns left onto Kenduskeag Trail and traverses several wooded knobs to reach the first open ledges along the ridge, with views south, west and northwest. The trail then crosses an open area of bog and ledge, with a look to the flat-topped summit ridge of Shelburne Moriah ahead. It dips to a small saddle, then climbs moderately over a series of ledges with views in various directions, enters the woods again briefly, then breaks out into the open again for the final climb to the summit, passing an excellent view ledge on the right. The trail reaches the open and somewhat flat summit at 5.6 mi., which is marked by a large cairn.

VIEW HIGHLIGHTS

Shelburne Moriah summit: The true summit is mostly open but views to the east are blocked by tree growth. However, by wandering around the nearby summit ledges, excellent views can be found in all other directions.

On the far left, looking southeast, is the long ridge of West Royce leading down to a gap with Mt. Meader on the opposite side. Meader Ridge extends to the right toward Eagle Crag and the Baldfaces, followed by Sable and Chandler Mountains and the Doubleheads, seen across the expanse of the Wild River Valley. Further right is the Moat Range and Mt. Chocorua with Black Mountain in Jackson at the head of the valley. The view then swings around to the east ridges of Mt. Hight leading up to that peak, followed by the Carter Range. The Moriahs are seen next with the northern Presidential Range peaks of Mts. Clay, Jefferson, Adams and Madison beyond.

Just shy of west is a look down to Pine Mountain in Gorham, seen over a shoulder of Middle Moriah. Higher and more distant, the Pliny and Pilot Ranges come into view above the closer Crescent Range. The Town of Gorham is visible below this range. To the right of The Horn in the distance is a section of the Pilot Range ridge, followed up by Rogers Ledge and Deer Mountain. Next to the right are Square Mountain, Greens Ledge and Round Mountain, with Goback Mountain and the Percy Peaks further out. Closer in this direction is Mt. Jericho seen over Mt. Hayes, which rises over Gorham. Cascade Mountain is visible to the right of and behind Hayes.

Continuing to the right of Hayes, the view moves up the Mahoosuc Range toward Trident Col, Bald Cap Mountain, and its ledgy sibling North Bald Cap, then upward to the broad mass of Mt. Success, with the prominent cliff known as The Outlook to its left. Mahoosuc Arm is seen to the right of Success, followed by Old Speck and Goose Eye and Baldpate Mountain in Grafton Notch. The long ridge of Old Blue Mountain leads right from Baldpate toward Sunday River Whitecap and Saddleback Mountain in the Rangeley Lakes region on the horizon. On the far right are numerous ridges which make up the eastern Mahoosuc Range followed by a very distant look out to Mt. Abraham and Spaulding and Sugarloaf Mountains.

East outlook: This open ledge 0.2 mi. east of the summit along Kenduskeag Trail affords views east and northeast which are not visible from the high point.

On the far left, the view begins with the Mahoosuc Range/Grafton Notch vista described above, then moves further right across a multitude of peaks in western Maine including Black and Wheeler Mountains, Mt. Blue,

Saddleback and Bald Mountains, Peabody Mountain, Mt. Zircon and peaks near Bryant Pond. Almost due east is Gammon Mountain on the opposite side of the Evans Notch area, with ledgy Caribou Mountain to the right of Gammon seen over nearby Howe Peak, over which the Kenduskeag Trail once continued. Haystack Mountain extends right from Caribou, then the view moves onto Butters and Red Rock Mountains and Miles Knob, with Albany Mountain in the back. Durgin Mountain is seen next to the right along with Speckled Mountain. East Royce is visible in front of Speckled, followed by West Royce and Mt. Meader.

ADDITIONAL ROUTES
Shelburne Trail (northern section), Kenduskeag Trail
10.8 mi. round-trip with 2,900 ft. elevation gain
This easier but lesser-used northeast approach, reached by a trailhead on Connor Brook Rd. (WMNF Forest Rd. 95) off US 2, 2.0 mi. west of the NH/ME border, starts out on unexciting logging roads, then makes a pleasant, moderate ascent to the height-of-land, followed by a rugged traverse with excellent views along Kenduskeag Trail.

Shelburne Trail (southern section), Kenduskeag Trail
9.2 mi. round-trip with 2,700 ft. elevation gain
This quiet, more remote and lesser-used approach from the south begins near Wild River Campground, and requires crossing the wide Wild River (difficult or impassable at high water; best attempted in late summer or early fall) at the start. This is a beautiful wilderness trek with stunning scenery along the eastern section of Kenduskeag Trail. This end of Shelburne Trail leaves Wild River Rd. (WMNF Forest Rd. 12) 0.6 mi. north of the campground.

OVERNIGHT OPTIONS
Rattle River Shelter, along with its three designated tent sites, is located 1.7 mi. in along Rattle River Trail. Water is available from the river 100 ft. away. This shelter can be busy during AT thru-hiker season.

Hikers approaching from the south can utilize the remote Wild River Campground at the end of Wild River Rd. off NH 113, near the southern end of Shelburne Trail. The campground offers 11 sites and one Adirondack-style shelter, water, and toilets. All sites are first come, first served; reservations are not accepted.

More information on both of these locations is available at fs.usda.gov.

WINTER

Shelburne Moriah by either of the two northern routes can be a difficult and challenging hike in winter mainly due to light use, long, strenuous, steep trail breaking up to the ridge, and challenging route-finding in open areas along Kenduskeag Trail. The ledges approaching the summit may require crampons if icy. The crossings of Rattle River and its branches may be difficult or impassable if not well frozen. The parking area for Rattle River Trail is plowed.

The parking area and access road for the northern Shelburne Trail approach is not plowed, but plowed parking may be available at the junction of US 2 and Connor Brook Rd. From this point, it's a 1.0 mi. walk into the summer trailhead. The first two miles of Shelburne Trail are usually well-tracked by snowmobiles.

The southern Shelburne Trail approach from Wild River Rd. is not possible in winter as NH 113 is gated through Evans Notch.

South Baldface/North Baldface

Elevations: 3,576 ft. / 3,597 ft.
Location: Town of Chatham and Township of Bean's Purchase
Map: CTA map, AMC map - Carter Range/Evans Notch
Locator map: 45/46

Note: These are two separate peaks for the purposes of the 52WAV list and can be climbed individually, but are commonly hiked together as a loop and are described as such below. Individual routes are also noted.

The loop over the bare rocky summits of the Baldfaces is one of the most spectacular trips in the White Mountains, offering miles of open ledge walking and stunning views in all directions. In this author's opinion, these two peaks are the crown jewels of the 52WAV. Still somewhat lesser-known to 4,000 footer peakbaggers due to their location away from the higher peaks, the Baldfaces are increasing in popularity both due to this list and their steep, rugged, beautiful scenery. Hungry hikers will also find plenty of lush blueberries in season.

There are several ways to approach the Baldfaces, and just about all of them involve steep, rugged climbing and substantial elevation gain. Only the approach to South Baldface which uses the southern section of Slippery Brook Trail allows for an easy ascent to the ridge, but the loop option over both peaks is impractical from this side.

Like other mountains in New Hampshire, the Baldfaces are no stranger to aviation disasters. On the afternoon of August 2, 1982, a single engine Piper Cherokee crashed into North Baldface about 1,000 ft. below the summit. The sightseeing flight out of Laconia Airport was bound for Portland, ME when it encountered thick clouds and a sudden thunderstorm which drastically reduced visibility. The pilot was killed upon impact, but the sole passenger survived. With no food or shelter and barefoot, she descended the mountain, working her way down along Wild River to a campsite where she was aided by campers, some 24 hrs. after the accident.

As with numerous other peaks around the state with bald in the name, these mountains were named for their treeless summits and expansive areas of open ledge, likely burned over by a fire in the early 1800s. Early trail guides state that the Baldfaces had acquired their current name by the mid-1800s and were popular with berry pickers at the time, which suggests a fire had occurred before then. The mountains would later experience another fire in 1903.

A lone hiker ascends the spectacular open northeast ridge of South Baldface with the summit beyond.

GETTING THERE
Parking is available at a large lot for Baldface Circle Trail on NH 113 in Chatham, just west of the Maine border, 25.0 mi. north of NH 16 in Conway and 12.7 mi. south of US 2 in Gilead, ME.

RECOMMENDED ROUTE
Baldface Circle Trail, Bicknell Ridge Trail
9.5 mi. clockwise loop with 3,600 ft. elevation gain

This route makes a very scenic loop over both Baldface peaks, ascending the ledges on South Baldface, with a descent along scenic Bicknell Ridge, and is often underestimated. It is very strenuous with steep and exposed scrambling up to South Baldface, along with other areas of scrambling along the ridge. While both peaks are relatively low by White Mountain standards, the significant elevation gain here is more than many 4,000 Footers, due mainly to the low trailhead elevation (520 ft.). Since this route is greatly exposed to the weather, hikers should use caution in rainy or stormy conditions. The steep ledges on South Baldface are not recommended for descent. Follow blazes and cairns carefully in open ledge areas.

From the parking area, cross NH 113 and walk north a short distance to the start of Baldface Circle Trail on the left. The yellow-blazed trail climbs a short bank, then proceeds easily with some rough footing to Circle Junction at 0.7 mi., where the trail splits; the northern section continues ahead and the southern section bears left (on the right, a short side path (sign) leads to Emerald Pool, a popular swimming hole along Charles Brook).

At Circle Junction, bear left to continue on Baldface Circle Trail, quickly passing a junction on the left with Slippery Brook Trail at 0.9 mi. The south branch of the loop joins an old logging road at easy grades to a junction on the left with Chandler Gorge Loop at 1.2 mi. This short loop trail leads to Chandler Gorge, a small flume with pool and cascades, then rejoins Baldface Circle Trail in 0.4 mi.

The main trail continues ascending along the old road, passing the upper junction with Chandler Gorge Loop, leaves the road at 2.5 mi., then reaches Last Chance Spring (unreliable) and Baldface Shelter a short distance beyond. The shelter is a good spot for a rest in preparation for the work ahead.

Baldface Circle Trail passes the shelter to reach the base of the South Baldface ledges. Climbing quickly becomes very steep and rugged over large, exposed, step-like slabs with several difficult scrambles and ever-increasing views. Follow markings on the ledges carefully. At 3.0 mi., the trail emerges on a magnificent, ledgy, completely open ridge with tremendous views including a look straight down into Charles Ravine. The trail swings left and ascends the ridge, moderately at first, then easily, to the somewhat flat shoulder of South Baldface and a junction at 3.2 mi. with Baldface Knob Trail, marked by a giant cairn and stone benches. Baldface Circle Trail bears right here and ascends moderately in the open over more ledgy steps and through scrub to the bare summit of South Baldface at 3.7 mi.

From the summit, the trail turns right and runs along the ridge between the peaks, mostly in the open, but dipping into sections of scrub. The trail descends to the deepest col along this section, climbs steeply to a shoulder where there is a brief break, then scrambles very steeply to the open summit of North Baldface at 4.9 mi.

From the summit, Baldface Circle Trail descends steeply in the open over ledges and slabs with excellent views east and northeast (the view looking straight up Meader Ridge from here is especially fine) to the upper junction with Bicknell Ridge Trail on the right at 5.8 mi.

This trail descends easily at first, then more steeply, over open ledges along the northern edge of Charles Ravine, offering excellent views south and east. Especially impressive is the rocky east ridge of South Baldface which was climbed earlier. At 6.9 mi., the trail passes a junction with Eagle Cascade Link on the left, then ruggedly descends back into the woods. Footing and grades improve as the trail crosses a branch of Charles Brook, then continues to the lower junction with Baldface Circle Trail at 8.3 mi. The area around this junction was minimally impacted by logging in 2019. Descend on this trail to return to Circle Junction and the trailhead.

VIEW HIGHLIGHTS

Both Baldface peaks provide what are perhaps the most magnificent views in the Evans Notch region from their bare, rocky summits. Both peaks also offer stunning looks down into and across the Wild River Wilderness to the east, a vast area of remote beauty.

South Baldface: Looking north from South Baldface are the Moriahs — Mt. Moriah, Middle Moriah and Shelburne Moriah — followed by Mt. Success and other peaks in the Mahoosuc Range, including Goose Eye Mountain and Old Speck. In the foreground, Meader Ridge extends out from North Baldface to Eagle Crag, Mt. Meader and the Royces. Further right is a look out to multiple layers of peaks in western Maine. To the northeast are Caribou and

Speckled Mountains, along with numerous other hills within the Caribou-Speckled Mountain Wilderness.

To the east and in the foreground are Deer Hill and Little Deer Hill, which are also accessible from the Baldface Circle trailhead. The southeast vista is mainly a flat expanse broken by the prominent ridge of Pleasant Mountain, and close by under Pleasant are the double summits of Eastman Mountain. More distant hills are visible as the view swings around to the south where the peaks of the Conway area appear, such as the Green Hills and Mt. Kearsarge North.

Across the broad Saco River Valley, the distant Ossipee Range can be seen, then the view moves around to the Moat Range, White Horse Ledge, the Doubleheads, and the Sandwich Range. Further right are the Osceolas, Mt. Carrigain, the Hancocks, and a distant Mt. Moosilauke, before Franconia Ridge and the Bonds come into view.

Looking west are the Wildcats and Carters, with Mt. Washington popping up behind Wildcat. The high, long ridge of the Carter Range extends right to dip behind nearby North Baldface, just a little over a mile away, to join the Moriahs. Far below, the deep Charles Ravine separates both Baldfaces.

North Baldface: The views from North Baldface are largely the same as those of South Baldface, although that peak's mass obstructs some of the perspective to the south. The trailless Sable and Chandler are more visible here, as is the unnamed 2,941 ft. bump known to bushwhackers as West Baldface. Perhaps the most awe-inspiring viewpoint on North Baldface is from open ledges to the east of and slightly below the summit, just off the trail. This high perch situated at the top of Charles Ravine's headwall offers a look down into and across the wide expanse of the valley. On the left, Bicknell Ridge descends east toward Chatham, and Meader Ridge continues north toward Eagle Crag and the Royces. Both ridges are dotted with numerous areas of open ledge. On the right side of the ravine, South Baldface's great northeast ridge plunges sharply into the valley below.

ADDITIONAL ROUTES
Baldface Circle Trail, Slippery Brook Trail, Baldface Knob Trail
10.3 mi. clockwise loop with 3,650 ft. elevation gain
This slightly longer alternate route, starting and ending at the Baldface Circle trailhead, bypasses the difficult South Baldface ledges and visits scenic Baldface Knob (3,025 ft.) on the ascent, a worthy destination in its own right.

The descent uses the northern section of Baldface Circle Trail, which is very steep and rough as it drops off the ridge.

INDIVIDUAL PEAK ROUTES

South Baldface via Baldface Circle Trail, Slippery Brook Trail (northern section) and Baldface Knob Trail
9.0 mi. round-trip with 3,150 ft. elevation gain

South Baldface via Baldface Circle Trail, Baldface Knob Trail and Slippery Brook Trail (northern section)
8.0 mi. counter-clockwise loop with 3,100 ft. elevation gain

South Baldface via Slippery Brook Trail (southern section) Baldface Knob Trail, Baldface Circle Trail
10.4 mi. round-trip with 2,100 ft. elevation gain

North Baldface via Baldface Circle Trail
9.8 mi. round-trip with 3,600 ft. elevation gain

North Baldface via Baldface Circle Trail and Bicknell Ridge Trail
9.7 mi. counter-clockwise loop with 3,600 ft. elevation gain

OVERNIGHT OPTIONS

Baldface Shelter is located along Baldface Circle Trail at the base of the steep South Baldface ledges. This shelter sleeps 6-8 and there is an additional designated tentsite nearby. The site has a composting toilet, and water is sometimes available from nearby but unreliable Last Chance Spring. More information is available at fs.usda.gov.

WINTER

The Baldfaces in winter are a serious undertaking most suitable for experienced hikers. It is strongly urged that the steep angled ledges ascending to South Baldface be bypassed using Slippery Brook and Baldface Knob Trails. These ledges are dangerous in icy or crusty conditions. Route-finding and strenuous trail breaking may be required along certain areas of the loop, and crampons may be needed along the open ledges. The parking area is plowed. NH 113 is gated north of the trailhead and just south of US 2 so the only driving approach in winter is from the south.

The already long approach to South Baldface via Slippery Brook Trail from the south becomes even longer in winter as Slippery Brook Rd. is only plowed to a point 3.5 mi. from NH 16, stretching out the total round-trip distance to a long 18 mi. While this is indeed a trek, the easy grades of this approach are suitable for experienced skiers at least part of the way.

Backcountry skiers may also be interested in Slippery Brook Glade, an area of new ski trails opened in 2018, located on a ridge just to the north of Slippery Brook Trail on the east slope of Baldface Knob. More information is available at granitebackcountryalliance.org.

South Moat Mountain

Elevation: 2,772 ft.
Location: Town of Albany
Map: AMC map - Crawford Notch/Sandwich Range
Locator map: 47

Hikers atop the highest point of South Moat Mountain.

South Moat Mountain rises at the southern end of the Moat Range, a high ridge most prominently seen from Conway, and its sharp, ledgy summit offers excellent views in all directions. For more information on this interesting mountain range, refer to the North Moat Mountain section.

GETTING THERE

Parking is available in a small dirt lot off Passaconaway Rd. in Albany. From West Side Rd. in Conway, 1.0 mi. north of NH 16, turn left onto Passaconaway Rd. and continue to the trailhead and parking area (sign) on the right at 3.2 mi.

RECOMMENDED ROUTE

Moat Mountain Trail

5.4 mi. round-trip with 2,200 ft. elevation gain

The start of the trail has been affected by logging in recent years and may be temporarily relocated at times; follow markings and signage carefully. Grades on this southern section of Moat Mountain Trail are mostly moderate with some steeper sections. Footing starts out generally good but becomes rougher higher up.

Yellow-blazed Moat Mountain Trail leaves the northern end of the parking area at a sign by a gate and meanders at easy grades through the woods, crossing a logging road at 0.1 mi. It hops onto another logging road and starts ascending easily, descends to cross a small brook at 0.3 mi., then ascends again, abruptly entering a pine forest at 0.7 mi. At 1.0 mi., the trail dips again to cross Dry Brook on a footbridge, swings right, and continues at easy grades to a point at 1.3 mi. where it turns left off the logging road.

Moat Mountain Trail, now a footpath, becomes steeper with a breather where it descends to cross a small brook before heading up again, becoming very steep and rough with rocky footing at 1.8 mi. It scrambles up wooded ledges to arrive at a vast area of open ledge dotted with boulders at 2.0 mi., where there is an excellent view of Mt. Chocorua. Above this point, the trail ascends more easily along a narrow rocky ridge, turns sharply right at the top of it, then winds its way fairly steeply over ledges and through belts of trees with ever-increasing views, to reach the open summit and its two ledgy knobs at 2.7 mi. The highest point of the peak is on the rightmost knob.

VIEW HIGHLIGHTS

South Moat's bare summit offers complete panoramic views in all directions, especially if you clamber up either of the two ledgy summit knobs. Looking north-northwest along the Moat Range is the nearby flat Middle Moat Mountain, with the bare peak of North Moat rising beyond. Extending right from between Middle and North Moat is the ledgy Red Ridge. The Presidential Range, Iron Mountain, and the Wildcat, Carter and Moriah

Ranges can also be seen beyond North Moat. Further right looks out to peaks in Jackson and the Evans Notch region beyond, including the Baldfaces. In the distance beyond Evans Notch are peaks in western Maine and the Rangeley Lakes area.

Looking northeast across the Saco River Valley are Kearsarge North, the Green Hills, and Mt. Cranmore with its ski trails on full display, with the village of North Conway below. Also visible is the prominent ridge of Pleasant Mountain in Maine, Conway Lake, and Sebago Lake.

To the south and southeast is Green Mountain and its fire tower in Effingham, the Moose Mountains, the Ossipee Range, the sharp horn of Mt. Chocorua, and just about all of the Sandwich Range spreading out to the right of it, including Mts. Paugus, Passaconaway, Whiteface, Tripyramid, and the rolling ridge of The Sleepers.

Further right are the more distant Mt. Tecumseh, the Osceolas, Mt. Moosilauke, Mt. Hancock, Mt. Tremont, Mt. Carrigain, and Vose Spur, the Bonds, the Twins, and the Willey Range.

ADDITIONAL ROUTE

Moat Mountain Traverse

9.7 mi. traverse with 3,350 ft. elevation gain

This complete north to south traverse of the range, starting at Diana's Baths in Conway and ending at the South Moat trailhead, follows Moat Mountain Trail across all three Moat peaks (North, Middle and South), with stunning views most of the way. This is one of the most scenic ridge walks in the Whites. See the North Moat Mountain section for details on the northern end of this trek.

WINTER

South Moat is an excellent intermediate winter hike in good conditions, although the steeper upper parts of the trail may be more difficult. The bare summit also offers no protection from the wind. Passaconaway Rd. is gated on the Kancamagus Highway side (where it is signed as Dugway Rd.), so hikers must approach from the Conway side. The parking area is plowed.

If doing the traverse from the north, the parking area at Diana's Bath is plowed and the first 0.6 mi. to the cascades is usually well broken out. Parking is prohibited along West Side Rd.; violators will be fined. Route-finding along the open ridge may be challenging in poor visibility and exposure to the weather is great.

Table Mountain

Elevation: 2,669 ft.
Location: Town of Bartlett
Map: AMC map - Crawford Notch/Sandwich Range
Locator map: 51

A hiker relaxes on Table Mountain's south ledges.

This mountain provides stellar views over the Swift River Valley and out to the Sandwich Range from atop open cliffs just southeast of its wooded true summit, reached by a well-beaten herd path. Because of its views, it was added to the 52WAV list in 2020.

In 1984, a campfire located in the saddle between Table and Bear Mountains led to a blaze which scorched 105 acres on the southern slopes of Table. According to a report in the Conway Daily Sun, smoke from the fire was first spotted by the fire warden manning the Green Mountain fire tower in Effingham. The fire burned for six days in steep, rugged terrain, where over 50 firefighters and USFS personnel did battle. Evidence of the fire can still be seen today via a prominent patch of light green sapling growth on the southeast shoulder of the mountain, as well as in areas of dead trees alongside Attitash Trail.

Aptly named, Table Mountain appears as a flat-topped peak when viewed from many perspectives. The name appeared on Arnold Guyot's 1860 map of the White Mountains, but was mistakenly applied to Table's higher neighbor Bear Mountain. This was corrected by the time Moses Sweetser published his comprehensive guidebook in 1876.

GETTING THERE

The easiest access to Table is from the western terminus of Attitash Trail on Bear Notch Rd. in Bartlett, 2.7 mi. south of US 302 in Bartlett Village and 6.6 mi. north of NH 112 (Kancamagus Highway). The small gravel parking area is marked by a sign and hiker symbol. Low clearance cars should use caution entering and exiting due to a washout. Also watch for fast-moving traffic as the parking area is along a curve.

RECOMMENDED ROUTE

Attitash Trail

To main ledges only: 3.8 mi. round-trip with 1,350 ft. elevation gain
To main ledges, true summit and east ledge: 4.3 mi. round-trip with 1,480 ft. elevation gain

A network of hiking trails once graced the Table/Bear Mountain area in the 1930s, but today only Attitash Trail remains. Marked with faded yellow and blue blazes, it provides an easy to moderate warm-up to the col between Bear and Table, then becomes quite steep up to the main ledges. Some sections on the ledges have loose, gravelly footing; use caution, especially on descent.

From the parking area, Attitash Trail ascends at easy grades along an old logging road, crossing a branch of Louisville Brook almost immediately. It continues up the old road and bears right onto another road at 0.3 mi. The trail traverses easily along the high bank of Louisville Brook down on the right; look for an interesting cascade at 0.6 mi. It crosses another branch of the brook at 0.7 mi., then bears left where the old road continues ahead and deteriorates. Here, the trail climbs a short steep section on log steps and enters a hardwood forest at 0.8 mi.

Attitash Trail continues an easy to moderate ascent and reaches the col between Table and Bear Mountain's east peak. The trail swings left here and begins a steeper ascent up the ridge via short switchbacks at first, then more steadily to the first open ledge viewpoint at 1.5 mi., with a look back to Bear Mountain and parts of the Sandwich Range. The trail bears left up the ledges, then struggles up an eroded gully with loose, gravelly footing and one small scramble. Use caution here, especially when coming back down. This leads to another flat outlook ledge on the right at 1.7 mi.

The steep ascent continues up through more ledgy areas mixed with gravelly pitches, passes an angled ledge on the right with views to the south, then reaches the main ledges atop high cliffs at 1.9 mi., where the best views can be found. Use caution with pets and children here. Behind this ledge on the left side of the trail, a well-worn path leads to an open ledge with standup views to the northwest.

For the side trip to the actual summit of Table from the main ledges, continue east along Attitash Trail for less than 0.1 mi. and look for an unmarked but obvious herd path on the left. This well-worn, narrow path ascends steeply at first, then easily, for 0.1 mi. to the somewhat flat and heavily wooded true summit of Table, which is marked by a green paint stripe on a tree in a small clearing.

To visit the east ledge from the summit, descend back to Attitash Trail, turn left for another 0.15 mi., and just after the trail begins to descend, turn right onto an unmarked side path which hops up two ledge steps and leads 10 yds. to a sunny open ledge with views to the east and southeast.

VIEW SUMMARY

Main ledges: The large flat ledges on the south side of the summit provide the widest views from the mountain, as well as ample space and sunshine for lounging. Starting on the far left is a vista of the long ridge of the Moat Range, starting with North Moat Mountain and moving across to Middle and South Moat. The lesser-visited "West Moat", a destination for bushwhackers, can be seen directly under South Moat. Moving to the right, the ridge leads out to a spur known as Haystack, with part of Douglas Mountain and the Burnt Meadow Mountains in Maine seen beyond. Closer in to the southeast, the remnants of the 1984 fire can be seen on the shoulder of Table. Continuing right is the backside of White Ledge in Albany, with the prominent Green Mountain in Effingham in the distance.

The majestic Mt. Chocorua lies to the south beyond the Swift River Valley along with its neighbor Mt. Blue and the Three Sisters; the main summit of Chocorua appears as a high, sharp cone from this vantage point. Mt. Paugus is seen to the right of Chocorua, followed by Wonalancet Hedgehog and Nanamocomuck Peak, before the ridgeline leads up to the massive bulk of Mt. Passaconaway. Below Nanamocomuck is the sheer cliff face on Square Ledge, with Hedgehog Mountain to the right. Continuing across the Sandwich Range are the rounded twin domes of the Sleepers and the triple-peaked Tripyramids. On the far right, Table's neighbor Bear Mountain comes into view with a rounded knob located at the end of the ridgecrest.

Northwest ledge: This ledge, accessed by a short side path from the main trail behind the main ledges, provides a vista to the northwest which is best seen while standing. Starting with Bear Mountain on the left, the view moves around to Owl's Cliff, the Hancocks, Mt. Tremont, the prominent Mt. Carrigain, and Bartlett Haystack. West Bond and Mt. Bond can be seen through the U-shaped Carrigain Notch. More restricted views from this outlook include Mt. Guyot, Mts. Lowell and Anderson, and Mt. Nancy.

East ledge: This ledge located to the east of the summit, just off Attitash Trail, provides an excellent view to Big Attitash Mountain (which appears here as a series of darkly-wooded humps) and the western slopes of the Moat Range. In the distance to the left of Big Attitash, Carter Dome and Mt. Hight are visible along with Iron Mountain, Jackson's Black Mountain, and Shelburne Moriah Mountain.

ADDITIONAL ROUTE
Moat Mountain Trail, Attitash Trail
To main ledges only: 9.6 mi. traverse with 3,200 ft. elevation gain
To main ledges, true summit and east ledge: 9.8 mi. traverse with 3,280 ft. elevation gain

This strenuous east to west traverse requires a car spot and starts at the northern terminus of Moat Mountain Trail at Diana's Baths along West Side Rd. in Conway. It climbs over wooded Big Attitash Mountain (the high point of which is several feet off the trail) on the way to Table. While it has received much-needed volunteer maintenance in recent years, Attitash Trail east of Table Mountain is lightly traveled and more primitive, may be difficult to follow at times, and is better suited for experienced hikers. See the North Moat Mountain section for parking details.

WINTER
Table is infrequently climbed in winter due to Bear Notch Rd. being gated 0.6 mi. south of US 302 and 1.0 mi. north of NH 112. During winter, the road is heavily used by snowmobiles. However, should you decide to hike Table in winter, parking is available in a plowed lot for snowmobilers just before the northern gate, 0.6 mi. from US 302. Round-trip distance to the main ledges, true summit and east ledge from this point is 8.3 mi. with 1,900 ft. elevation gain. Attitash Trail makes for a mostly moderate snowshoeing

route, with the steep climb up to the main ledges being more difficult. This section may require crampons in icy or crusty conditions. Approaching from the east via Diana's Baths is possible, but would likely require strenuous long-distance trail breaking, as Attitash Trail east of Table is rarely traveled in winter. The parking area at Diana's Baths is plowed.

Table Mountain's sunny ledges.

Northern New Hampshire

The Horn

Elevation: 3,900 ft.
Location: Township of Kilkenny
Map: AMC map - North Country/Mahoosuc Range
Locator map: 06

Mt. Cabot and The Bulge as seen from The Horn.

Located along Kilkenny Ridge in the Pilot Range between Mt. Cabot and Unknown Pond, The Horn is one of the highest and most remote 52WAV peaks, offering excellent views of many surrounding North Country mountains from its uppermost table-like summit ledge.

The Horn was officially trailless until the long-distance Kilkenny Ridge Trail was constructed in the 1980s, although bushwhackers had been visiting more frequently by then, since it had become a New England Hundred Highest peak in 1968.

The Horn was likely named for its sharp appearance resembling an animal's horn from many vantage points. In the late 1800s it was also briefly known as South Peak.

GETTING THERE

Limited roadside parking is available near the end of Mill Brook Rd. (WMNF Forest Rd. 11) in Stark, 4.5 mi. south of NH 110. If there is no room to park at the trailhead, alternate parking is available in the turnaround a short distance further at the end of the road.

RECOMMENDED ROUTE
Unknown Pond Trail (northern section), Kilkenny Ridge Trail, The Horn Spur

8.4 mi. round-trip with 2,170 ft. elevation gain

This lesser-used northern approach to The Horn is an attractive walk through birch forest to secluded Unknown Pond, which features a scenic view of the peak from its eastern shore. Grades are moderate with mostly good footing. The section of Kilkenny Ridge Trail between the pond and The Horn is steeper and rougher and can sometimes be difficult to follow.

From Mill Brook Rd., yellow-blazed Unknown Pond Trail ascends easily along its namesake brook at first, crossing the Stark/Kilkenny town line (marked by a wooden post) at 1.0 mi., then more moderately through a long stretch of birches with limited views through the trees. The trail then rises to a wet area, crosses its height-of-land, and then descends gradually to a junction at 2.2 mi. with Kilkenny Ridge Trail on the right at the northern edge of Unknown Pond.

Turning right, yellow-blazed Kilkenny Ridge Trail starts out level and passes a short side path on the left which leads to the shore of the pond and a view to The Horn. It descends to a saddle, then angles up moderately along the northwest side of The Horn to a junction at 3.9 mi. with a spur trail on the left (sign) in the col between The Horn and The Bulge.

Turn left and ascend moderately along this 0.3 mi. spur trail, narrow and brushy in places, over several scrambles to the base of The Horn's summit ledges. The final pitch up a vertical wall seems impossible to climb but well-beaten paths around to the left allow hikers to easily walk up the back of the ledge to the highest point, which is indicated by a USGS benchmark embedded in the flat ledge.

VIEW HIGHLIGHTS

The Horn acts as the watchtower over the remote Kilkenny region, with the widest views attained from the uppermost summit ledge.

The vista begins with the great mass of Mt. Cabot dominating the southwest view with the rounded hump of The Bulge in front. Looking west beyond The Bulge is the Town of Lancaster and the Connecticut River Valley beyond, with views out to Mts. Abraham and Ellen, Camel's Hump, the Worcester Range, and Mt. Mansfield on the horizon. Further right are Burke, Belvedere, and East Haven Mountains in Vermont's Northeast Kingdom, along with East Mountain and its derelict Air Force station on the summit, as well as Jay Peak. Back at The Bulge, a ridge extends right over the trailless Pilot Range, with the high point of Hutchins Mountain in the middle.

Beyond the Pilot Range, views deep into Vermont continue before swinging around to the Nash Stream Forest area where Goback Mountain, Sugarloaf Mountain, Bunnell Mountain, the Percy Peaks, and Long Mountain can be seen. Also visible is Devil's Slide in Stark. Further right and best seen while standing is a distant view to Magalloway Mountain in Pittsburg, and on very clear days the mountains along the Quebec border are visible. Continuing to the right are looks into western Maine, including Azicohos Mountain, and closer in are Rogers Ledge and Square Mountain further north along the Kilkenny Ridge Trail. Both are noted for their high granite cliffs. Maine's East Kennabago and West Kennebago Peaks can be spotted above these cliffs. Further right and just a mile away is the unofficially named Unknown Pond Ridge.

Numerous other peaks in Maine are visible before the view swings over to the Grafton Notch region and Baldpate Mountain, before jumping over to Old Speck, which begins a look along the Mahoosuc Range including Mahoosuc Arm, Fulling Mill Mountain, Goose Eye Mountain, Mt. Carlo, and Mt. Success. The Mahoosucs continue to the right over Bald Cap Mountain, Cascade Mountain, and Mt. Hayes before disappearing down into Gorham. Further right beyond Gorham the three major peaks of the Moriah Range — Shelburne Moriah, Middle Moriah, and Mt. Moriah — come into view before moving on to the Carter Range.

The Presidential Range rises opposite the Carters with the rounded summit of North and South Weeks below and in front with a long ridge extending right toward Mt. Waumbek from South Weeks. The Middle and South Peaks of Terrace Mountain can be seen below Waumbek before the view arrives back at Mt. Cabot.

ADDITIONAL ROUTE

Unknown Pond Trail (southern section), Kilkenny Ridge Trail, The Horn Spur, Bunnell Notch Trail, York Pond Trail

11.6 mi. counter-clockwise loop with 3,300 ft. elevation gain

This long and strenuous loop option starting near the end of York Pond Rd. in Berlin, 2.0 mi. west of the Berlin Fish Hatchery, combines a visit to The Horn with a hike over the unassuming bump known as The Bulge, as well as Mt. Cabot, the northernmost NH 4,000 footer. The southern section of Unknown Pond Trail can be overgrown, wet and muddy in places, and the Kilkenny Ridge Trail between Unknown Pond and Mt. Cabot can sometimes be difficult to follow.

OVERNIGHT OPTIONS

Unknown Pond Tentsite, located on the southeast side of the pond just off the southern section of Unknown Pond Trail, features six first come, first served tent sites, an outhouse, and a reliable water source. More information is available at fs.usda.gov.

Cabot Cabin, located 0.4 mi. southeast of Mt. Cabot's summit along Kilkenny Ridge Trail, is a rustic shelter maintained by the USFS and the Jefferson Boy Scouts with first come, first served bunks and a small sitting area. The cabin once had a wood stove but it was removed long ago for safety reasons. Semi-reliable water is available from the old fire warden's spring located 0.2 mi. down a quasi-abandoned, steep and very overgrown side path off Kilkenny Ridge Trail, 0.2 mi. above the cabin. The sign at this side path was missing in 2017 but the junction was marked by a small cairn. Don't expect luxury at the cabin but it does provide basic accommodations for an overnight stay. Be sure to store food securely as mice are often present.

WINTER

Mill Brook Rd. is gated in winter so hikers bound for The Horn must approach via the southern section of Unknown Pond Trail, starting near the end of York Pond Rd. in Berlin. This is a 10.6 mi. round-trip with 2,270 ft. elevation gain. Kilkenny Ridge Trail can be especially difficult to follow and very strenuous in unbroken snow. Crampons may be needed on The Horn's summit ledges if icy.

If doing the complete loop over all three peaks the section between Mt. Cabot and York Pond Rd. is heavily traveled and usually well packed down. Cabot Cabin, while no longer heated, still offers shelter from the wind. The southern parking area for Unknown Pond Trail may not be plowed reliably but the York Pond Trail parking is, a short distance further up York Pond Rd. (use caution when entering and exiting this lot as it slopes down slightly). The Berlin Fish Hatchery gate on York Pond Rd. is left open and is usually frozen solid within snow and ice throughout the winter. The road itself is plowed to the trailhead but is often icy and not always sanded.

Magalloway Mountain

Elevation: 3,385 ft.
Location: Town of Pittsburg
Map: There is no formal trail map for Magalloway. The peak appears on the Cohos Trail map, but the trails are not depicted. Also refer to the USGS Magalloway Mountain quad.
Locator map: 09

Mt. Magalloway is the northernmost 52WAV peak and as such many hikers put off the long, remote drive to Pittsburg. But Magalloway has much to offer, being one of the highest peaks in the North Country. Its distant location far from civilization offers a true wilderness feel and its summit fire tower and high east-facing cliffs provide panoramic views over this sparsely populated region. Since the drive to Magalloway is long but the actual hike is short, many hikers include this peak with other destinations in the Connecticut Lakes region. The mountain is heavily wooded but nearly all of its east face is dominated by an expansive talus slope and high, craggy cliffs. These features are best seen from Magalloway Rd., east of the peak.

In 1910 the New Hampshire Timberland Owners Association built a lookout tower at the summit, one of the first such structures in the state. Over the years the tower has been replaced several times and the current active tower was constructed in 1935. Also a name given to a river in the area, Magalloway is a Malecite word meaning "the shoveler", which describes how caribou shovel snow from side to side with their hooves when foraging for food.

GETTING THERE

Parking is available at the end of remote Tower Rd. in Pittsburg. In mid-2019 the former signage along the route in from the highway directing hikers to the tower was reported as missing. From US 3, 4.7 mi. north of the dam at First Connecticut Lake, take Magalloway Rd. southeast. This is primarily a privately-owned logging road (although suitable for any vehicle) so watch out for fast-moving logging trucks who have the right of way. In 2019, a logging operation was underway along this road. Bear left at two forks — the first at 2.3 mi. and the second at 2.9 mi. At 5.3 mi. turn right onto the rougher and narrower Tower Rd. (no road sign). High clearance is strongly recommended for this road as conditions change frequently; it is not uncommon to encounter exposed culverts. At 6.3 mi. bear right and continue to the end of the road and parking, 8.4 mi. from US 3.

The Magalloway Mountain fire tower.

ROUTE

Coot Trail, Overlook Trail, Bobcat Trail
2.2 mi. clockwise loop with 900 ft. elevation gain
This short loop over Magalloway uses the steep, eroded Coot Trail (the old access road for the fire tower) for the ascent and the more gradual Bobcat Trail for the descent (which also has better footing), and includes a side a trip to the east cliffs via Overlook Trail. Both Coot and Bobcat Trails leave from the parking area at the end of Tower Rd.

From the end of Tower Rd., Coot Trail enters the woods (the trail sign was reported missing here in mid-2019) and immediately begins climbing southwest along the old jeep road, quickly passing a cabin on the right. Footing becomes rough and grades are steep in places with several short bypasses around washed out sections. At 0.6 mi. the trail reaches the junction with Bobcat Trail on the right; look back here for a view out to First Connecticut Lake. Above this junction, the footing and grades become easier as Coot Trail ascends gently to the grassy summit clearing, Magalloway Cabin, and fire tower at 0.8 mi. When entering the clearing, a somewhat obscure side path departs right and descends 0.1 mi. to the old fire warden's spring which is not reliable.

Behind the cabin, a side path (sign: "Overlook Trail") descends easily north for 0.2 mi. along the precipitous east cliffs which offer spectacular views. Use caution with pets and children here as the trail is literally on the edge of the cliffs in places. Beyond the 0.2 mi. mark this side path continues to descend but becomes narrower and more overgrown the further you go.

Doubling back to the junction with Bobcat Trail at 1.4 mi. along this loop, that trail descends steeply at first then moderately, passing a view to Second Connecticut Lake on the right at 1.6 mi. Grades eventually ease as the trail descends with muddy footing in its lower section to end at Tower Rd. a short distance west of Coot Trail.

VIEW HIGHLIGHTS

Fire tower view: Magalloway's summit doesn't provide many views from the ground but a climb up to the fire tower offers expansive vistas in all directions into three states and two countries.

The view north and northwest is dominated by dozens of small peaks in southern Quebec with the international border being about 20 mi. away. Just about due north on the far horizon is Mont Mégantic, an ancient volcanic ring dike similar to the Ossipee and Pawtuckaway Mountains in southern New Hampshire.

Nearby to the northeast is Stub Hill, a frequent target of bushwhackers, with the long Diamond Ridge lower and in front of it. Swinging around to this angle brings peaks in western Maine into view, including Kennebago Divide, Snow Mountain, East Kennebago Mountain, Mt. Abraham and Saddleback Mountain.

Looking southeast, the Grafton Notch area and the Mahoosuc Range come into view, including Old Speck, Goose Eye Mountain and Mt. Success, followed by the Carter-Moriah Range and Mt. Washington, just about due south. To the right of Washington Mt. Cabot can be seen before the view comes around closer to the Northeast Kingdom of Vermont. Here, East Mountain and Monadnock Mountain (not the one in NH) are visible before the vista arrives back in Canada.

East cliffs: The vista from atop Magalloway's eastern cliffs along Overlook Trail is largely the same as the eastern views described above but from this perspective you also get a look down to the cliffs and great talus slope on the mountain's east face. Also from the cliffs is a view down to the Middle Branch of the Dead Diamond River and Magalloway Rd. as it disappears into the remote wilderness, headed toward Maine.

OVERNIGHT OPTIONS

The cozy Magalloway Cabin, located at the summit, is available for overnight stays with advance reservations required. Heat is provided via a wood stove and supplied firewood and an outhouse is located behind the cabin. It is recommended that hikers carry in their own water as the old fire warden's spring is unreliable. More information is available at nhdfl.org.

WINTER

While it has been done, Mt. Magalloway is rarely hiked in winter due to Magalloway Rd. being closed to vehicle traffic as a major snowmobile corridor. A winter hike requires snowshoeing or skiing over 8 mi. into the trailhead from US 3 and back out again in addition to the hike itself, turning this relatively easy 2.2 mi. loop into a nearly 19 mi. journey. Experienced bushwhackers can shorten this distance by utilizing off-road shortcuts.

Mt. Hayes

Elevation: 2,573 ft.
Location: Town of Shelburne
Map: AMC map - North Country/Mahoosuc Range
Locator map: 17

Mt. Hayes, located north of Gorham and just east of the Shelburne town line, is the southernmost peak in the Mahoosuc Range, a chain of rugged and scenic peaks extending into New Hampshire from western Maine. It offers excellent views of the Presidential and Carter Ranges from open ledges a short distance south of its mostly wooded and nondescript summit. The Appalachian Trail passes over Hayes, turning north along Mahoosuc Trail 0.2 mi. north of the summit.

In the late 1800s, the Mascot Lead Mine operated on the southwest slope of Mt. Hayes. Though the mine was short-lived, it later became better known as one of the few places in the state where bats hibernate. The internal temperature of the mine stays in the cool 50s and it is estimated that some 1,700 bats gather here to spend the winter. Hikers can visit the mine opening by carefully climbing a steep and loose talus slope above Mascot Pond, which is reached by a spur path off Mahoosuc Trail. However, there is no venturing inside the mine as the entrance is barricaded for both human and bat safety.

The mountain was named in honor of Margaret Hayes, first proprietor of the White Mountains Station House in Gorham during the mid-1800s. Centennial Trail is named as such due to its construction by Appalachian Mountain Club in 1976, which was its 100th year of operation.

Mt. Madison in the distance as seen from Mt. Hayes' south ledges.

GETTING THERE

Parking for a few vehicles is available at the Centennial Trail trailhead on Hogan Rd. in Shelburne, 0.2 mi. west of North Rd. Alternate parking is available at the junction of Hogan and North Rds., 0.5 north of US 2. In early

2019 Hogan Rd. was passable to the trailhead by any vehicle, but the road is usually rough. If it is not possible to reach the trailhead parking area the alternate parking area should be used.

RECOMMENDED ROUTE

Centennial Trail (Appalachian Trail), Mahoosuc Trail
7.2 mi. round-trip with 2,200 ft. elevation gain

Centennial Trail, a segment of the AT, ascends at mostly moderate grades to Mahoosuc Trail at the ridge. The short section of this route along Mahoosuc Trail descends easily over ledges with limited views, first over the true summit, then to the more open ledges 0.3 mi. further.

Centennial Trail, blazed in standard AT white markings, starts climbing at moderate grades before reaching a steeper section which ascends over rock steps, then it eases to cross a small brook at 0.7 mi. Above the brook the trail continues a moderate climb, passing several overgrown or restricted viewpoints, descends briefly, then makes a long, easy ascent to reach the informally-named "East Hayes" at 2.8 mi., a ledgy knob with restricted views. Centennial Trail turns right and descends slightly from this knob to a shallow saddle then makes a short and easy climb to a junction with Mahoosuc Trail at 3.1 mi.

Turning left (the route of the AT turns right and heads north), Mahoosuc Trail descends easily over ledges for 0.2 mi. to the actual and somewhat flat summit of Mt. Hayes, marked by a small cairn in a clearing, where there are restricted views. The trail continues descending easily another 0.3 mi. to reach the fully open ledges at the southwest end of the ridge.

VIEW HIGHLIGHTS

The large open ledges south of the summit of Mt. Hayes invite a long stay. This viewpoint is notable for its look down to Gorham and the Androscoggin River with an impressive backdrop of the northern Presidential Range peaks of Mt. Madison and Mt. Adams rising beyond. Lying low in front of Madison is the Pine Mountain, described separately in this guide. Mt. Washington, Boott Spur and Slide Peak can be seen to the left of Adams. Further left across Pinkham Notch the view jumps over to the Wildcats and Carters with the three Moriah peaks next in line. To the left of Shelburne Moriah, several peaks in the Caribou-Speckled Mountain Wilderness region in Maine are seen, including Gammon, Caribou, Haystack and Butters Mountains.

Swinging back to Mt. Adams the view drops right toward Mt. Bowman and Cherry Mountain then onto the Crescent Range in Randolph before the Pliny Range peaks of Mt. Waumbek and Mt. Weeks appear with Mt. Cabot further back.

ADDITIONAL ROUTE
Mahoosuc Trail
7.2 mi. round-trip with 1,740 ft. elevation gain
This southwestern approach from a parking area under the railroad bridge on NH 16 in Gorham, 0.3 mi. north of US 2, offers optional side trips to Mascot Pond and Leadmine Ledge along the way but the poorly-marked walk in from the highway to the trailhead can be confusing as it follows a maze of bike paths and roads on private property. This section of Mahoosuc Trail is also lightly used and maintained. As of 2019 the southern terminus of Mahoosuc Trail on Hogan Rd. could not be reached by vehicle due to a washed out bridge 1.3 mi. west of North Rd.

WINTER
Centennial Trail is a good route for snowshoeing with mostly moderate grades and protection from the weather. Crampons may be needed on the open ledges along Mahoosuc Trail if crusty or icy. Hogan Rd. is not maintained in winter but the parking area at the junction of Hogan and North Rds. is plowed.

If approaching from NH 16 the parking area under the railroad bridge is plowed with room for a few cars. The already maze-like route from the highway to the trailhead can be even more difficult to follow unless it has been broken out.

Mt. Martha (Cherry Mountain)

Elevation: 3,557 ft.
Location: Town of Carroll
Map: RMC map, AMC map - Franconia/Pemigewasset
Locator map: 21

Mt. Martha is one of two named summits (the other being Owl's Head; 3,258 ft.) of Cherry Mountain, a prominent north-south ridge located west of the

Presidential Range. A fire tower was once located atop the summit from 1939 to 1968, the concrete footings of which are still present. While the peak was more open in the past, tree growth has sprung up over the decades; two outlooks still provide good views.

On July 10, 1885 torrential rains unleashed a great slide of *"a million tons of boulders, trees and mud"* which fell from the northern slopes of Owl's Head and *"tumbled a tortuous two miles"*. It was early on a Friday morning when the slide occurred — around 6am — and farmers had already begun their chores for the day. As the slide hurtled down the mountain it created a wide swath of destruction in its wake but perhaps the worst casualty was the farm of Oscar Stanley. His house and barn were *"smashed like eggshells"* by the debris. Oscar survived but most of his animals did not and 40 acres of his best farmland was destroyed. The Cherry Mountain Landslide would prove to be a double disaster for him as the structures were being rebuilt after a fire five weeks earlier. At the time, the slide became quite the tourist attraction and excursion trains were run to bring in curious viewers from all over.

Another moment of tragedy was on November 22, 1948 when a small plane crashed into the side of Cherry Mountain, killing the pilot and his two passengers. The aircraft had just left Whitefield Airport in poor weather bound for Bedford, MA. Because of the conditions, the pilot turned the plane around in an attempt to return to the airport, but instead collided with the lower slopes of the mountain.

Jeremy Belknap's 1791 map of New Hampshire labels Cherry Mountain as Pondicherry Mountain, no doubt a reference to the nearby pond. This name also appears on Philip Carrigain's 1816 map of the White Mountains. In the early 1900s the Mt. Martha name started appearing on topographic maps and is commonly believed to be in honor of the nation's original First Lady. The naming conventions regarding Cherry Mountain have at times caused confusion with hikers with one name given to the entire mountain and two other names to the primary summits. For the purposes of this list it's the Mt. Martha summit that must be climbed but many hikers combine it with Owl's Head for its excellent views. That peak gets its name, along with at least four other mountains in the state, including the infamous 4,000 Footer, from its sharp bird-of-prey appearance.

GETTING THERE

A large parking area and trailhead is located along NH 115 in Carroll, 1.9 mi. north of US 3 and 7.7 mi. south of US 2, directly opposite Lennon Rd. It should be noted that there are two trailheads providing access for Cherry Mountain located along NH 115. The directions above are for the southernmost one (Owl's Head Trail begins at a trailhead and parking area 5.6 mi. north of US 3 and 3.9 mi. south of US 2 in Jefferson).

Approaching the summit of Mt. Martha in winter.

RECOMMENDED ROUTE
Cherry Mountain Trail (western section), Mt. Martha Spur
Mt. Martha only: 3.8 mi. round-trip with 1,900 ft. elevation gain
Include side trip to Owl's Head: 5.4 mi. round-trip with 2,450 ft. elevation gain
The western section of Cherry Mountain Trail offers a mostly moderate ascent with steeper terrain closer to the ridge. Footing is a mix — generally good lower down but some rougher sections as you ascend. Mt. Martha Spur is eroded in places with a steep section near the top.

From the parking area Cherry Mountain Trail ascends easily at first then moderately along an old logging road, passing a clear-cut area on the left which affords some views through the trees. The trail dwindles into a footpath and becomes steeper with rocky footing in places, then at 1.7 mi. it reaches the ridge at a T-junction where it turns right and descends 3.6 mi. along a snowmobile trail down the eastern side of the mountain to Cherry Mountain Rd.

At this junction, Mt. Martha Spur turns left and ascends the snowmobile trail moderately for 0.2 mi. to a junction with Martha's Mile on the right (this superbly-maintained trail descends moderately to a col then climbs moderately with two short but steep scrambles to the outlook ledges on Owl's Head where there is a excellent vista of the Presidential Range — well worth the 0.8 mi. one-way side trip).

Opposite this junction on the left is a cleared outlook to the southeast. Continuing straight a few yds., the spur trail reaches the mostly wooded summit of Mt. Martha and makes a loop through the old fire tower footings.

VIEW HIGHLIGHTS

Northeast outlook: Mt. Martha has no expansive vistas but two outlooks just off the summit provide good views in opposite directions. Across from the junction with Martha's Mile, a cleared outlook provides the main attraction — a view northeast to the entire Presidential Range stretching from Mt. Madison to Mt. Webster in Crawford Notch. The Dartmouth Range can be seen lower and in front of the Presidentials.

Southwest outlook: From the fire tower footings at the summit, a well-beaten side path descends a short distance west to a ledge with views southwest toward Mt. Carrigain, the Twins-Bonds Range, Mt. Garfield, Franconia Ridge and Cannon Mountain.

Owl's Head: Mt. Martha's sibling is reached by Martha's Mile as noted above. The true summit of the peak is wooded with a few restricted viewpoints, but open ledges just below the summit provide one of the most scenic vistas in the White Mountains. The view here of the Presidential Range is similar to that of the one on Martha but totally open and unencumbered by trees. Additional views open up to the left of the Presidentials to the Crescent Range and the Grafton Notch area in Maine. Just next door to the south is the main mass of Mt. Martha with the deep Walker Valley far below. Extending to the left of Martha is an eastern ridge which culminates in an area known as The Humps before descending toward Cherry Mountain Rd.

ADDITIONAL ROUTES

Cherry Mountain Trail (eastern section), Mt. Martha Spur
7.6 mi. round-trip with 1,500 ft. elevation gain
This lightly used, quiet, and longer approach from Cherry Mountain Rd. (WMNF Forest Rd. 14) follows a snowmobile trail the entire way but offers

easy grades and generally good footing through attractive forest, especially along the beautiful wooded ridge. This route can be wet and muddy at times, but as far as snowmobile trails go this is a very pleasant walk. Parking is available in a small pull-off opposite the trailhead on Cherry Mountain Rd. in Carroll, 3.2 mi. north of US 302.

Owl's Head Trail, Martha's Mile
6.4 mi. round-trip with 2,550 ft. elevation gain
This route, starting at the northern trailhead on NH 115, first makes the steep climb up and over Owl's Head with its magnificent views, before moving onto to Mt. Martha. The lower section of this trail can be wet, muddy, and difficult to follow and the upper section is quite steep. See driving directions above for Owl's Head Trail.

Cherry Mountain Trail (eastern section), Mt. Martha Spur, Martha's Mile, Owl's Head Trail
7.0 mi. traverse with 1,600 ft. elevation gain
This point-to-point hike requires a fairly long car spot between opposite sides of the mountain. It begins at the Cherry Mountain Rd. trailhead and ends at the Owl's Head trailhead on NH 115, passing over the Mt. Martha and Owl's Head summits.

Cherry Mountain Trail (western section), Mt. Martha Spur, Martha's Mile, Owl's Head Trail
5.1 mi. traverse with 2,000 ft. elevation gain
This hike requires a short car spot and connects both of the trailheads on NH 115, passing over both the Mt. Martha and Owl's Head summits.

WINTER
While the distance is short the western section of Cherry Mountain Trail can be a real workout in deep unbroken snow as grades become steeper closer to the ridge. Route-finding may also be difficult in places. Mt. Martha Spur sees heavy snowmobile traffic and is always well packed down; be alert for fast-moving sleds. Deep snow improves the two outlooks near the summit and opens up a third one to the north. The parking area off NH 115 is not plowed but limited roadside parking may be available if snowfall is lean; be sure to get all four wheels out of the travel lanes. Space for one or two cars may also be available across the street at the plowed intersection with Lennon Rd.

The eastern approach from Cherry Mountain Rd. is not feasible in winter as the road is gated 2.8 mi. south of the trailhead. Parking is not always available outside the gate and the road is not always plowed up to it. Beyond the gate both Cherry Mountain Rd. and the eastern portion of Cherry Mountain Trail are heavily used by snowmobiles.

The northern trailhead on NH 115 for Owl's Head Trail is also not plowed but is sometimes packed down by high clearance vehicles if snow depths are light. Roadside parking here is possible depending on snowfall amounts. Due to the parking issues this approach is hiked less in winter.

Mt. Starr King

Elevation: 3,915 ft.
Location: Town of Jefferson
Map: RMC map, AMC map - North Country/Mahoosuc Range
Locator map: 31

Mt. Starr King lies along the western end of the Pliny Range, a chain of hills and mountains north of US 2 in Jefferson. Often combined with its more popular 4,000 foot neighbor Mt. Waumbek, Starr King is a worthy destination on its own for an intermediate hike. The actual summit is wooded but a nearby outlook from a clearing offers good views. This clearing was also home to a cabin constructed in the 1940s and removed sometime around 1980. A stone fireplace is all that remains, which has become a well known landmark and photo op for White Mountain hikers. An early 1936 AMC guide mentions that a USGS tower was located at the summit of Starr King, which featured panoramic views in all directions.

The Reverend Thomas Starr King, a Unitarian minister from Boston and author of the 1859 book *"The White Hills: Their Legend, Landscape and Poetry"*, was a frequent visitor to the Jefferson area and the peak was named in his honor. King Ravine in the Presidential Range also bears his name.

GETTING THERE

Parking is available in a small dirt lot off Starr King Rd. in Jefferson, 0.2 mi. northeast of US 2. Starr King Rd. is 0.2 mi. east of NH115A and 3.6 mi. west of NH 115. The entrance to this lot has historically been rough for low clearance vehicles. When driving up this road keep left at all forks and then bear right to reach the parking area. As of early 2019, Starr King Rd. was heavily posted as no parking due to overflow issues.

All that remains of a former cabin on Starr King is this stone chimney.

ROUTE

Starr King Trail

5.2 mi. round-trip with 2,300 ft. elevation gain

This yellow-blazed trail is a direct route to the summit of Mt. Starr King, with the option to continue a mile further to Mt. Waumbek. Grades are moderate the whole way and footing is generally good. In 2019, Randolph Mountain Club crews made much needed repairs and improvements to this heavily-used trail which sees high foot traffic by hikers bound for Mt. Waumbek.

From the parking area the trail follows a logging road for a short distance, turns left off it, then after a brief ascent, turns right onto another logging road, soon passing the round foundation of an old spring house on the right. At 0.4 mi. the trail turns right off the road, then turns right again at 0.8 mi. and begins a steady moderate ascent up the mountain's southwest ridge. The trail traverses the west side of the ridge, passing a small spring on the left at 2.1 mi., then makes a steady climb to the wooded summit; the highest point is a ledge with a USGS benchmark on the right. Just beyond, the trail descends easily to the cabin clearing.

VIEW HIGHLIGHTS

The main vista on Starr King is from the cabin clearing where an outlook provides a good view southeast to the Presidential Range.

WINTER

Starr King Trail is heavily traveled in winter by hikers headed for both Mt. Starr King and Mt. Waumbek so it is usually broken out quickly after a storm. Moderate grades with no tricky sections make for excellent snowshoeing and the route is protected from the wind. For winter hiking, this is one of the easiest ascents in the White Mountains. The trailhead parking area on Starr King Rd. is not plowed, but alternate winter parking is available diagonally across from Starr King Rd. on the south side of US 2 in a plowed dirt lot, requiring a 0.3 mi. walk to the trailhead. Use caution when entering or leaving this lot as the entrance slopes down and can be icy. Additional parking is also available at the nearby Old Corner Store/Irving gas station in (please give them your business as a thanks!) and at a large pull-off along US 2, 0.2 mi. east of Starr King Rd.

Mt. Success

Elevation: 3,592 ft.
Location: Township of Success
Map: AMC map - North Country/Mahoosuc Range
Locator map: 32

Mt. Success is one of the gems of the Mahoosuc Range, a chain of peaks stretching from New Hampshire into Maine, and is located just west of the border of the two states. Its open ledges and sub-alpine meadows offer sweeping views in most directions. The Appalachian Trail also passes over the summit and many hikers symbolically finish the 52WAV list on this aptly-named peak.

Of interest to both hikers and aviation buffs is the wreckage of a DC-3 which crashed a short distance south of the summit in 1954. Northeast Airlines Flight 792, bound for Berlin from Boston, encountered heavy snow squalls which effectively reduced visibility to zero. Having to rely on instrument navigation only, the plane suddenly encountered turbulent weather and a severe downdraft which caused it to collide with the mountain shortly after 11am. A large piece of the fuselage, wing and other wreckage can still be found along the AT boundary corridor, reached by a herd path off Mahoosuc Trail. Use caution when visiting the crash site due to sharp metal debris. If you do visit please honor and respect the site. Please also keep in mind that this wreckage is located on federal land and it is illegal to remove any artifacts or debris.

Originally known as Ingalls Mountain and still indicated as such on some maps, the mountain was renamed to Mt. Success in 1936 to avoid confusion with the smaller Mt. Ingalls (2,242 ft.) further south in Shelburne. Its current name is derived from being located in the township of Success which was founded in 1773. Mt. Success is the highest point within the township.

The view from The Outlook on Mt. Success.

GETTING THERE

The former parking area for Success Trail was located in a field at the end of a side road, 0.4 mi. off Success Pond Rd. in Success, but this side road is now closed indefinitely due to damage from a 2017 storm. Hikers must now park roadside at the junction of these two roads, where limited room is available. From Hutchins St. in Berlin, follow Success Pond Rd. for 5.4 mi. to the junction with the side road on the right (new trail signage was placed here in 2018) where there is room to park just before and after. Alternate parking is available at pull-offs a short distance before this point. Success Pond Rd. is somewhat notorious for its rough conditions and while high clearance is recommended, the road is usually passable by any vehicle at (sometimes very) slow speeds. The first mile in from Hutchins St. is typically the roughest as that section is also heavily used by ATVs which often dislodge softball-sized rocks from the road surface.

RECOMMENDED ROUTE
Success Trail, Outlook Loop, Mahoosuc Trail
6.0 mi. round-trip with 2,080 ft. elevation gain
This route offers a moderate ascent up to the ridge via Success Trail with a side trip along the way to The Outlook. Footing is mainly good aside from a few rougher sections. Success Trail also has a stretch of ledgy slabs which are mossy and may be slippery in wet conditions. Mahoosuc Trail is rougher in general with several steep ups and downs along the ridge, and one chimney section that is sometimes more difficult to ascend.

From the parking on Success Pond Rd., pass through a row of boulders and around and exposed culvert and walk easily up the side road, bearing right at a fork, to a large open field which served as the former parking area at 0.4 mi., where the trail enters the woods at the far end (the trail sign just inside the trees).

Success Trail ascends easily at first then moderately along an old logging road, climbing the aforementioned mossy slabs in one section (a bypass is available on the left) to a junction on the right at 1.6 mi. with an easy 0.3 mi. loop trail which leads to The Outlook, a high open ledge with excellent views to various peaks of the North Country. From the ledges the loop trail turns left and runs along the edge of The Outlook's high cliffs (watch blazes carefully here) before turning left again to descend easily back to Success Trail, 100 yds. above the lower loop junction.

Success Trail now ascends more easily then descends gradually to cross a small brook, where artifacts of an old logging campsite are on display. The trail continues easily through a wet area, then climbs somewhat steeply to a junction with Mahoosuc Trail at 2.4 mi.

Turning right, white-blazed Mahoosuc Trail descends slightly and then makes an immediate steep ascent over ledges, one of several rough pitches along this section. The trail then drops off a small chimney-like section which can be tricky if wet; hikers with long legs have an advantage here. After an easier stretch the trail again makes a steep and rough climb, swinging left near the top, to arrive at the open summit of Mt. Success at 3.0 mi. The summit consists of two bumps of similar height; the slightly higher southwest bump on an uplifted ledge is considered to be the high point and is marked with a USGS benchmark and trail sign. Just below this ledge to the south is an expansive sub-alpine meadow traversed by bog bridges where cotton grass blooms in late summer.

VIEW HIGHLIGHTS

The Outlook: These high cliffs are one of the premier perches in the North Country, offering extensive vistas south, west and northwest. High on the left is the main mass of Mt. Success, which blocks out any views toward Maine. Far below is a deep ravine carved into the western face of Success, with a broad valley beyond where the cliffs of North Bald Cap rise prominently on the other side. Between the right slope of Success and North Bald Cap, North Baldface barely pops up on the horizon, followed to the right by Shelburne Moriah and the rest of the Moriah ridge which extends over the Carters to Pinkham Notch. On the other side of the Notch, the Presidential Range rises up with Mt. Adams appearing in front of Mt. Washington. To the right of North Bald Cap is the Crescent Range, followed by Mt. Waumbek, Terrace Mountain, Mt. Cabot, and The Horn, all seen beyond the Town of Berlin. Wandering around the ledges in that direction opens up additional views to the northern Kilkenny peaks and the Nash Stream Valley.

Summit view: The vista from Mt. Success' summit just about doubles that of the Outlook, forming an almost 360-degree panorama. Some views are partially blocked by scrub and the main mass of the mountain itself. Starting in the northeast is a look up the Mahoosuc Range toward Mt. Carlo, Goose Eye Mountain, and Old Speck. To the right of Goose Eye is Puzzle Mountain, with Saddleback Mountain peering over its right shoulder. Further right and closer in is Lary Brook Mountain and Bear Mountain which are connected by a bumpy ridge. Beyond are numerous peaks deep within Maine. To the southeast, the Evans Notch area comes into view with a good look at East and West Royce and the Baldfaces. The Moriahs and Carters are seen to the right of the Baldfaces, before the view jumps across Pinkham Notch to the Presidential Range.

Once again Mt. Adams is seen in front of Washington, with Mt. Hayes visible under Adams. Further right is Cherry Mountain, the Pliny Range peaks of Waumbek, Weeks and Terrace, followed by Mt. Cabot and The Horn. The view then spreads right across the upper Kilkenny Region before arriving at the cluster of peaks in the Nash Stream Valley, including the Percy Peaks, Long Mountain, and Bunnell Mountain. Just shy of north is a distant look to Vermont's Monadnock Mountain, and extremely remote Magalloway Mountain is just barely visible due north on very clear days. To the right of Magalloway are several distant Maine mountains before the view comes back around to the Mahoosucs.

ADDITIONAL ROUTES

Austin Brook Trail, Mahoosuc Trail
12.0 mi. round-trip with 3,350 ft. elevation gain
This route provides a longer, rougher and steeper approach to Mt. Success from the south which is more suitable for backpackers or strong day hikers, starting on North Rd. in Shelburne, 0.6 mi. west of Meadow Rd. The section of Mahoosuc Trail north of Gentian Pond involves long stretches of sustained and strenuous steep climbing.

Carlo Col Trail, Mahoosuc Trail, Success Trail, Outlook Loop
9.2 mi. clockwise loop with 2,950 ft. elevation gain
This interstate route, which requires a car spot to connect the 2.7 mi. distance between the Success and Carlo Col trailheads along Success Pond Rd., makes for a steep, rough and remote almost-loop hike which connects the open summits of Mt. Carlo (3,576 ft.) in Maine and Mt. Success in New Hampshire.

OVERNIGHT OPTIONS

For backpackers approaching Mt. Success from the south, first come, first served Gentian Pond Shelter is located a short distance south of the Austin Brook Trail/Mahoosuc Trail junction. This three-sided shelter and tent platforms lie along the Appalachian Trail, so expect to share them with thru-hikers in season. A privy is nearby and water is available from the pond, but filtering is strongly recommended due to algae. More information is available at fs.usda.gov.

If doing the loop via Carlo Col Trail, Carlo Col Campsite is located off that trail, 0.2 mi. north of Mahoosuc Trail. The site offers a shelter, tent platforms, privy and bear boxes. Water is available from a nearby stream. More information is available at outdoors.org.

WINTER

Mt. Success is seldom hiked in winter, mainly due to difficulty in reaching the primary trailhead. Success Pond Rd. is a privately-owned logging road which does not receive regular maintenance. In recent years the road has been plowed but this cannot be guaranteed. Even if it is plowed, high clearance and AWD/4WD is still recommended due to ruts and ice and depending on snow banks, roadside parking at the trailhead may be nonexistent. Alternate parking may be available before the trailhead at pull-offs.

If you can reach the trailhead and can park, Success Trail offers moderate snowshoeing up to the ridge. Sometimes snowmobiles break out the lower part of the trail and travel as far up as The Outlook, which may require crampons in crusty or icy conditions. Use caution here as the dropoff is significant. Mahoosuc Trail will likely require arduous trail breaking and route-finding, and the short chimney section may be tricky if filled in with ice. Mt. Success' exposure on top offers little protection from the wind. Deep snowpack opens up additional views along sections of Mahoosuc Trail and at the summit.

The southern approach from North Rd. in Shelburne is an unlikely route mainly due to its distance, light use, and lack of parking.

North Percy Peak

Elevation: 3,415 ft.
Location: Town of Stratford
Map: TCTA map, AMC map - North Country/Mahoosuc Range
Locator map: 38

The striking gumdrop-shaped North Percy Peak and its symmetric sibling South Percy Peak are located within Nash Stream Forest in New Hampshire's North Country, and are the dominant landscape features in the greater Stark and Groveton area. The steep exposed granite slabs — which look impossible to climb from some perspectives — and open scrubby summit of North Percy offer spectacular views of the surrounding North Country as well abundant blueberries in season. The Percy Peaks also inspired the logo for the Cohos Trail, a 170 mi. route stretching from Crawford Notch to the Quebec border.

Chartered in 1774, the nearby town of Stark was originally named Percy after Hugh Percy, 1st Duke of Northumberland (also the origin of the neighboring town of Northumberland). The town was later renamed Stark in 1832 in honor of General John Stark, a hero of the battles of Bunker Hill and Bennington. In commemoration of the latter conflict, it was General Stark who wrote the famous words "Live Free or Die" in 1809, which would later become New Hampshire's official motto. A village within the town of Stark still bears the Percy name. The Percy Peaks and Percy Pond also appeared on Philip Carrigain's 1816 map of the White Mountains.

The symmetrical gumdrop of North Percy Peak as seen from South Percy Peak.

GETTING THERE
Roadside parking for several vehicles is available along gravel Nash Stream Rd. in Stratford. From NH 110 in Groveton, 2.6 mi. east of US 3, take Emerson Rd. north for 1.4 mi. then bear right onto Northside Rd. for 0.7 mi. Turn sharply left onto Nash Stream Rd. and continue 2.7 mi. to a parking area on the right just before the bridge over Slide Brook. Hikers are requested to park at an angle off the road.

RECOMMENDED ROUTE
Percy Peaks Trail, South Percy Spur, Percy Loop Trail, Nash Stream Rd.
6.8 mi. counter-clockwise loop with 2,550 ft. elevation gain (includes side trip to South Percy Peak)
This counter-clockwise loop hike uses the steeper and rougher Percy Peaks Trail (blazed in orange) for the ascent and the easier, more gradual Percy Loop Trail (blazed in red and yellow) for the descent, with a short side trip to South Percy Peak (3,234 ft.) via an unofficial but well-beaten side path. The entire loop is closed with a short walk along Nash Stream Rd. Footing is rugged in places on Percy Peaks Trail, with sections of steep and angled ledge. The upper slabs of the summit cone are very steep and exposed and offer excellent traction when dry (but may be dangerous if wet). Percy Loop

Trail is more rocky and rugged in its upper half, but the lower portion is easy walking along an old logging road. The side path to South Percy is steep, narrow, and rough, although very short.

From the parking area, continue up Nash Stream Rd. to cross the bridge over Slide Brook, then turn right onto Percy Peaks Trail (sign) and enter the woods. The trail ascends easily, crossing a small stream at 0.3 mi., then it follows sections of old logging roads mixed with footpaths alongside Slide Brook. The trail turns sharply left at a large glacial boulder, swings out onto a relocated section, then makes a steep and rough ascent to reach the the lower slabs of North Percy at 1.2 mi., but does not ascend them. It bears right and makes a steep climb alongside the slabs, then turns left and crosses them. The trail then ascends the south side of the mountain, steeply at times, along side-sloping ledges where footing is rough. After dropping off a ledge, grades ease as the trail reaches a junction with Old Summer Club Trail (a section of the Cohos Trail) on the right at 1.7 mi.

For the side trip to South Percy Peak, turn right onto Old Summer Club Trail and descend easily for 0.1 mi. to a junction with an unofficial side path on the right (sign: "To South Percy"), where the main trail swings left. This narrow rugged path climbs steeply for 0.3 mi. over several scrambles to the more wooded summit of South Percy Peak, where there is a hiker register. Just past the summit are several open ledges with excellent views.

From the junction with Old Summer Club Trail, Percy Peaks Trail bears left and then left again to a junction with Percy Loop Trail on the right. Turning sharply left, Percy Peaks Trail climbs moderately and scrambles up an eroded slot to reach the start of the steep exposed slabs at 2.6 mi. The trail then breaks out into the open with several twists and turns; hikers should follow blazes and cairns carefully, but slight variations in the route may be necessary for the best footing. The steepest slabs are at the start of this section, then grades ease as the trail reaches the broad, somewhat flat summit at 3.0 mi. The high point is marked by a USGS benchmark and an iron pin which is likely a remnant of when the peak was used as a station by the United States Coastal Survey in the 1870s.

Carefully make your way back down the slabs to the junction with Percy Loop Trail and bear left to descend easily at first, then more moderately over rougher and rockier terrain, to a junction with Trio Trail (a section of the Cohos Trail) on the right at 4.1 mi. Percy Loop Trail continues a moderate descent to a junction with an old logging road, where it turns left. The trail descends along this road and a second road at easy to moderate grades, passes a Cohos Trail register on the right, then meets Nash Stream Rd. at 5.7 mi. Turn left and follow the road for a 1.1 mi. walk back to the parking area.

VIEW HIGHLIGHTS

North Percy Peak: The summit area of North Percy is somewhat flat, but by exploring the various open ledges you can get the full panorama. Please take care to not trample fragile vegetation.

Close by, directly to the south, is South Percy Peak, with The Horn, The Bulge, and Mt. Cabot in the distance beyond, and Mts. Carrigain and Hancock further right, followed by the Franconia Ridge high peaks. The view then swings around toward Cannon Mountain, the Kinsmans, and Mt. Moosilauke, before extending off to a multitude of small peaks and hills in western New Hampshire and Eastern Vermont.

Mt. Ellen in the Green Mountains can be seen in the far distance just shy of west, followed by the Northeast Kingdom peaks, including Burke, East Haven, and East Mountains, with Jay Peak appearing just about to the northwest. Closer in the triple-summited ridge of Savage, Goback, and Teapot Mountains comes into view, as does Castle Mountain and its West Peak, followed by Sugarloaf, Bunnel, Gore and Fitch Mountains.

Looking due North is a fantastic view straight up the valley of Nash Stream, where Deer Mountain, Muise Mountain, Mt. Kent, Dixville Peak, and Kelsey Mountain are visible. Further right, the vista becomes quite distant to peaks in Maine before disappearing behind Long Mountain's ridge.

The view emerges on the other side toward Cambridge Black Mountain, with Old Speck and the Mahoosuc Range stretching to the right. Down in front under the Mahoosucs is Bald Mountain in Stark, dropping to the low bump of Victor Head and Christine Lake. Above Victor Head and far on the horizon, the peaks of the Evans Notch region appear, before views move onto the Moriahs, Carters, and Wildcats. The Presidential Range follows next, capped off by Mt. Washington, before the view comes back to Mt. Cabot.

South Percy Peak: While not nearly as bare as North Percy, ledges a short distance past the summit provide views from the west to the northeast and are largely the same as those seen from that peak. The most impressive view here is a look back at North Percy and its bare granite ledges which appear impossibly steep to climb from this vantage point. For peakbaggers, South Percy is also part of the NH 3,000 Footers hiking list, as well as the NH 500 Highest list.

ADDITIONAL ROUTE
Pond Brook Falls Trail, Trio Trail, Percy Loop Trail, Percy Peaks Trail
12.6 mi. round-trip with 2,000 ft. elevation gain
This longer northern route to North Percy only, starting 2.9 mi. further up Nash Stream Rd. from the Percy Peaks Trail, uses sections of the Cohos Trail which provide access to the attractive Pond Brook Falls and Percy Loop Campsite. This hike requires a car spot between the Pond Brook Falls and Percy Peaks trailheads.

OVERNIGHT OPTIONS
Percy Loop Campsite is located along Trio Trail, a short distance east of its junction with Percy Loop Trail, and features a tent platform and privy. The water source is the brook at the trail junction. Campfires are not permitted.

WINTER
North Percy is challenging in winter. Extreme caution must be used on the open slabs if icy. Crampons and an ice axe may be required; there is also an avalanche danger. The side path to South Percy is narrow and could be hard to follow if unbroken. Since these peaks are infrequently hiked in winter, strenuous trail breaking will likely be required.

Nash Stream Rd. is gated in winter, although parking is plowed by the gate 0.5 mi. from Northside Rd. for snowmobile traffic. A longer and more difficult approach is from the south via Christine Lake, where limited plowed parking may be available at the end of Christine Lake Rd. in Stark. Total round-trip distance to both peaks from this point is 9.0 mi. with 2,700 ft. elevation gain. Refer to the Cohos Trail map for the route, which uses a combination of snowmobile trails and a section of Old Summer Club Trail.

Pine Mountain (Gorham)

Elevation: 2,404 ft.
Location: Town of Gorham
Map: AMC map - Carter Range/Evans Notch
Locator map: 39

One of many geographic areas with "pine" in the name around the state, this Pine Mountain is an under-appreciated gem. It lies low in Gorham between the towering northern Presidential peaks to its south, and the long, rugged Mahoosuc Range to the north. Pinkham Ledge, on the south side of the mountain, offers a spectacular panorama out to the high peaks which line both sides of Pinkham Notch. Excellent views are also available from other easterly outlooks, all reached by short side paths. The true summit is wooded and was also the location of a series of fire towers which collectively were in service from 1910 to. 1967. The final tower was demolished in 1975, but the concrete footings still remain today. Pine Mountain was added to the 52WAV list in 2020.

The summit is located on property owned by the Horton Center, a faith-based camp and retreat operated by the New Hampshire Conference of the United Church of Christ (Congregational). The Center owns a 100-acre tract on the mountain, with a large camp situated on the northern plateau.

> **Important:** Hikers are welcome on the mountain but are requested to not disturb any Horton Center activities which may be occurring. Public access to the Horton Center grounds is prohibited.

Once known as Camel's Hump and Camel's Rump, the peak takes its current name from the fine stands of pine trees which stood on its slopes before most were destroyed by fires. While the US Board on Geographic Names lists fifteen Pine Hills in New Hampshire, this is one of only two Pine Mountains in the state, the other being in Alton in the Lakes Region.

GETTING THERE

Parking is available at the trailhead for Pine Link Trail on Pinkham B Rd. (WMNF Forest Rd. 207) in Gorham, 2.5 mi. southeast of US 2 in Randolph, and 1.9 mi. northwest of NH 16 in Martin's Location. Pinkham B Rd. is a mix of pavement and dirt with some rough sections and therefore requires careful and slow driving. The trailhead is located just west of the height-of-land along the road, directly opposite Pine Mountain Rd. and the main entrance to the Horton Center. Do not park on Pine Mountain Rd. if the lot is full.

RECOMMENDED ROUTE

Pine Mountain Rd., Ledge Trail, Pine Mountain Trail, Pine Mountain Loop
4.0 counter-clockwise loop with 1,000 ft. elevation gain

This route provides an easy warm-up followed by a steep and rugged climb to Pinkham Ledge and the summit. The route is described here in the counter-clockwise direction, as it is easier to ascend the steep scrambles on Ledge Trail than it is to descend them. Use caution in wet or icy conditions and be aware of vehicles along Pine Mountain Rd.

Pine Mountain Rd. leaves opposite the parking area (trail sign, sign for Horton Center) and runs at easy grades with minor ascents and descents, passing through a gate (which may be closed to vehicles at times, but foot traffic is allowed) at 0.1 mi. Just as the road begins a steadier ascent, yellow-blazed Ledge Trail departs on the right (sign) at 0.9 mi.

Ledge Trail, a footpath, ascends moderately with rougher footing through an area of boulders, turns sharply right at a switchback, then traverses steeply-sloping ledges with a view up to Pinkham Ledge on the left. It dips back into the woods, then climbs a steep, exposed ledge with a drop off on the right and excellent views south. The best way up if wet is along the left edge. At the top of this ledge, Ledge Trail bears left into the woods, ascends moderately, swings left to skirt the base of a cliff, then right to begin a steep, rocky scramble. The trail climbs up through a small gully, then scrambles up a steep ledge which is easier than it looks. At the top, the trail turns sharply left and ascends up angled slabs to reach Pinkham Ledge and the most impressive views on the mountain (follow blazes on the slabs for the best route) at 1.3 mi. At the south end of the ledge is a memorial bench for Carol Williams Horton carved out of the granite; a prime seat to take in the vista. Ledge Trail turns right here, ascends easily along the ridge and ends at the wooded summit clearing and old fire tower footings at 1.5 mi. The highest point is a large boulder on the right.

Continuing straight ahead, yellow-blazed Pine Mountain Trail ambles easily along the ridgecrest via the old tractor road which was used to access the fire tower. It quickly passes a short side path on the right for Angel View, the first of three east-facing open ledge outlooks (in 2019, the former sign was missing at this junction). The main trail passes a second short side path to Gorham View (sign) on the right, and then a third to Chapel View (sign) on the right, which leads 60 yds. to an Adirondack-style shelter (public use prohibited) and log bench on an open ledge. Pine Mountain Trail descends easily, then moderately, to a well-signed four-way junction at 1.8 mi., where it turns right. Pine Mountain Loop turns sharply left here and the old tractor road continues ahead toward the Horton Center (no public access).

Turning right here, Pine Mountain Trail descends easily and bears left onto a series of bog bridges under a power line (in reverse, bear right here at a trail sign) and runs level for a short distance to another four-way junction at 2.0 mi. Here, Pine Mountain Trail continues ahead and descends to the northern trailhead in Gorham. An unmarked path turns left (no public access), and a spur trail to Chapel Rock turns right.

Important: Chapel Rock is off-limits to the public during the months of June, July and August while the Horton Center camp is in operation. Please respect this by visiting Chapel Rock in the off-season only.

The cliffs in this area may also be used by rock climbers from the Horton Center at times, and hikers should share the trail with climbers.

From this junction, backtrack along the route above, returning to the junction with Pine Mountain Loop at 2.4 mi. At this junction, bear left up wooden steps onto yellow-blazed Pine Mountain Loop (sign), which diverts hikers away from the Horton Center grounds, and is a section of the original route of Pine Mountain Trail. It climbs slightly then descends easily, angling across the slope on bog bridges, to reach a junction with Pine Mountain Rd. at 2.6 mi. Turn left here for an easy 1.4 mi. walk back to the parking area.

Striated ledges on Pine Mountain point the way to Pinkham Notch.

VIEW HIGHLIGHTS

Pinkham Ledge: This is the most impressive vista on the mountain with a panoramic 180-degree view, stretching from the high peaks of the Carter-Moriah Range over the Presidential Range and all the way around to the Crescent Range. The sun-soaked stone bench here at the end of the ledge invites a relaxing stay to take in the views.

The vista begins on the far left at the end of the Carter-Moriah Range with fellow 52WAV peak Shelburne Moriah Mountain and its trailless neighbor Middle Moriah, followed by the main peak of the family, Mt. Moriah. The ridgeline dips then climbs over Imp Mountain and makes its long traverse over the Carters before dropping steeply into U-shaped Carter Notch, only to ascend steeply up the other side and over the wild and rugged Wildcats. Further right, the view descends into Pinkham Notch then rises to Mt. Washington and onto the enormous mass of Mt. Madison, the most prominent feature seen front and center from this viewpoint. To the right of Madison, the view moves out to the distant Cherry Mountain and its double summits of Mt. Martha and Owl's Head, before jumping across US 2 and ending at Mts. Randolph and Crescent in the Crescent Range.

Angel View: This small ledge just off Pine Mountain Trail provides an eastern view starting with the Mahoosuc Range on the left, before dropping down to the town of Gorham, with the Shelburne peaks of Middle Mountain, Mt. Crag, and formerly-trailed Mt. Evans rising beyond. From the US 2 corridor, the vista rises to the right over the Moriahs and Carters to deep Carter Notch.

Gorham View: Looking down on the town of Gorham, this open ledge offers essentially the same views as Angel View, although from a slightly more southern perspective.

Chapel View: This small ledge viewpoint features a log bench and Adirondack shelter to take in the wide views, which stretch from the Mahoosuc Range on the left to the Wildcats on the right. This ledge also provides an excellent look at the cliffs on the north side of Chapel Rock.

ADDITIONAL ROUTE

Pine Mountain Trail, Ledge Trail

5.8 mi. round-trip with 1,870 ft. elevation gain

This longer northern approach starts at a trailhead in a gravel pit, reached by a dirt road which extends past the end of Promenade St. in Gorham. It follows a former abandoned route of Pine Link Trail, which once connected the northern Presidential Range peaks with an old route of the Appalachian Trail in Gorham. Along with the summit, this route also includes visits to the eastern outlooks and Pinkham Ledge (Pine Mountain Trail ends at the viewless summit and fire tower clearing; continue south along Ledge Trail for 0.1 mi. to reach Pinkham Ledge).

WINTER

In winter, Pinkham B Rd. is only maintained to a point 0.5 mi. from US 2 and 0.4 mi. from NH 16 (near the entrance to Barnes Field Campground). Limited roadside parking may be available at these points depending on snowfall amounts and plowing. Approaching from NH 16 is more feasible and if there is parking at this location this route adds 2.8 mi. round-trip and 420 ft. elevation gain to the hike.

Both Pinkham B Rd. and Pine Mountain Rd. offer easy snowshoeing, especially if packed down by snowmobiles. Snowmobiles may also occasionally travel to the summit of Pine via the old tractor road section of Pine Mountain Trail. The steep grades of Ledge Trail make for difficult and challenging snowshoeing and full crampons may be required on the open ledges in icy or crusty conditions.

The parking area for Pine Mountain Trail from the north is not plowed so hikers are encouraged to use public parking in downtown Gorham; a plowed lot used by snowmobilers is located at the corner of Church and Railroad St. From here, walk south on Church St., then turn right onto Promenade St. to the trailhead. This adds 0.8 mi. round-trip to the hike. Limited parking may be available at the plowed end of Promenade St. just past the last house, but this cannot be guaranteed (if space is available, do not block the private driveway here). This would add about 0.4 mi. round-trip to the hike. This approach offers mostly easy to moderate grades for snowshoeing although route-finding may be difficult due to poor trail markings.

Rogers Ledge

Elevation: 2,965 ft.
Location: Township of Kilkenny and Town of Stark
Map: AMC map - North Country/Mahoosuc Range
Locator map: 41

The remote, wild and uninhabited Kilkenny Region as seen from Rogers Ledge.

Rogers Ledge is the first peak that hikers will encounter when traveling south along the remote Kilkenny Ridge Trail, a long-distance backcountry route created in the 1980s for backpackers seeking solitude away from the more crowded areas of the White Mountains. It's the highest of a group of isolated peaks located in the northern part of the uninhabited township of Kilkenny, and its most striking feature is a high granite cliff on its south face. From atop this broad cliff is a vast 180-degree panorama of the Kilkenny highlands and various mountain ranges beyond, including the Mahoosucs, the Moriahs and Carters, the Presidentials, and the Pliny and Pilot Ranges. Due to its remote location away from the more popular hiking areas of the Whites, Rogers Ledge sees relatively light foot traffic but the somewhat long trek offers stunning scenery and quiet, beautiful forests. Along with The Horn, this is one of the premier viewpoints in the Kilkenny region. As such, Rogers Ledge was added to the 52WAV list in 2020. Rogers Ledge's neighbors Square Mountain and Greens Ledge are similar in terrain with their own cliffs, but neither is accessible by trail.

In 1903, a devastating forest fire burned over 25,000 acres in the Kilkenny region, including the area around Rogers Ledge. The blaze was initially sparked in the town of Stark and quickly spread to surrounding Milan, Berlin, Randolph, and Kilkenny. Logging slash was abundant in this area and coupled with weather conditions, the fire burned rapidly until all of its fuel had been consumed. In the more than a century since, the forest has healed itself well, and today's birch stands surrounding the peak serve as a reminder of the conflagration.

Rogers Ledge and its trailless North Peak were once known as the Peaked Hills (with Rogers Ledge being called South Peak at that time), and these names appeared on AMC maps for several decades starting in the late 1800s. Between that time and the 1940s and 1950s Rogers Ledge was given the offensive name "Nigger Nose" for reasons unknown, which then replaced the former designation on maps and in trail descriptions.

The retired Rev. Robert McConnell Hatch, an experienced tramper in the Kilkenny region, was so disturbed by this inappropriate naming that he undertook an effort to have it changed. He proposed naming the peak after Major Robert Rogers (1727-1795), an American colonial frontiersman who served in the British army during both the French & Indian Wars and the American Revolution. During the former conflict, Rogers trained and led the famous Rogers' Rangers, who were experts in raiding and close combat behind enemy lines.

Hatch's proposal was rebuffed by authorities at first, but was later boosted through a collaboration with the Argus-Champion Editor Edward DeCourcy and an endorsement by the Automobile Legal Association. The ALA suggested naming Rogers Ledge after the late President John F. Kennedy, but the choice of honoring Major Rogers ultimately prevailed and the name change was made official by the U.S. Board on Geographic Names in November, 1964. In the summer of 1965, Rev. Hatch and a hiking companion trekked out to the peak to affix a brass plaque at the top of the cliff indicating the new name; this plaque is still in place today (when entering onto the cliff, turn left for a few yds. and it is on the left, partially obscured by a tree).

GETTING THERE

To reach the northern terminus of Kilkenny Ridge Trail at South Pond Recreation Area in Stark, turn south onto South Pond Rd. from NH 110, 10.0 mi. east of US 3 in Groveton or 14.4 mi. west of NH 110 in Berlin. In 0.7 mi. bear right at fork, pass through a gate (open daily 10am to 8pm in season) and continue to the main parking area at 1.8 mi. There is a per vehicle per day fee which is sometimes waived for day hikers. More information is available at fs.usda.gov or by calling the WMNF Androscoggin District Office at 603-466-2713. (Note: Pets are not permitted at this recreation area.)

RECOMMENDED ROUTE
Kilkenny Ridge Trail
To Rogers Ledge only: 8.2 mi. round-trip with 1,850 ft. elevation gain
Include trip to Devil's Hopyard: 9.4 mi. round-trip with 2,000 ft. elevation gain
This approach from the north is on the longer side but the ascent is very gradual and easy the whole way. Footing is generally good overall, but there are some rocky stretches and the trail can be muddy and wet at times. Kilkenny Ridge Trail is marked by yellow blazes of various ages, visibility and type (paint, plastic). In late 2019, the upper 1.5 mi. or so had some brushy sections with spruce growing into the trail, but the route was still easy to follow despite it being lightly traveled and remote.

From the main building and WMNF kiosk at the parking area, turn right and walk along the west shore of the pond through the picnic area to the start of Kilkenny Ridge Trail (sign) where mileages begin. The first 0.2 mi. of the trail is a well-graded, handicapped-accessible path with several viewpoints along the shore. Footing becomes slightly rougher beyond that point as the trail continues mostly level to cross Devil's Hopyard Stream on a footbridge, then it reaches the junction with Devil's Hopyard Trail on the right at 0.7 mi. Turn right here on this unblazed and somewhat obscure trail for an optional side-trip into a narrow steep-sided gorge whose floor is strewn with very slippery, moss-covered boulders. An impressive feature of this gorge is the underground stream which can be clearly heard beneath the boulders but not seen. This side trail ends at 0.7 mi. next to a high rock wall on the left and an "end of trail" sign; the mileage indicated on the trail sign at the junction with Kilkenny Ridge Trail is to the "start" of the gorge.

> **Warning:** Use caution and allow extra time when in the gorge due to the slick, rough, awkward footing and several scrambles, all of which can be potentially hazardous. This trail is also not recommended for dogs.

From the trail junction, Kilkenny Ridge Trail continues straight ahead to cross Cold Stream (may be difficult at high water) at 0.9 mi., then begins a long, gentle ascent up a shallow valley through a beautiful hardwood forest. At 2.0 mi., the trail crosses an unnamed stream not shown on most maps. At times of high water it may be difficult to get over right where the trail crosses, but just a few yds. upstream it is much narrower. Conifers start to mix in as the gradual ascent continues, and at 3.2 mi. the trail crosses the Stark/Kilkenny boundary, marked by a wooden post on the right.

Climbing becomes more moderate up a rocky section as the trail ascends steadily through a forest of birch and ferns, slowly curving left. It merges onto a narrow ridge and makes the final moderate ascent to a wooded area behind the main ledge. Turn right onto any of the beaten paths in this area to emerge on a high, broad, table-like shelf atop a granite cliff at 4.1 mi. Use caution with pets or children on this ledge due to the precipitous drop. Back on the main trail, continue a short distance to the high point of Rogers Ledge on the right, which is marked by a USGS benchmark on an open ledge where Kilkenny Ridge Trail turns left and descends for points south.

VIEW SUMMARY

Main ledge: The broad shelf atop the south cliff of Rogers Ledge is roomy enough for several hikers to spread out and soak up the sun while enjoying a panoramic 180-degree panorama across the vast Kilkenny region. Aside from the City of Berlin, not too many signs of human civilization are visible from this vantage point.

Starting on the far left is the long line of peaks within the Mahoosuc Range starting with Old Speck, the highest peak, on the left. Moving right, the ridge runs over Mahoosuc Arm, Mahoosuc Mountain, Fulling Mill Mountain, Goose Eye Mountain's cluster of peaks, Mt. Carlo, Mt. Success, and Bald Cap Mountain, which all rise beyond the City of Berlin. Closer in is the low Deer Ridge, then back out to the Mahoosucs is Cascade Mountain. Berlin's Jericho Mountain is seen over Deer Ridge as is Mt. Hayes. Continuing right are the three peaks of the Moriah Range — Shelburne Moriah, Middle Moriah and Mt. Moriah — followed up by Imp Mountain and North and Middle Carter Mountains. Below the Carters is Black Crescent Mountain. The Carter Range continues to the right over South Carter, Mt. Hight, and Carter Dome, before dropping steeply into the prominent gouge of Carter Notch. On the right side of the notch, the Wildcat Range rises abruptly before the view swings over to the Presidential Range, stretching from Mt. Madison to Mt. Pierce, with the closer Mt. Crescent and Mt. Randolph underneath the Presidentials.

Across the broad valley below Rogers Ledge rises Unknown Pond Ridge, with Kilback Pond seen down below. Poking just above the ridge are a part of Mt. Cabot, the steep cone of The Horn, and the rounded bump known as The Bulge. On the far right is a wide view of the trailless Pilot Range extending northwest from Mt. Cabot. The sharp summit of Hutchins Mountain lies just about in the center of the range.

Summit view: The high point of Rogers Ledge rests on a partly open ledge which provides a more restricted view of the southeast and south portions of the vista described above.

ADDITIONAL ROUTES
Mill Brook Trail, Kilkenny Ridge Trail
From Mill Brook trailhead: 8.4 mi. round-trip with 1,600 ft. elevation gain
From Berlin Fish Hatchery gate: 9.2 mi. round-trip with 1,600 ft. elevation gain
This southern approach, while around the same mileage as coming in from the north, offers a similarly gradual hike up the valley of Cold Brook to Rogers Ledge, starting at the Berlin Fish Hatchery off York Pond Rd. in Berlin (see the Horn section for driving details). Except in winter when it's open all the time, the fish hatchery gate is open 8am to 4pm. In 2020, it was reported that the gate will now be locked daily at 4pm. If you think your hike will fall outside these hours and want to stay on the safe side, parking is available in a pull-off just before the gate. From here, it's a 0.4 mi. walk up the road to the trailhead. For more information, contact the Hatchery at 603-449-3412.

Rogers Ledge Traverse
8.3 mi. traverse with 1,850 ft. elevation gain
This north to south traverse, using Kilkenny Ridge Trail and Mill Brook Trail, journeys through some of the most remote areas of the Kilkenny region, starting at South Pond Recreation Area and ending at the Berlin Fish Hatchery. This route requires a somewhat lengthy car spot.

Kilkenny Ridge Traverse
23.2 mi. traverse with 7,700 ft. elevation gain
This long backcountry trek, best suited for experienced backpackers, traverses the entire Kilkenny Ridge Trail north to south starting at South Pond Recreation Area and ending at the Starr King trailhead in Jefferson (see Mt. Starr King section for details). The last 2.6 mi. is along Starr King Trail. In addition to Rogers Ledge, this trip allows for visits to 52WAV peaks The

Horn and Mt. Starr King, 4,000 footers Mt. Cabot and Mt. Waumbek, Terrace Mountain (North Peak, South Peak), and all three summits of Mt. Weeks. Due to the great driving distance between trailheads, it is advised to arrange a car spot prior to the day of the hike.

OVERNIGHT OPTIONS

Backpackers in this remote region can utilize Rogers Ledge Tentsite, which is located on a side path off Kilkenny Ridge Trail, 0.5 mi. south of Rogers Ledge. This free primitive camping area offers four tent pads and an outhouse. Water is available from a small brook 0.1 mi. south along Kilkenny Ridge Trail.

WINTER

With its mostly easy grades and plowed road access, the approach from the south via Mill Brook Trail provides the easiest winter route to Rogers Ledge for experienced snowshoers. The Berlin Fish Hatchery gate is left open all winter and plowed parking is available at the trailhead. If unbroken, Mill Brook Trail will likely involve route-finding due to it not being well-blazed. The northern approach from South Pond is possible, but due to the road being gated 0.7 mi. south of NH 110, this option requires an additional 1.1 mi. road walk each way, stretching this route out to 10.4 mi. round-trip. Limited parking is usually available near the gate.

Sugarloaf (Stratford)

Elevation: 3,703 ft.
Location: Town of Stratford
Map: TCTA map
Locator map: 50

Sugarloaf (not to be confused with Middle Sugarloaf in Twin Mountain, another 52WAV peak) is situated at the northern end of Nash Stream Valley, and its ledgy summit, which once bore a fire tower from 1910 to 1976, provides excellent vistas to the south and west. A unique feature of the summit is an antique cast iron stove, presumably hauled up from the old fire warden's cabin, which seems to change location with each visit. Sugarloaf is located within a group of the tallest peaks in the region, and provides a good perspective over the broad valley of Nash Stream. Due to its remote location and distance from major roads, the mountain also provides a sense of isolation, being far removed from the busier trails of the White Mountains, seen far to the south.

Like other similarly-named mountains in the state, the mountain was likely named due to its shape resembling the cone-shaped "loaves" in which sugar was once sold.

The bare and ledgy summit of Sugarloaf.

GETTING THERE

Limited roadside parking is available near the end of a private driveway on Nash Stream Rd. in Stratford; please do not block access to either the road or driveway. Nash Stream Rd. may be rough at times but is passable by any vehicle. From NH 110 in Groveton, take Emerson Rd. north for 1.4 mi. then bear right onto Northside Rd. for 0.7 mi. Turn sharply left onto Nash Stream Rd. and continue 8.2 mi. to the trailhead on the left. The former signage here was difficult to see but has been made more prominent as of 2017.

ROUTE

Sugarloaf Mountain Trail

4.2 mi. round-trip with 2,200 ft. elevation gain

This somewhat steep and unrelenting route makes a direct ascent up the eastern slope of Sugarloaf and mostly follows the old jeep road for the former fire tower, which has rocky and eroded footing in places. The toppled remains of the former fire warden's cabin lie about a half mile below the summit. The trail starts on private property and hikers should respect all signage while staying on the marked trail. While the distance is short, Sugarloaf Mountain Trail's significant elevation gain and consistent ascent make it a strenuous climb.

From Nash Stream Rd., the trail starts up the driveway and passes a private cabin on the right, crosses a small stream, then passes through a gate and a clearing. It bears right at a fork at 0.1 mi. (sign: "Sugarloaf Mt. Trail") where Cohos Trail diverges left and ascends moderately to a four-way junction with a snowmobile trail at 0.4 mi. Above this junction, the trail climbs a long, consistently steeper section of the old road to reach a grassy clearing and the remains of the old fire warden's cabin at 1.6 mi. Slightly uphill and opposite the cabin at a fork a short side path diverges left to an unreliable spring. Bearing right at the fork to the spring, the trail passes through a brushy area above the clearing (turn around for a restricted view east), and continues a stiff climb to reach Sugarloaf's northeast ridge, where grades finally ease. The trail swings left and ascends easily along the ridge, with one final steeper pitch to the partly open summit, marked by a USGS benchmark and summit sign which has been in a fragile state of disrepair in recent years.

VIEW HIGHLIGHTS

The vista from Sugarloaf's ledgy summit stretches nearly 180-degrees from northeast to south but you need to wander around a little bit to get the complete picture. There are also some looks west by descending past the summit to another set of open ledges.

Looking to the northeast is the valley which holds Nash Stream Bog (a wetland area created when a dam which held Nash Pond Bog back gave way) and beyond to Dixville Peak, as well as dozens of distant mountains in Maine. Swinging around to the east, Old Speck in Grafton Notch is visible, followed by the Mahoosuc Range. To the southeast across the broad Nash Stream Valley below is the aptly-named Long Mountain and the distinctive shape of the Percy Peaks. Seen between and above Long and the Percys are the Moriah, Carter, Wildcat, and Presidential Ranges, with Mt. Washington being the highest point on the horizon. To the right of Washington, The Horn, Mt. Cabot, and Mt. Waumbek come into view, as do Mt. Carrigain, the Hancocks, South Twin Mountain, and Franconia Ridge.

The ledges just past the summit open up views looking west to a nearby ridge containing the multiple summits of Lightning, Teapot, Goback, and Savage Mountains.

WINTER

Sugarloaf is not a feasible winter hike due to Nash Stream Rd. being closed to vehicles 0.5 mi. north of Northside Rd. (although it is plowed to this point), turning this normally short hike into a nearly 20 mile epic. Nash Stream Rd. is heavily used by snowmobiles and there are no other trailed approaches to the mountain.

A hiker and his canine companion head up the Sugarloaf Mountain Trail.

Delisted Peaks

Black Mountain - Middle Peak

Elevation: 2,756 ft.
Location: Town of Jackson
Map: AMC map - Carter Range/Evans Notch

This Black Mountain — not to be confused with Black Mountain in Benton, a current 52WAV peak — is a long, bumpy ridge running north to south in Jackson. The popular Black Mountain Ski Area is located on the southernmost slopes and hiking trails reach its Middle Peak and historic Black Mountain Cabin. The true summit on the northernmost bump was once reached by a trail, but is now only accessible via a lengthy and scratchy bushwhack. In 2001, Black Mountain was added to the 52WAV list to replace the vanishing views on Carr Mountain. Unfortunately, Black Mountain's Middle Peak has suffered the same fate as Carr's, and as a result it too was removed from the list in 2020.

GETTING THERE

A small parking area with room for several vehicles is located at the end of Melloon Rd. in Jackson. From Main St. in Jackson, take Carter Notch Rd./NH 16B north, passing picturesque Jackson Falls on the right. At 3.6 mi., turn right onto narrow Melloon Rd. and continue 0.3 mi. to the parking area on the left. Please do not block the adjacent private driveway and chain gate.

RECOMMENDED ROUTE
Black Mountain Ski Trail, Black Mountain Summit Spur
3.4 mi. round-trip with 1,500 ft. elevation gain
Black Mountain Ski Trail, constructed in 1934 by the Civilian Conservation Corps, provides a direct route to Black Mountain Cabin. From there a footpath continues to the ridge and summit. Footing is generally good although occasionally wet in places. Despite being a ski trail, grades are never overly steep. In summer it can be quite brushy. The trail begins on private property; please stay on the trail and respect all posted signage.

ADDITIONAL ROUTE

East Pasture Ski Trail, Black Mountain Summit Spur, Black Mountain Ski Trail, Black Mountain Cutoff

4.9 mi. counter-clockwise loop with 1,310 ft. elevation gain

This loop from the end of Black Mountain Rd. offers an easier, more remote-feeling, and longer approach up the eastern side of the mountain with a view of the Doubleheads along the way, using a wide, gentle cross-country ski trail for most of the ascent, and hiking trails to reach the summit and cabin. To reach the trailhead, follow the driving directions described in the North Doublehead section of this guide, but turn left onto Black Mountain Rd. just after the Black Mountain Ski Area and continue 0.5 mi. to a roadside parking area on the right.

WINTER

As the name implies, Black Mountain Ski Trail is heavily used in winter by both hikers and skiers. It is recommended that hikers wear snowshoes to preserve the trail and stay to the side, being mindful of fast-moving skiers. Deep snow improves the summit viewpoints a bit. The parking area at the end of Melloon Rd. is plowed.

East Pasture XC Ski Trail is also a ski trail in winter, so the same recommendations apply as above. The parking area at the end of Black Mountain Rd. is plowed.

Carr Mountain

Elevation: 3,454 ft.
Location: Town of Wentworth
Map: AMC map - Moosilauke/Kinsman Ridge

Lesser-known to most hikers, Carr Mountain is a massive 8.5 mi. long ridge, stretching from Rumney to Wentworth to Ellsworth to Warren. A mountain with a long and rich history, Carr once bore a fire tower at the summit which was in service from 1929 to 1948, the concrete footings and stairs of which remain today. One of the original 52WAV peaks, Carr was removed from the list in 2001 due to decades of diminishing views. While Carr no longer offers the vistas it once did, its wild character and beautiful forests make it a worthwhile hike for those seeking a quieter destination within the WMNF.

GETTING THERE
Parking for several vehicles is available in an expanded lot (sign) on the west side of Stinson Lake Rd. in Rumney, 6.8 mi. north of NH 25. This lot was expanded in 2019. Stinson Lake Rd. was also rebuilt and is now paved (formerly dirt) all the way to the new parking area.

RECOMMENDED ROUTE
Three Ponds Trail, Carr Mountain Trail (eastern section)
6.8 mi. round-trip with 2,300 ft. elevation gain
This route offers an easy to moderate climb up the eastern side of Carr Mountain through wild and attractive forests. The upper section is lightly blazed, may be difficult to follow, and in 2018 was suffering from severe erosion. Footing is generally good with some rougher sections higher up.

ADDITIONAL ROUTE
Carr Mountain Trail (western section)
5.8 mi. round-trip with 2,600 ft. elevation gain
This lightly traveled approach from Clifford Brook Rd. in Warren incorporates old logging roads which moderately ascend the western side of the mountain. This half of Carr Mountain Trail is lightly maintained, may be difficult to follow in areas, and is recommended for experienced hikers. This route also allows for a short side trip to Waternomee Falls, a 15 ft. waterfall 0.2 mi. from the main trail. From NH 25 in Warren, turn into the Warren Fish Hatchery and Wildlife Center, turn right onto Fish Hatchery Rd. road for 0.1 mi., then turn left onto Clifford Brook Rd. for 0.6 mi. to a signed parking area on the right.

WINTER
Carr Mountain Trail from the east is a beautiful winter hike through deep, dark woods, with moderate grades making for good snowshoeing. Expect to share Three Ponds Trail and the lower 1.4 mi. of Carr Mountain Trail with snowmobile traffic at times. If not well frozen, the crossing of Sucker Brook along Carr Mountain Trail can be difficult.

The western half of the trail from Warren is lesser-used in winter and may require significant trail breaking. Route-finding may also be needed due to sparse blazing. Clifford Brook Rd. gets plowed as does the designated parking area (although the latter may not be plowed right away). Do not park by the house at the end of the road.

Hibbard Mountain

Elevation: 2,944 ft.
Location: Town of Jackson
Map: WODC map, AMC map - Crawford Notch/Sandwich Range

Hibbard Mountain is a nondescript peak, unlabeled on some maps, located just north of Mt. Wonalancet on the eastern side of The Bowl, a great glacial cirque encircled in part by Mts. Whiteface and Passaconaway. Its wooded summit, easy to pass right over without noticing, once featured a wide view across and down into this cirque, but tree growth has now mostly eliminated the vista. However, a good but limited south-facing viewpoint is located a short distance south of the summit. Hibbard Mountain was removed from the 52WAV list in 2020.

GETTING THERE

The parking area and trailhead are located at the end of Ferncroft Rd. in Albany. This trailhead, located on private land, is very popular and is often overflowing due to hikers bound for Mts. Whiteface and Passaconaway. Due to heavy use, a possible expansion is being proposed for the future. Beyond the turn for the designated parking area, parking is not allowed along the main road. Please observe all posted signs and do not obstruct access to nearby private residences. An outhouse is also located at the far end of the parking lot. From Center Sandwich, take NH 113 east for 3.7 mi., bearing left onto NH 113A (use caution with oncoming traffic here as the intersection is somewhat obscured) and continue 6.7 mi. to picturesque Wonalancet Village. At a sharp right turn in the road, turn left onto Ferncroft Rd. and continue to the trailhead and parking on the right in 0.5 mi.

RECOMMENDED ROUTE

Old Mast Rd., Wonalancet Range Trail

5.6 mi. round-trip with 2,140 ft. elevation gain

This route to Hibbard is a mix of easy and difficult climbing with a steep and rough ascent over Mt. Wonalancet on the way. Other than that stretch, grades are moderate and footing is generally good. The first 0.8 mi. of this route is located on private land.

ADDITIONAL ROUTE
Old Mast Road, Walden Trail, Wonalancet Range Trail, Short Cut
5.9 mi. counter-clockwise loop with 2,200 ft. elevation gain
This loop hike, also starting at the Ferncroft trailhead, is a much more rugged alternative, ascending the very steep and rough Walden Trail to a south-facing viewpoint near the summit of the unofficially-named Wonalancet Hedgehog (3,144 ft.) on the way to Hibbard.

WINTER
Hibbard Mountain isn't heavily hiked in winter, so trail breaking is a possibility. Short Cut is recommended as a bypass to the steep, rugged climb and sloping ledge on Mt. Wonalancet which can be potentially dangerous in icy conditions. Beyond Wonalancet, easy to moderate grades make for good snowshoeing although route-finding may be difficult in place if the trail is unbroken. Deep snow improves the view over the trees at Hibbard's summit. The parking area at Ferncroft is plowed but can be rutted and icy.

Iron Mountain

Elevation: 2,723 ft.
Location: Town of Jackson
Map: AMC map - Carter Range/Evans Notch

Iron Mountain is a steep-sided peak whose mostly viewless summit once bore a fire tower from 1941 to 1948, the remains of which are still present today. The wooded true summit doesn't offer much in the way of views but spectacular vistas can be found on the scenic south cliffs which are located on a southern shoulder. Note that these cliffs are on the opposite side of the mountain from the trailhead, and visiting them requires climbing back over the summit on the return trip. The name of the mountain comes from the old iron mines on the southern slopes which can be visited via a short side path. From the 1930s to around 1975 the Iron Mountain Slope ski area operated on Ducks Head, a low eastern subpeak. The ski trail originated at the site of the former Iron Mountain House, located approximately where Red Fox Bar & Grille is today on NH 16. The slopes have since been reclaimed by nature but bushwhackers can still find relics and old equipment from the former rope tow in the woods. Iron Mountain was removed from the 52WAV list in 2020.

GETTING THERE

A small parking area is available on Iron Mountain Rd. in Jackson. From NH 16, take Green Hill Rd. west for 1.2 mi. to where it becomes Iron Mountain Rd. In 0.2 mi. bear left at a fork where WMNF Forest Rd. 325 diverges right, and begin a steep climb as the road becomes rougher and narrower, reaching a small parking area on the right (sign) at 1.4 mi. This parking area and the first 0.3 mi. of Iron Mountain Trail are located on private land which is protected by a conservation easement held by Upper Saco Valley Land Trust; please respect the property.

ROUTE

Iron Mountain Trail

Summit only: 1.6 mi. round-trip with 800 ft. elevation gain
Include south cliffs: 3.2 mi. round-trip with 1,200 ft. elevation gain

Iron Mountain was once graced with three trail approaches but today only one maintained route remains. Iron Mountain Trail offers a rugged, eroded climb to the summit from the north with a good viewpoint along the way. From the summit the trail descends down the opposite side of the mountain to the south cliffs. Sections of this trail on the north side of the mountain may be relocated in the future by USFS due to ongoing severe erosion. In general markings are poor on this trail with yellow and some silver blazes being very faded. Small cairns also mark the route from the summit down to the south cliffs along with a few informal signs at junctions.

WINTER

Iron Mountain is infrequently hiked in winter mainly due to difficulty in parking as Iron Mountain Rd. is not plowed (but is partly tracked out by snowmobiles). Where Green Hill Rd. ends and Iron Mountain Rd. begins, 1.2 mi. from NH 16, there is a small plowed pull-off on the right, but unfortunately it is signed as no parking. If snow amounts are light, there may be room to park roadside along Green Hill Rd. but do not block access or driveways for the adjacent private residences. If parking is available, a steep 1.4 mi. uphill road walk is required to reach the trailhead. Total round-trip distance to the summit from this spot is 4.4 mi. with 1,620 ft. elevation gain. To extend the trip to the south cliffs, the round-trip distance is 6.0 mi. with 2,020 ft. elevation gain. Crampons may be required on the sloping south cliffs if conditions are icy or crusty.

Mt. Wolf

Elevation: 3,478 ft.
Location: Town of Lincoln
Map: AMC map - Moosilauke/Kinsman Ridge

Mt. Wolf, located along the rugged and somewhat remote Kinsman Ridge, is the dominant peak along the ridge's southern half, and is not often visited by day hikers as a sole destination. It once offered expansive views east toward Franconia Ridge from its eastern summit knob, but over the decades this vista has diminished due to tree growth. Because of this, Wolf was removed from the 52WAV list in 2010. The true summit and hiker register are located on the wooded western knob, which is accessible via a short herd path off Kinsman Ridge Trail. Although it's no longer big on views, Mt. Wolf still offers a wild, rugged and remote hiking experience.

GETTING THERE

A large parking lot for Beaver Brook Trail/Appalachian Trail (WMNF fee area) is located near the height-of-land on NH 112 in Kinsman Notch, 6.8 mi. west of I-93.

RECOMMENDED ROUTE

Kinsman Ridge Trail (Appalachian Trail)

9.2 mi. round-trip with 3,150 ft. elevation gain

This route to Mt. Wolf from the south is steep and rugged, with several ascents and descents along the ridge. This approach also involves 700 ft. of climbing on the way back. Grades vary and footing is often rough. The optional short side trip to the true summit is technically a bushwhack, although a fairly well-worn herd path now leads to the high point.

ADDITIONAL ROUTE

Reel Brook Trail, Kinsman Ridge Trail (Appalachian Trail)

9.6 mi. round-trip with 2,500 ft. elevation gain

This alternate route from the west is reached by a rough side road (high-clearance recommended) off NH 116 in Easton, 3.7 mi. north of NH 112, and provides a generally easy ascent to Kinsman Ridge, combined with a more rugged approach south toward Mt. Wolf.

WINTER

Mt. Wolf is one of the tougher and seldom-visited winter treks as the steep and rugged Kinsman Ridge Trail on the southern end doesn't see much snowshoe traffic, which would likely require strenuous trail breaking. Kinsman Ridge Trail can also be difficult to follow in areas of more open woods if not broken out and its white blazes tend to blend in with the surrounding forest. However, deep snow vastly improves the view over the trees from the outlook atop the eastern summit knob and may also create a bit of a view from the true summit. The large parking area for Beaver Brook Trail in Kinsman Notch is plowed.

The access road to the Reel Brook trailhead is not plowed in winter and there usually isn't room along NH 116 to park, making this route less feasible in winter.

Square Ledge (Albany)

Elevation: 2,620 ft.
Location: Town of Albany
Map: WODC map, AMC map - Crawford Notch/Sandwich Range

This Square Ledge, different than the similar Square Ledge in Pinkham Notch, is located at the end of a ridge which stretches east from 4,000 footer Mt. Passaconaway. While Square Ledge's true summit is wooded, two viewpoints still offer good views. Despite its somewhat low elevation, the hike to Square Ledge lies in a rugged and wild area of the Sandwich Range Wilderness, resulting in a trek that may be more strenuous than the numbers suggest. Square Ledge was removed from the 52WAV list in 2020.

GETTING THERE

Parking for Oliverian Brook Trail is available in a large lot off the Kancamagus Highway (NH 112), 1.0 mi. west of Bear Notch Rd.

RECOMMENDED ROUTE

Oliverian Brook Trail, Square Ledge Branch Trail, Square Ledge Trail, Passaconaway Cutoff
8.4 mi. clockwise loop with 1,550 ft. elevation gain

This loop offers an easy ramble in and out of a remote wilderness area with a steep and rugged ascent over Square Ledge in the middle. The loop is best done in the clockwise direction in order to ascend the much steeper east side, rather than descend it.

ADDITIONAL ROUTE
Old Mast Rd., Square Ledge Trail
7.4 mi. round-trip with 2,250 ft. elevation gain
This southerly route via the Ferncroft trailhead, while shorter, involves more elevation gain due to some climbing on the return trip. See the Mt. Paugus section for details on parking at Ferncroft.

WINTER
The approach from the Kancamagus Highway via Oliverian Brook Trail is the best winter route to Square Ledge and is an excellent snowshoeing trip with a few short, steep pitches to keep things interesting. That said, the Oliverian Brook Trail parking lot may not always be plowed, but sometimes room for a few vehicles is available near the start of the access road to it. The approach from the Ferncroft side is not recommended for inexperienced hikers in winter, due to the very steep climb up the east side of Square Ledge which could generate significant ice. The parking area at Ferncroft is plowed but is often rutted and icy.

West Royce Mountain

Elevation: 3,204 ft.
Location: Township of Bean's Purchase
Map: CTA map, AMC map - Carter Range/Evans Notch

The Royces are a pair of steep rugged peaks located on the west side of Evans Notch, are separated by a state line, and lie at the northern end of the Baldface-Royce Range. West Royce is just inside New Hampshire, while East Royce (which has the better views and is accessible via a spur trail) is just inside Maine. West Royce also had a fire tower from 1940 to 1948, the concrete footings of which remain just off trail a short distance south of the summit. The east face of the mountain is graced with high, exposed granite cliffs which are most prominently seen from East Royce. West Royce was removed from the 52WAV list in 2020.

GETTING THERE
Parking for East Royce Trail is available in a small lot off NH 113 (signed as a New Hampshire highway but actually located in Maine here) in Batchelder's Grant, ME, 9.0 mi. south of US 2 in Gilead, ME.

RECOMMENDED ROUTE
East Royce Trail, Royce Connector, Royce Trail
West Royce only: 5.2 mi. round-trip with 1,850 ft. elevation gain
Include trip to East Royce ledges: 5.8 mi. round-trip with 2,310 ft. elevation gain
This route makes a steep and rough ascent to the ridge with an out-and-back side trip to the summit of West Royce and an optional side trip to East Royce.

ADDITIONAL ROUTE
Burnt Mill Brook Trail, Royce Trail
5.4 mi. round-trip with 2,400 ft. elevation gain
This northwestern approach starting on Wild River Rd. (WMNF Forest Rd. 12), while more remote to get to, offers an easier ascent up to the ridge than the steeper and rougher Evans Notch route. The trailhead and parking area are located 2.7 mi. south of ME 113.

WINTER
The East Royce trailhead is inaccessible in winter due to NH 113 being gated through Evans Notch. Hikers looking to approach West Royce in winter must do so using longer Royce Trail from the south (8.6 mi. round-trip with 2,750 ft. elevation gain). The two crossings of Cold River may be difficult or impassable if not well frozen. West Royce is not frequently hiked in winter, so strenuous, steep trail breaking may be required. There is usually plowed parking at the junction of NH 113 and the access road to Basin and Cold River Campgrounds. A short walk north along the highway is required to reach the trailhead.

The Burnt Mill Brook Trail approach is not possible in winter as Wild River Rd. is inaccessible due to NH 113 being gated through Evans Notch.

References

Author not provided. *Time has changed Table Mountain.* Conway, NH: Conway Daily Sun, 2017.

Clark, Jeremy. *New England Trail Conditions.* newenglandtrailconditions.com

Compton, John. *1HappyHiker.* 1happyhiker.blogspot.com

Conrad, David E. *The Land We Cared For, A History of the Forest Service's Eastern Region.* Milwaukee, WI: U.S. Forest Service, 1997.

Davis, Jeremy. *New England Lost Ski Areas Project.* nelsap.org

Dingman, Clay. *Cardigan Mountain Trails.* cardiganmountaintrails.blogspot.com

Dickerman, Mike. *Stories from the White Mountains: Celebrating the Region's Historic Past.* Charleston, SC: The History Press, 2013.

Doan, Daniel and Ruth Doan MacDougall. *50 More Hikes in New Hampshire, 6th Edition.* Woodstock, VT: The Countryman Press, 2014.

Goodale, Christine L. *Fire in the White Mountains — A Historical Perspective.* Ithaca, NY: Cornell University, 2003.

Ignasher, Jim. *New England Aviation History.* newenglandaviationhistory.com

Julyan, Robert and Mary Julyan. *Place Names of the White Mountains.* Hanover, NH: University Press of New England, 1993.

Lord, Dick. *Mt. Willard Section House.* upward-concepts.com

Lyons, Shirley Elder. *Over The Hill Hikers and How They Grew and Grew and Grew.* Portsmouth, NH: Peter E. Randall Publisher, 2010.

Moultonborough Historical Society. moultonboroughhistory.org

Nilsen, Kim. *50 Hikes North of the White Mountains.* Woodstock, VT: The Countryman Press, 2012.

Over The Hill Hikers. overthehillhikers.blogspot.com

Pitcher, Frederick. *Monadnock Trails.* monadnocktrails.com

Searles, Karl. *Live Free and Hike: A NH Day Hiker's Blog.* livefreeandhikenh.blogspot.com

Smith, Robert Hanaford Sr. *An 1885 Landslide.* The Weirs Times. 2016.

Smith, Steven D. and Mike Dickerman. *The 4000-Footers of the White Mountains, A Guide and History, 2nd Edition.* Littleton, NH: Bondcliff Books, 2012.

Smith, Steven D. *Mt. Chocorua, A Guide and History*. Littleton, NH: Bondcliff Books, 2006.

Smith, Steven D. *Paths & Peaks*. mountainwanderer.com/paths-peaks.php

Smith, Steven D. *Southern New Hampshire Trail Guide, 4th Edition*. Boston, MA: Appalachian Mountain Club, 2015.

Smith, Steven D. *White Mountain Guide, 30th Edition*. Boston, MA: Appalachian Mountain Club, 2017.

Soldati, Fabio. *Peakfinder*. peakfinder.org

Sweetser, Moses Foster. *The White Mountains, A Handbook For Travellers, 7th Edition*. Boston, MA: Ticknor & Co., 1886.

Weingart, Paul D. *Kilkenny Unit Plan, White Mountain National Forest, Eastern Region*. Laconia, NH: White Mountain National Forest, 1975.

WhiteMountainHistory.org. whitemountainhistory.org

Wonalancet Out Door Club. *Guide to Wonalancet and the Sandwich Range of New Hampshire (Replica of 1901 Edition)*. Littleton, NH: Bondcliff Books, 2002.

About The Author

Ken MacGray is a freelance writer and hiker living in southern New Hampshire after previous life in the media industry. He has always been a hiker but didn't find his true passion for it until later in life and has completed the NH 4,000 Footers and finished almost three rounds of the 52WAV, among other hiking accomplishments.

Notes